THE STRUGGLE FOR
AUSTRALIAN INDUSTRIAL
RELATIONS

For Rebecca

THE STRUGGLE FOR AUSTRALIAN INDUSTRIAL RELATIONS

Braham Dabscheck

Melbourne

OXFORD UNIVERSITY PRESS

Oxford   Auckland   New York

OXFORD UNIVERSITY PRESS AUSTRALIA
Oxford New York
Athens Auckland Bangkok Bombay
Calcutta Cape Town Dar es Salaam Delhi
Florence Hong Kong Istanbul Karachi
Kuala Lumpur Madras Madrid Melbourne
Mexico City Nairobi Paris Singapore
Taipei Tokyo Toronto

and associated companies in
Berlin Ibadan

OXFORD is a trade mark of Oxford University Press

National Library of Australia
Cataloguing-in-Publication data:

Dabscheck, Braham.
        The struggle for Australian industrial relations.

    Bibliography.
        Includes Index.
        ISBN 0 19 553486 7.

    1. Industrial relations—Australia. I. Title.

331.0994

Edited by Cathryn Game
Cover photograph from Andrew Chapman
Photography
Typeset by Syarikat Seng Teik Sdn. Bhd.
Printed through Bookpac Production Services, Singapore
Published by Oxford University Press,
253 Normanby Road, South Melbourne, Australia

CONTENTS

TABLES

ACRONYMS

ABL	*Australian Bulletin of Labour*
ABS	Australian Bureau of Statistics
ACTU	Australian Council of Trade Unions
AFR	*Australian Financial Review*
AIDA	Australian Industries Development Association
AIRC	Australian Industrial Relations Commission
AJLL	*Australian Journal of Labour Law*
ALP	Australian Labor Party
AMWU	Amalgamated Metal Workers' Union
BCA	Business Council of Australia
BCB	*Business Council Bulletin*
CAI	Confederation of Australian Industry
CPI	Consumer Price Index
ILO	International Labour Organisation
JIR	*Journal of Industrial Relations*
NILS	National Institute of Labour Studies
NWC	National Wage Case
OECD	Organisation for Economic Cooperation and Development
SMH	*Sydney Morning Herald*

ACKNOWLEDGMENTS

In preparing this book I received help from a number of individuals and organisations who provided me with documents and information. I have also benefited from conversations over the years with various individuals who have acted as a sounding board and/or provided me with ideas for further analysis and investigation. They are too numerous to name individually. However, I would like to thank all of them for aiding me in the preparation of this book. I would also like to express my thanks for the skill and dedication of the staff at the library of the University of New South Wales for helping me to track down documents and sources that seemed impossible to find. Thanks also to the Economics Department at the University of Wollongong for providing me with facilities to conduct my research and writing in the second half of 1993 during a period of study leave, and to the University of New South Wales for enabling me to have study leave. Brian Brooks, Bradon Ellem, Peter Gahan and Tom Sheridan provided useful comments on an early draft of chapter 1, for which I am most thankful. Any errors or omissions, of course, are my responsibility alone. Alan Fettling of Oxford University Press has been a constant source of encouragement during this project. Finally, I would like to thank two people in particular for their help in the writing of this book. First, Marie Kwok for processing several drafts and the final manuscript. Marie is an easygoing and agreeable person to work with. The second is Pam Bedwell for her love, humour and understanding.

PREFACE

....

The struggle of [people] against power is the struggle of memory against forgetting.

> Kundera, M. (1982), The Book of Laughter and Forgetting,
> *Faber & Faber, London, p. 3.*

Where there are more wills than one, there must come collision of will—and disputes; and even if the directors of industry were to be elected there still would be need for regulation. Regulation has come to stay.

> Higgins, H. B. (1920), 'A new province for law and order—III', Harvard
> Law Review, *December, p. 136.*

....

April 30 1975 stands out as the most intellectually stimulating day of my life; the day I discovered how little I understood or knew about Australian industrial relations. The event that triggered this realisation was a decision by the then Australian Conciliation and Arbitration Commission[1] to introduce a system of industrial relations regulation, known as wage indexation, in an attempt to respond to and overcome the industrial relations and economic problems of the mid 1970s.[2] Under wage indexation the commission assumed major responsibility for the conduct and operation of industrial relations.[3]

In the late 1960s and early 1970s university classrooms were full of discussions of how Australia's experiment with industrial tribunals was coming to an end; of how collective bargaining would replace arbitration as a method of industrial relations regulation. The late 1960s and early 1970s were a period of full employment in which unions, in the words of Woodward, had been 'given the economic whiphand'.[4] Having taken on and effectively destroyed the penal powers (against industrial action) contained in the *Conciliation and Arbitration Act* 1904[5] unions increasingly, or so it seemed, negotiated directly with employers outside or apart from the regulatory umbrella provided by industrial tribunals.[6] Scholars and students stood on each other's shoulders softly chanting the mantra 'Arbitration is dead'.

The propelling of the commission to the centre stage of Australian industrial relations after 30 April 1975 demonstrated not only that announcements concerning arbitration's death were somewhat premature but also that the commission would play a central role in the future course of Australian industrial relations. If nothing else, 30 April 1975 would seem to have demonstrated that industrial tribunals provide a, if not the, key to understanding Australian industrial relations. Whether one studies industrial tribunals because they form part of the landscape of Australian industrial relations, feels the need to offer applause or hurl brickbats, perceives them as agents of progress or constraints that need to be overcome, they have invariably been associated with the major episodes of Australian industrial relations.

In the period between 1890 and 1910 the various colonial, State and Commonwealth Governments brought into being various systems of industrial tribunals and wages boards to regulate relationships between employers, on the one hand, and workers and unions, on the other hand.[7] These regulatory bodies were created in response to the perceived chaos associated with a series of major industrial clashes and the prolonged depression of the 1890s. Employers championed the cause of 'freedom of contract', or what some in our more 'enlightened' times would refer to as 'individual bargaining', in routing unions in a number of bitter and drawn-out disputes. Moreover, at the turn of the century there was no welfare state to help the needy.

The creation of industrial tribunals and wages boards resulted from the activities and energies of middle-class intellectuals; of lawyers, judges and politicians—people outside the economic struggle of capital and labour—who rejected *laissez-faire* economics and believed that there was a need for the state to assume a prominent role in the regulation of employment relationships.[8] These individuals sought to harness the power of the state to create new institutions in attempting to alleviate human suffering and re-establish the moral basis of society.

Henry Bournes Higgins, a lawyer and parliamentarian, a delegate to the conventions that produced the Australian Constitution, a member of the High Court of Australia (1906–29) and the second president of the Commonwealth Court of Conciliation and Arbitration (1907–21), epitomises the Australian approach to industrial relations at the turn of the twentieth century.[9] In fashioning industrial tribunals Higgins and his contemporaries seem to have brewed an antipodean amalgam of Catholic social thought, the ideas of the Fabians, Sidney and Beatrice Webb, and North American Progressivism.

In 1891 Pope Leo XIII published an encyclical letter, *Rerum Novarum* (The Workers' Charter), which argued that the state needed to assume a greater role in the affairs of workers and employers. *Rerum Novarum* maintained 'that wages ought not to be insufficient to support a frugal and well-behaved wage-earner'.[10] The Webbs, in their quest to enhance social efficiency and end moral degradation, argued for the establishment of a national minimum wage.[11] Roe has provided a series of illuminating studies in which educated middle-class people were associated with major reforms that he links to the Progressive movement, which was a major feature of North American political life at the beginning of the twentieth century.[12]

Higgins was aware of *Rerum Novarum*,[13] and met the Webbs during their 1898 sojourn in Australia.[14] Following a reading of *Industrial Democracy*, it might be reasonable to suggest that Higgins' approach to industrial regulation and, in particular, the concept and method of calculating the basic wage (the minimum wage for an adult unskilled male labourer designed to sustain a family of five) were simply borrowed or adapted from the Webbs.[15] Between 1915 and 1920 Higgins published a series of articles concerning his work as an industrial relations regulator in the *Harvard Law Review*, a journal at the centre of North America's intellectual milieu.[16] In the first of these articles Higgins, in an oft-quoted passage, stated that industrial tribunals would usher in

> a new province for law and order . . . the process of conciliation, with arbitration in the background, is substituted for the rude and barbarous processes of strike and lockout. Reason is to displace force; the might of the State is to enforce peace between industrial combatants as well as between other combatants; and all in the interests of the public.[17]

While Higgins was a strong advocate and staunch defender of industrial tribunals—particularly of attacks directed at his court—we need to be wary of overstating the role he believed they should perform. In his hands industrial tribunals would determine minimum terms and conditions of employment[18]—the most famous example being the 1907 *Harvester* judgment, which established such a wage for an adult unskilled male labourer[19]—and provide a vehicle for the resolution of industrial disputes. Higgins stated that the 'ideal of the Court is a collective agreement settled, not by the measurement of economic resources, but on lines of fair play'.[20] He also said:

> The Court leaves every employer free to carry on the business on his own system, so long as he does not perpetrate industrial trouble or endanger industrial peace; free to choose his employees on their merits and according to his exigencies; free to make use of new machines, of improved methods, of financial advantages, of advantages of locality, of superior knowledge; free to put the utmost pressure on anything and everything except human life.[21]

Throughout the twentieth century different groups and organisations have competed with each other in suggesting and offering various proposals to reform industrial relations. Australia has continually experimented with and developed new approaches in attempting to improve industrial relations. It is as if Australia is a social science laboratory in which reformers of different hues have been given free reign to develop, experiment and test their various views concerning the best way to conduct industrial relations. Members of industrial tribunals, at both the Commonwealth and State levels, regularly enunciate new principles and develop new schemes to confront the myriad problems of industrial relations regulation. Governments are continually commissioning reports or conducting inquiries. Academics tap out tomes. Employers, unions and other groups are forever offering suggestions and advice concerning reform. Both Commonwealth and State Governments are continually introducing and/or revising legislation in a never-ending search for an industrial relations nirvana. For example, the major piece of legislation at the Commonwealth level has been amended on about a hundred occasions in the last ninety years.

Until recently at least, most of the proposed and actual reforms have been predicated on a continuing role for industrial tribunals.[22] Since about the mid 1980s, however, proposals for reform have become more hard-edged and fundamental, attacking the very basis of Australian industrial relations. An increasing number of individuals and groups want to replace the system of industrial tribunals with something called enterprise bargaining. The New South Wales, Victorian, Tasmanian and Western Australian Governments have introduced legislation that has sought to diminish, if not extinguish, the role of industrial tribunals and unions. In mid 1992 the Federal Labor Government enacted legislation that reduced the ability of the commission to vet enterprise agreements negotiated between employers and unions. In the March 1993 federal election the Coalition campaigned on a policy of abolishing compulsory arbitration.

The aim of this book is to document and provide a critical commentary on the major issues and developments of the late 1980s and early 1990s; to examine the struggle for Australian industrial relations. The book is written as a sequel to my 1989 work, *Australian Industrial Relations in the 1980s*. It will focus on the major issues, events and debates of Australian industrial relations in these years culminating in the passage of the *Industrial Relations Reform Act* 1993. In this period Australia has moved away from a centralised to an increasingly decentralised system of industrial relations regulation. Three major issues have been associated with this transformation: a diminution in the hitherto prominent role played by the commission, the development and adoption of different models of enterprise bargaining, and a massive campaign of amalgamations, which has rationalised the structure of unions.

Chapter 1 will provide a discussion of theoretical issues. It will first examine general issues of studying industrial relations and link the predeliction of scholars to eschew theoretical discourse to the inter- or multi-disciplinary nature of industrial relations scholarship. The chapter will then construct a general theory of Australian industrial relations. This theory will be built around the analytical device of an orbit of interaction and will provide the basis for analysing the major issues and events of the late 1980s and early 1990s in Australia.

Chapter 2 provides a context in which to analyse these developments. The chapter will provide a brief account of the early Accords, or agreements negotiated between the Australian Labor Party and the Australian Council of Trade Unions. The original Accord rested on the supposition that centralisation provided the best means for Australia to overcome and respond to various economic and industrial relations problems. The chapter will examine developments in the mid 1980s that resulted in a movement away from tenets of centralisation contained in the Accord. It will also examine issues associated with the relationship between industrial relations structure and economic performance.

The early Accords were predicated on the commission playing a major role in regulating industrial relations and determining wages. In the late 1980s and early 1990s the role and stature of the commission were increasingly challenged and undermined. Chapter 3 examines the forces and events associated with a reduction in, or redefinition of, the role of the commission. The chapter is divided into two sections. The first examines High Court decisions during the 1980s that served to undermine the protection hitherto afforded to the commission by section 51, paragraph XXXV of the Australian Constitution. The second provides a detailed account of various strains and clashes between the Accord partners and the commission concerning industrial relations regulation.

Chapter 4 examines various issues of enterprise bargaining. It begins with a presentation and detailed critique of evidence and proposals developed by the Business Council of Australia. It then presents the various models developed by State Governments concerning enterprise bargaining. The third section examines the federal, or Accord, model of enterprise bargaining.

In 1987 the ACTU embarked on a massive campaign of union amalgamations in an attempt to improve the quality of services provided by unions for members, enhance recruitment possibilities and withstand attacks from those opposed to unions. Various issues associated with this rationalisation strategy are the subject matter of chapter 5. The chapter discusses the number of unionists and level of unionisation in Australia. It also outlines details of the program of amalgamation/rationalisation and evaluates the strategy.

An epilogue draws together the major themes of the struggle for Australian industrial relations in the late 1980s and early 1990s.

1

A GENERAL THEORY OF AUSTRALIAN INDUSTRIAL RELATIONS

. . . because it relies on existing social science theories, it is virtually impossible for industrial relations to contribute to the evolution of theory in the social sciences . . . this should be one of the more important goals of industrial relations research, but it is obviously difficult to accomplish if researchers simply apply established social science theories to industrial relations issues.

Cappelli, P. (1985), 'Theory construction in IR and some implications for research', Industrial Relations, *Winter, p. 105.*

The 'national wage structure' seems to consist of little islands of rationality in a sea of anarchy.

Ross, A. M. (1956), Trade Union Wage Policy, *University of California Press, Berkeley, p. 73.*

Industrial relations involves the interaction of countless individuals, groups and organisations. These entities have different goals, aspirations and views that spring from their respective locations within industrial relations. In interacting with each other and seeking the realisation of their respective goals they will make pronouncements designed to further their particular interests. In so doing they will have a penchant for exaggeration, a tendency to place interesting, novel not to say biased interpretations on events and evidence. They will seek to present their respective positions in the best possible light, to demonstrate how the various proposals that they are offering will not so much serve their own interests but, more importantly, enhance the well-being of others, if not the national or public interest.

The industrial relations discourse of practitioners[1] seems to be invariably characterised by exaggeration and hyperbole. It is as if we are forced to tiptoe our way through mush—the continual outpourings of those involved in industrial relations. Howard, for example, has observed that 'there can be few fields of enquiry so doctrine-ridden, and rich in doctrinal clashes, as that of industrial relations'. He has also stated: 'Industrial relations . . . is a subject widely held, by usually ill-informed commentators, relying on dubious evidence and a fund of prejudices, to be of critical importance to our society'.[2]

A potential role that presumably could be performed by scholars is to provide analyses that do not suffer from the problems identified by Howard. Scholarship is synonymous with the traditions of science. Scholars accept nothing *a priori*. They are unimpressed by the (non-scientific) status or power bases of those who make statements or offer profound insights. Scholars subject anything and everything to rigorous testing and critical scrutiny in ascertaining its usefulness in providing explanations of the real world. Scholarship might be able to clear a path through the mush that is industrial relations.

In reviewing Australian research Gurdon concluded, in a critical vein, that it 'has had little inherent direction and has tended to follow the headlines'.[3] The first half of this observation assumes that there should be an inherent direction to guide research, that it should be conducted in accordance with a master plan, as presumably determined by a powerful entity. It is conceivable, however, that such a master plan would stifle innovation and creativity and censor methods and findings inconsistent with the dictates of the said plan.

The second half of Gurdon's observation—following the headlines—could be interpreted as a strength, rather than a weakness, of Australian research. By engaging in issues and debates of immediate or high public interest scholars can conceivably provide a more scientific analysis of such issues than would otherwise have occurred. This phenomenon could be interpreted as the industrial relations equivalent of the exchanges that occur between evolutionists and creationists.

Scholarship, then, has the potential to transform industrial relations discourse from its doctrinaire base, to provide scientifically based insights to aid understanding, insights different from the preoccupations and interests of the various (other) individuals, groups and organisations involved in industrial relations. In saying this it should be noted that others can seek to utilise the skills of scholars in pursuing their own interests. People who were once scholars often find themselves attracted to the employ of (non-scholastic) others. Moreover, scholars might be enticed and/or hawk their services to conduct short-term consultancy research. Such sponsored research provides an aura of respectability and authority, which might not otherwise be present, to aid sponsors in the pursuit of their goals. However, we need to be wary of consultancy-based research. It might produce little more than sophisticated doctrine. Niland has observed that the 'nature of research is strongly influenced by the nature of sponsorship. Pressures on researchers to come up with the "right" results can be as subtle as they are powerful'.[4]

An illustration of this can be provided by the following extract from Drago et al., people associated with the National Institute of Labour Studies, who were commissioned to produce research on behalf of the Business Council of Australia. The context of this extract is that the BCA wanted to claim that Australia's traditional reliance on awards and occupational unionism was less likely to induce 'shared interests' at the workplace than systems based on enterprise bargaining. In comparisons made between multi-union Australian and non-union American firms Drago et al. found what they described as

> a curious anomaly in the data: American managers seem more innovative in terms of motivating employees through both pay incentives and participative management, yet Australian employees are more satisfied and committed to their organisations . . . the Australian industrial relations system . . . provides . . . an atmosphere where both high job

satisfaction and commitment to organisations and peers flourish . . . The system may also act to protect employees from poor styles of supervision.[5]

What they refer to as 'a curious anomaly in the data' contradicts accepted norms of social science research. When there are contradictions between data and a hypothesis the traditional approach of scholars is to reject the hypothesis (as it is not supported by the data) and to experiment with and/or develop alternative hypotheses (which are not inconsistent with the data). In this instance Drago et al. decided to reject, or attack, their own data.

DEVELOPING A SCIENTIFIC APPROACH

As a first step in attempting to enhance the development of a scientific approach to industrial relations research it might be prudent to return to basics and note the scholar's traditional distinction between positive and normative statements. *Positive statements* are concerned with *what is* whereas *normative statements* are concerned with *what ought to be*. Positive statements, by definition, are concerned with what is happening in the real world and hence can be tested, or falsified, by reference to facts.[6] Normative statements, on the other hand, simply reflect the desires or value judgements of different individuals and groups. In terms of the discussion above concerning the pronouncements of practitioners industrial relations is sinking under the weight of normative statements. Differences about values, about what ought to happen, cannot be resolved by reference to facts. While differences between protagonists over 'ought statements' often make for heated, spirited, if not interesting exchanges, there is no scientific method available to resolve such disputes, which are avoided by scholars as a result.

It might appear that positive statements are conservative and concerned with maintenance of the status quo while normative statements are radical and designed to bring about change.[7] A number of comments will be offered here in defence of positive statements. First, it is possible to construct positive statements that are concerned with change and seek to develop an understanding of dynamic phenomena. For example, propositions could be developed concerning what will result from legislative changes or the factors of importance in increasing or decreasing union membership, and so on. Second, it is much easier to give vent to one's biases and make profound statements about what ought to happen than it is to develop an understanding of how the real world operates.[8] Third, and most importantly, it is only by attempting to develop an understanding of 'what is' that we can ever hope to initiate action that will enable us to move towards and realise a desired objective. In travelling somewhere it is helpful to know where we are before embarking on the journey.

Scholars in industrial relations often express misgivings about the intellectual depth and robustness of their discipline. It is as if they are gripped by a fear that it lacks the respectability apparently afforded to older, more established disciplines. Almost forty years ago Dunlop, in his seminal work, *Industrial Relations Systems*—which is generally regarded as heralding the birth of the discipline of industrial relations—observed 'that far too much of the writing concerned with industrial relations . . . has lacked intellectual rigour and discipline'.[9] Despite the growth, if not explosion, in industrial relations scholarship since the publication of *Industrial Relations Systems*,[10] this pessimistic view is continually endorsed, or rather re-endorsed, by commentators on the discipline's development.

In 1969 Somers, in introducing a book of readings on industrial relations theory, said, 'Even its most devoted supporters must confess that industrial relations has not yet achieved a status comparable to the traditional academic disciplines or to the established professional fields'.[11] In a separate essay in that volume he expressed his feelings of disquiet more forcibly and warned

> that the survival of industrial relations as a separate discipline and its growth as a respectable field of study require a broad conceptual or theoretical framework serving to integrate the disparate strands of thinking and research now roughly juxtaposed under the banner 'industrial relations'.[12]

In 1980 Hyman commented that industrial relations

> forms an area of study with no coherent theoretical or disciplinary rationale, but deriving from a directly *practical* concern with a range of 'problems' confronting employers, governments and their academic advisers in the pursuit of labour stability.[13]

Taylor and Bray, in an introduction to critical essays on Australian industrial relations, observed: 'Industrial relations has always experienced considerable difficulty in carving out space for itself in the academic world'.[14] Blain and Plowman, in surveying Australian research conducted between 1970 and 1986, concluded that 'a weakness of the overall literature is the disproportionate attention given to description. It tends to concentrate on collecting facts and gives relatively little weight to theoretical analysis and explanation'.[15] Lansbury and Westcott reached a similar conclusion in reviewing Australian research post 1986.[16]

In some ways these feelings of disquiet could be regarded as surprising given the apparent promise of Dunlop's notion of an industrial relations system. Dunlop hoped to upgrade industrial relations scholarship from the collection of 'mountains of facts' and 'the preoccupation, if not the obsession, with labor peace and warfare'[17]. Dunlop defined an industrial relations system as consisting

> of three groups of actors—workers and their organisations, managers and their organisations, and governmental agencies concerned with the work community. These groups interact within a specified environment comprised of three interrelated contexts: the technology, the market or budgetary constraints, and the power relations in the larger community and the derived status of the actors. An industrial relations system creates an ideology or a commonly shared body of ideas and beliefs regarding the interaction and roles of the actors which helps to bind the system together.[18]

He also argued: 'The establishment of . . . procedures and rules . . . is the centre of attention of an industrial relations system . . . the establishment of these rules is the major concern or output of the industrial relations sub-system of industrial society'.[19]

Much ink has been used in criticising Dunlop's notion of an industrial relations system, criticisms that will not be rehearsed here other than for the identification of two issues. First, in Dunlop's hands change is exogenous—changes in his three contextual variables affect actors resulting in alterations to the rules that govern their interactions.[20]

Shalev has questioned the appropriateness of separating the internal and external. He has argued that the 'social, economic, and political environment can be more fruitfully seen as interacting with, and therefore as analytically inseparable from labour relations *per se*'.[21] Technological change is not something that occurs in a vacuum external to Dunlop's actors. Its introduction results from decisions made by those within an industrial relations system. Legislation and/or political decisions pertaining to industrial relations do not appear out of thin air; numerous individuals, groups and organisations become involved in and seek to influence decisions so made.[22] Industrial relations actors learn about their economic well-being through their interactions with customers, suppliers, creditors and banks. It is not as if information concerning markets is produced by an invisible force. As Guille has commented, 'Industrial battles are fought on the bourse floor as well as the foundry floor: industrial relations as an academic study is trivialised if such connexions are not emphasised'.[23]

Moreover, Dunlop's model of exogenous change produces actors who seem to be lifeless and lacking in motivation. He tells us little about what actors want—other than a need to make rules. Dunlop's actors might indeed read scripts prepared for them by others, but they do not seem to be participating in a drama.

The second issue concerns the location or space within which an industrial relations system operates. Dunlop said: 'The concept of an industrial relations system is deliberately variable in scope; it may be used to characterize an immediate work place, or enterprise, a sector or a country as a whole.'[24] He also said that:

> The usage which has been developed recognises that a group of allied systems may be integrated into a larger sector or into a national system. In turn many systems may be subdivided into specialised smaller systems depending upon the purpose at hand.[25]

Dunlop also noted that: 'Work places and enterprises which themselves constitute isolated systems may attach themselves to larger systems, or those with marginal identification to a system may break away and develop their own rules, distinctive in some respects'. Moreover, he wished

> to avoid the twin errors of regarding . . . all work places in an industrial society as neatly divided or assigned into a small group of permanent industrial relations systems, and . . . envisaging each work place as somehow autonomously establishing rules which have little or no relation to others determined in an industrial society.

Nevertheless, Dunlop concluded that:

> It is sufficient for the present purposes to hold that the world of actual industrial relations experience has sufficient stability and order to warrant the use of the concept of an industrial relations system as a fruitful instrument in organizing and understanding the establishment of the rules of the workplace.[26]

Because he saw the real world of industrial relations characterised by stability and order Dunlop regarded the combination, intermingling and breaking up, or integration and disintegration, of different industrial relations systems as being issues of marginal concern. This is most unfortunate because these issues—analytical loose ends, as it were— are rich in theoretical possibilities.[27] How are we to explain the switching mechanism that produces the combining and breaking up of systems? How and why do such systems combine or fall apart? What is the relationship of these various systems to each other? Are issues of concern to a particular actor subdivided, as it were, between and across different systems? For example, some issues relevant to different actors will be determined by numerous pieces of legislation,[28] the decisions of courts and tribunals, negotiations between unions and employers, and between workers and immediate supervisors. The unravelling of real-world industrial relations could be akin to the slicing of a multilayered cake.

The potential integration and disintegration of different systems means that, in attempting to understand a particular issue, there can be more than three groups of actors whose actions would need to be analysed.[29] The problem with a three-actor model is that there are a limited number of ways in which actors can interact.[30] The theoretical significance of an *n* actor model is that there are many permutations and combinations of interaction.

The 'strategic choice' model of Kochan, McKersie and Cappelli and Kochan, Katz and McKersie has followed Dunlop in identifying different locations at which decisions are made.[31] In doing so they have focused on decision-making in different parts of the corporation. Their other significant contribution is that management (or should it be capital?) makes key decisions in responding to product market pressures. The product market was one of Dunlop's contexts,[32] and all first-year economics students know that labour markets are influenced by product markets. A major problem with the strategic choice model is that it is even weaker than Dunlop concerning the role of the various organs constituting the state and other groups and organisations involved in industrial relations.[33]

The inability of industrial relations to develop a theoretical core of its own stems from the interdisciplinary or multidisciplinary nature of industrial relations scholarship. While all disciplines grow and progress from analogies and the crossfertilisation of ideas from other disciplines, industrial relations finds itself inhabiting a peculiar epistemological place. As all introductory students are told (in their first lecture!) the study of industrial relations involves or combines contributions from more established disciplines. Attention is usually directed to the traditional social sciences of politics, sociology, economics and psychology as well as history and law.

This list of relevant disciplines is not complete. Few industrial relations courses pay any attention to accountancy, which presumably informs the decisions of enterprises. A minority of scholars, such as those with a concern for socio-technic systems and the work of Taylor and scientific management, have considered engineering in their musings. Occupational health and safety issues involve knowledge of physics, chemistry, biology and anatomy.

It is as if one needs to combine knowledge from all disciplines to be able to unravel the mysteries of industrial relations. Yet, as Hills has noted, 'Few students today can become renaissance persons due to the tremendous expansion, elaboration, and testing of theory in each of the social sciences'.[34]

The interdisciplinary or multidisciplinary crossroads that is industrial relations has produced an intellectual paralysis among scholars. It seems so much easier to borrow insights from other disciplines than to develop industrial relations theories by themselves. It is as if those who work in academic industrial relations are sitting back, watching and waiting for others to provide them with intellectual nourishment. Adams has observed that

> a major reason for the widespread opinion about the absence of industrial relations theory may be that much of the theory taught in industrial relations programs, discussed at industrial relations meetings and used to guide industrial relations research is considered by many

scholars to be something other than industrial relations theory. If one classifies as industrial relations only those theoretical constructs unclaimed by other fields then it is probably true that the set is sparsely populated.[35]

A logical extension of this view is that what has been traditionally regarded as the discipline of industrial relations constitutes nothing more than a hollow shell. Cappelli has observed that: 'As industrial relations scholars moved towards the application of existing social science theories, industrial relations began to disappear as a unique field and an independent discipline'.[36] Could the discipline of industrial relations be nothing more than a mirage in the imagination of a motley group of scholars?

Because industrial relations is seemingly devoid of theories of its own, many scholars feel the need to move over into other more prestigious disciplines. If there is nothing to keep you at home, you will look elsewhere for excitement. Somers has noted: 'Because industrial relations lacks a unifying theme, the feeling is that it is not really a field at all and that greater contributions can be made by co-operation with one's codisciplinarians under an established theoretical framework'.[37] Moreover, as the discipline lacks any core of its own, it is easily subject to invasion by outsiders—whether it be econometricians looking for new data sets to practise their skills or those who are in the vanguard of the unitarist heaven apparently offered by human resource management.[38]

Voos has stated: 'There is a wide range of theoretical discourse in industrial relations, but at the same time, abstract theory *per se* does not play a dominant, or even a particularly central, role in our field.'[39] This situation needs to be rectified. There is a need for industrial relations scholars to pursue abstract theorising—to help the discipline escape the theoretical tundra in which it finds itself. An attempt at such abstraction will now be made in developing a model of Australian industrial relations.

To conceive of a model of Australian industrial relations begs the question, what type of model? At the risk of being accused of presenting a caricature, industrial relations scholars essentially use micro models. The majority of scholars focus on the workplace, the employment relationship or job regulation.[40] This produces a tendency to conceive industrial relations in literal and narrow terms. Associated with this micro workplace focus, scholars experience difficulties in incorporating the various organs that constitute the state, let alone other non-workplace institutions embroiled in industrial relations. Dufty and Fells, for example, claim that 'the key "industrial relations" is that between the individual employer and the individual worker', and 'that the focus of industrial relations should be at the point of production—the workplace'.[41] A literal interpretation of this 'ought' statement would seem to suggest that organs of the state and trade unions fall outside the scope of industrial relations scholarship.

Hills has said: 'A total industrial relations system can certainly be envisioned for a given country, but it is hard to conceptualise anything similar to the measurable flows of consumption, investment or government expenditures so important to the study of macroeconomics'.[42] In making this statement he appears to be unaware of Marxist and corporatist writers who have employed 'macro' terms in their respective discussions of industrial relations. Marxists, of course, base their analyses around the notion of class. Hyman, for example, argues that:

> capitalist social relations of production reflect and reproduce a structured antagonism of interests between capital and labour . . . capitalism simultaneously organises workers collectively (since the capitalist labour process is essentially collective in character), and hence generates the material basis for effective resistance to capital and the priorities of the capitalist mode of production. What is conventionally studied as industrial relations may thus be conceived as a fetishized representation of the class struggle and the various forms in which it is (at least temporarily) contained, fragmented and routinized.[43]

Corporatism analyses society in terms of the interaction between three lumps or aggregates: the state, capital and labour. Corporatism implies that all three are monolithic and that peak representative bodies can control and discipline their constituent parts in pursuit of the national interest. The major problems with both these approaches, despite the antithesis of their intellectual positions, is where the entities aggregated push and pull in different directions (and/or disintegrate), and in ignoring the actions of groups and organisations not included in the aggregates that also become involved in industrial relations.[44]

THE THEORY OUTLINED

It is possible to develop models that do not fall into the traps identified above. The model developed here will focus on the interconnections and interdependencies between the various individuals, groups and organisations that play a part in the phenomenon of real-world Australian industrial relations. To distinguish it from macro models it will be described as a general theory of industrial relations.[45]

In presenting this theory a new analytical construct will be developed to conceptualise the basic element, or entity, of industrial relations. The term *interactor* is the fundamental building block of this new theory. It is derived from the relations or interactions inherent in the words, or notion, *industrial relations*. In industrial relations, as in life, no person is an island. An *interactor* is defined as any individual, group or organisation involved in real-world industrial relations. The formal propositions of the theory will now be presented.

Proposition 1: Australian industrial relations comprises *n* interactors

Following on from the definition of an interactor it is possible to identify a large number of different interactors—whether they be supervisors, managers, employers, employer organisations, workers, work groups, unions, union confederations, political parties, industrial tribunals, courts, other state instrumentalities, the media, academe, medical, women's, feminist, Aboriginal, immigrant, ethnic, youth, church, religious and other groups. Moreover, it might also be necessary to include interactors who have the appearance, so to speak, of being non-Australian. To the extent that decisions made by interactors overseas have an impact on Australian industrial relations they would need to be included in our analysis—whether it be unions, head office of a multinational corporation, international money market operators, overseas competitors and customers, foreign governments and international organisations.

Proposition 2: Interactors interact in orbits of interaction

Interactions take place in what will be described as orbits of interaction.[46] A myriad of different orbits can be distinguished; their membership, composition and type is only limited by the imagination and ingenuity of interactors to find each other. Different orbits of interaction can be created by the various interactors listed in proposition 1.

Proposition 3: There is no limit on the number of interactors within a particular orbit

Given the term *interactor* the minimum size, or number, of interactors within a particular orbit must be equal to two. A particular individual, group or organisation can interact with another individual, group or organisation. It is possible to conceive—if not observe in reality—orbits with larger numbers of interactors. For example, the orbit of a large firm could contain shareholders, directors, managers, supervisors, workers, unions, suppliers, banks, customers, courts, industrial tribunals and other governmental regulatory agencies.[47] The creation of a piece of legislation will involve many interactors, ranging from political parties, government, government departments, regulatory agencies, unions, employers, consultants and so on.

Proposition 4: An interactor can inhabit more than one, or many, orbits

An interactor can inhabit more than one or many orbits; an interactor is not confined to a single unique orbit. A union, for example, can have a presence in orbits involving other unions, workplaces, enterprises, political parties, governments, courts, industrial tribunals, regulatory agencies, occupational health and safety, equal employment opportunity, training, education and so on. We can conceive of other interactors—those listed (and others) in proposition 1—being present in a wide variety of similar, and dissimilar, orbits.

Proposition 5: Orbits interact with each other

Orbits of interaction interact with each other. Orbits do not travel through the space that is Australian industrial relations in splendid isolation. They are continually bumping into and colliding with each other. The worker–employer relationship, which is seen by some to be the essential condition or requirement of industrial relations scholarship, is hemmed in by legislative decree, the decisions of courts and industrial tribunals,[48] not to mention the activities of unions and employer organisations, let alone the dictates of finance capital. To be able to understand what is happening in a particular orbit it is necessary to learn about its relationship with other orbits.

The significance of this, coupled with proposition 4, is that interactors can use their presence in particular orbits to place pressure on, or alter the behaviour of interactors in another, or other, orbits. For example a large, or multinational, corporation can threaten to close a particular part of its operation—and move finance elsewhere and/or open up a new plant—unless the workers concerned (with or without union representation) agree to reductions in income and/or changes in work practices.[49] Or, in taking this analysis away from an enterprise or corporation focus, interactors can make use of their presence in political, legislative, legal or tribunal orbits in an attempt to force other interactors to behave, or not behave, in particular ways. An employer, for example, could seek a court order to stop workers in their enterprise orbits from striking. A union can attempt to secure legislation in attempting to force employers to upgrade standards of occupational health and safety.

Proposition 6: Interactors are motivated by the desire to enhance their authority within orbits of interaction

What is the motivation of interactors? What is their reason for existence? The answer to these questions will be provided by borrowing from conflict theory and the work of Dahrendorf. He argues:[50]

> authority is a universal element of social structure . . . Authority relations exist wherever there are people whose actions are subject to legitimate and sanctioned prescriptions that originate outside them but within a social structure . . . the existence of domination and subjection is a common feature of all possible types of authority and, indeed, of all possible types of association and organisation . . . Empirically, group conflict is probably most easily accessible to analysis if it is understood as a conflict about the legitimacy of relations of authority.[51]

Following Dahrendorf interactors are motivated by the desire to be authoritative. The continuing struggle that occurs between interactors[52] is over the distribution of authority within orbits—those with authority wish to maintain, or extend, their position while those without, or possessing limited, authority wish to lift themselves up from their lowly position. Interactors want to prevail in the interactions that occur. All interactors are constrained maximisers—constrained by those with whom they interact. This struggle over authority is the engine driver of change.

Following propositions 4 and 5, interactors, in attempting to enhance their authority within a particular orbit, will move backwards and forwards across different adjacent orbits. They will activate those whom they perceive as enhancing, and avoid or seek to block access to those who are inimical to, their interests.

Proposition 7: Interactors, or those in a particular orbit, can create new interactors and hence new orbits

The world of industrial relations is replete with interactors participating in acts of creation. A decision is made to open a new business and employ staff to perform necessary tasks. This in turn results in the creation of, at least, enterprise–work-group interactors and an enterprise–work-group orbit. Workers decide to create or join a union, which transforms the nature of the orbit in which enterprise–worker negotiations have been conducted. The colonial governments of the nineteenth century created the interactor known as the Commonwealth Government and set off a chain reaction of new orbits. Governments (both State and Commonwealth) brought into being courts, industrial tribunals and other regulatory agencies, which, in turn, ushered in the creation of new orbits. Employers form employer associations, and unions form union confederations. Both participate in different bargaining, political, legal and tribunal orbits.

Proposition 8: Interactors, or those in a particular orbit, can destroy other interactors and hence create new orbits

If interactors can create they can also destroy. The history of Australian industrial relations is riddled with examples of destruction. Enterprises can be destroyed when customers and suppliers decide to take their trade (interactions) elsewhere. 'Downsizing' and making workers redundant seems to be the natural offspring of that continuing love affair between employers and efficiency. As Hyman has said, 'Employers require workers to be both dependable and disposable'.[53] Employers and others seek to bring about the destruction of unions and the creation of union-free orbits.[54] Unions and other employers seek to drive 'cut-throat' and 'unscrupulous' employers out of business. Unions seek the destruction of rival unions and/or union confederations propose programs of rationalisation, which involve the death of small unions. In the 1956 *Boilermakers'* case the High Court of Australia saw fit to destroy the Commonwealth Court of Conciliation and Arbitration.[55] The existence of industrial tribunals, and other regulatory agencies, is opposed by those who sing the praises of the market and/or favour collective or, more recently, enterprise bargaining. Any and all inter-actors are continually subjected to tests of relevance and competition from other interactors.[56]

In examining a particular orbit it is possible to conceive of what could be described as an equilibrium—a sort of suspension of time—in which a particular episode of interaction, or the struggle over author-ity, had played itself out. Such a situation would be analogous to examining the positions of different teams on a league ladder after a particular round of a sporting competition. The detritus of such an episode would be the pronouncements and documents of interactors that provide the basis for much of industrial relations scholarship. It is conceivable that all orbits could be simultaneously experiencing stasis, simultaneously suspended in time. Such a situation will be described as one of general equilibrium.

Stasis, or rest, however, is illusory in industrial relations. The strug-gle between protagonists over authority is relentless, involving both the destruction and creation of new interactors, pushing and pulling orbits into new forms and arrangements. Following chaos theory this is a model in which butterflies of different hues can flap their wings and produce storms of wondrous complexity.[57] The most famous but-terflies in Australia, of course, were the nineteenth-century middle-class intellectuals who brought about the creation of industrial tribunals.

CONCLUSION

Industrial relations is not a discipline with a tradition of developing its own theoretical insights or indulging in abstract thought. The major reason for this was linked to the interdisciplinary or multidisciplinary nature of industrial relations scholarship. Scholars have borrowed from or relied on ideas generated by other disciplines. It was argued that it was necessary for industrial relations scholars to escape from this theoretical tundra.

Differences between micro, macro and general theories, or models, of industrial relations were examined. An attempt has been made to develop a general theory of Australian industrial relations. The theory was built on the analytical construct of an orbit of interaction. An *inter-actor* was defined as any individual, group or organisation that becomes involved in industrial relations; an *orbit* is where such interactors interact. What is popularly understood as Australian industrial relations comprises the totality of these orbits. Within a particular orbit interactors constrain and are constrained by each other. Similarly, all orbits constrain and are constrained by other orbits. To understand a particular orbit it is necessary to learn about its relationship—interactions—with other orbits. To know the part it is necessary to know the whole; to know the whole it is necessary to know the parts.

The dynamic in this general theory is the authority struggle between interactors. Orbits are in a continual state of flux, or evolution, as they travel through the space and time that is Australian industrial relations. Orbits swirl around, overlap, intertwine and bump into each other, breaking up and combining in an increasing variety of new and different forms. Interactors can be destroyed and new ones created. Interactors make use of their membership in adjacent orbits to enhance their authority in a particular orbit(s). This theory will be employed to examine the major developments in Australian industrial relations in the late 1980s and early 1990s.

2

FROM CENTRALISATION
TO . . .

It is believed that a centralised approach to wage fixation is the
most equitable means by which the objectives can be met. It is recog-
nised that if a centralised system is to work effectively as the only
way in which wage increases are generated, a suppression of sec-
tional claims is essential except in special or extraordinary circum-
stances proved before the centralised wage fixing authority. This
Summit therefore proposes that the parties should as a matter of
priority develop the option of a return to a centralised system under
the auspices of the Australian Conciliation and Arbitration
Commission.

National Economic Summit Conference Documents and
Proceedings *(1983), Vol. 2* Record of Proceedings, *AGPS,*
Canberra, p. 197.

. . . corporatism in twentieth-century Britain appears to be little
more than a technique of economic management operating within
capitalism and developed during periods of national *economic dif-*
ficulty. When international *slumps have overtaken the British*
economy corporatist structures have been easily and painlessly
dropped.

Booth, A. (1982), 'Corporatism, capitalism and depression in
twentieth-century Britain', British Journal of Sociology, *June, p. 200.*

This book is concerned with providing a critical commentary on major issues and events in Australian industrial relations in the late 1980s and early 1990s. Before embarking on this task, however, it will be useful first to provide a context in which to analyse these developments.

While there is always a problem in knowing how far back one should go in searching for an appropriate reference point it might be convenient to begin the discussion with an analysis of the Accord, or agreement, negotiated between the Australian Labor Party and the Australian Council of Trade Unions in the run up to the March 1983 federal election. The Accord constituted a quasi-corporatist agreement designed to bring about economic growth and recovery consistent with industrial relations and equity considerations. The Accord maintained that a centralised system of wage determination and industrial relations regulation provided the best means for achieving such goals.

The chapter will then examine various strains on the Accord that resulted in a movement away from, or weakening of the tenets of, centralisation. This will be followed by an investigation of issues associated with the relationship between industrial relations structure and economic performance.

THE ACCORD: CONSENSUS AND ALL THAT

At the beginning of 1983 the Australian economy was experiencing stagflation with both inflation and unemployment rates in excess of ten per cent. When Coalition Prime Minister Malcolm Fraser called a snap federal election on 3 February 1983 the ALP and the ACTU negotiated an agreement, known as the Accord, which, while it did 'not pretend to be a panacea for all the current economic problems',[1] was portrayed as providing the best solution to bring about economic growth and recovery. The ALP, under its new leader, former ACTU president Bob Hawke, portrayed itself as a champion of consensus and cooperation in contrast to the confrontationist and conflict-based approach of the Fraser Government. During the election campaign Hawke pledged that, if the ALP was elected on 5 March, he would hold a national economic summit conference of governments, employers, unions and various interest groups to devise a cooperative program with which to turn the economy around.

The Accord pledged the Labor Party to a wide range of economic and social policies it would pursue if successful at the forthcoming election. The centrepiece of the Accord was its advocacy of a wages and incomes policy as offering

> by far the best prospect of enabling Australia to experience prolonged higher rates of economic and employment growth, and accompanying growth in living standards without incurring the circumscribing penalty of higher inflation, by providing the resolution of conflicting income claims at lower levels of inflation than would otherwise be the case.[2]

The Accord recommended the adoption of a centralised system of wage determination in which wage rises would be linked to changes in prices, a system known as wage indexation. In advocating a centralised system the Accord stated that 'the maintenance of real wages is agreed to be a key objective . . . over time', wage and salary earners should share in increased national productivity, and 'there should be no extra claims except where special and extraordinary circumstances exist'.[3]

A significant problem that confronted the Accord partners (other than the ALP winning the March 1983 election—which it did) was that they, or rather more correctly the Commonwealth Government, did not possess the power to implement a wages and incomes policy. The Australian Constitution has traditionally limited the ability of the Commonwealth Government to become directly involved in industrial relations and to use legislation to implement a wages and incomes policy. (Since the negotiation of this original Accord a series of High Court decisions have significantly altered the constitutional basis of Australian industrial relations.) The major industrial relations power available to the Commonwealth has been section 51, paragraph XXXV, of the Constitution, which enables it to make laws with respect to 'Conciliation and arbitration for the prevention and settlement of industrial disputes extending beyond the limits of any one state'. Section 51, paragraph XXXV, is an indirect power forcing the Commonwealth Government to delegate powers of conciliation and arbitration to industrial tribunals charged with the responsibility of preventing and settling interstate industrial disputes.

Most discussions of the Accord have been concerned with whether it represents an antipodean version of neo-corporatism. Little, if any, attention has been directed to the question of the Australian

Conciliation and Arbitration Commission endorsing the wages side of the Accord.[4] Implicit in most writings on the Accord is the view that the commission should simply act as a cipher, rubber-stamping agreements negotiated between the ALP and the ACTU. Various people who have staffed the major federal tribunal have consistently maintained and guarded their, and the tribunal's, independence from the government of the day as well as unions, employers and other interested parties. One of the members of the tribunal perceived its independence so strongly that he referred to himself and his colleagues as the 'economic dictators of Australia'.[5] An issue that needs to be considered here is the relationship between the Accord and the commission. Given the constitutional protection afforded to the commission, the implementation of the wages component of the Accord was contingent on endorsement by the commission.

Interestingly, from April 1975 to July 1981 the commission had operated a system of wage indexation that was similar in essentials to the wages and incomes policy at the heart of the Accord. Wage indexation was developed in response to the economic and industrial relations problems of the mid 1970s. In the original wage indexation decision of 30 April 1975 the commission said it would be prepared to link wage rises to movements in prices in national wage cases if, and only if, wage rises from other sources were kept to a minimum. Throughout the six-year life of wage indexation the commission was involved in a continuing struggle with unions, employers and governments to obtain a consensus to ensure its survival. On three occasions—December 1978, June 1979 and January 1981—the commission indicated that it was on the verge of abandoning indexation because of the lack of support from the parties. In the early 1980s Australia experienced a short-lived mining and resources boom. In this more buoyant economic environment increasing numbers of employers were prepared to increase wages by amounts that exceeded the commission's wage indexation guidelines. After a series of such increases, in both private and public sectors, in July 1981 the commission, given its previous warnings, brought wage indexation to an end.

In *Australian Industrial Relations in the 1980s* I argued that the commission believed that a centralised system of wage determination based on wage indexation constituted the best means to respond to Australia's various economic and industrial relations problems.[6] The commission had abandoned wage indexation in light of the inability of the parties to demonstrate that they possessed the 'collective responsibility' to make such a system work. Before the 1983 election the ALP and the ACTU, with their knowledge of industrial relations and an ability to ascertain the desires of the commission, from reading its previous decisions, calculated that the commission was prepared to rerun the wage indexation experiment of 1975–81.

The ALP and ACTU would be able to take credit for a decision the commission itself wished to put in place; for the commission, the Accord demonstrated that two major institutions possessed the responsibility to sustain a centralised wage determination system based on wage indexation. Following the Labor Party's victory in March 1983, the major function of the National Economic Summit Conference, for the commission, was for the Accord partners to deliver, or demonstrate, that business, employer groups and State Governments also possessed the responsibility to complete wage indexation's resurrection.

The National Economic Summit Conference was held on 11–14 April. With the exception of Queensland Premier Sir Joh Bjelke-Petersen, it adopted a fifty-six-point communiqué that essentially endorsed the Accord. Business and employer groups decided not to oppose the 'consensus' being developed by the new Labor Government. Prominent businessman Sir Peter Abeles, a close friend of Prime Minister Bob Hawke, pointed out that business and employer groups 'felt during the early days of this Conference as though we had been invited to play singles tennis against a championship doubles combination'.[7] Following a national wage case the commission, in September 1983, duly reinstated wage indexation and quoted extensively from both the Accord and the summit communiqué to demonstrate to itself and those with whom they interact that there now existed the collective responsibility to sustain such a system.

INITIAL STRAINS ON CENTRALISATION

In reintroducing wage indexation in the national wage case of September 1983 the Australian Conciliation and Arbitration Commission said it would only countenance granting six-monthly CPI-based increases if increases in wages or other benefits from other sources were kept to a minimum. The commission was spectacularly successful in this quest, notwithstanding a small number of unions that refused to commit themselves to the Accord and the commission's principles and employers who were prepared to grant additional entitlements to their workforces following negotiations with unions.[8] In the June 1986 national wage case the commission reported that, between September 1983 and December 1985, 96 per cent of all award wage increases resulted from its national wage case determinations.[9]

The major argument advanced in support of the Accord, and its heralding of a centralised system of wage determination, was that it provided the best prospect for economic growth and recovery. The economy would constitute a crucial, if not the ultimate, test of the Accord. As is indicated by table 2.1, during 1983–84 and 1984–85 the economy experienced growth rates in excess of five per cent and falls in both inflation and unemployment. In these years at least the performance of the Australian economy would have provided succour for supporters of the Accord.

Notwithstanding the economic growth that seemed to flow from the Accord, in the mid 1980s Australia was beset by external economic problems: deterioration in the balance of payments and the terms of trade, a depreciating currency and increases in the level of international debt. Given these international economic problems criticism was directed at wage indexation, and pressure to abandon it mounted. The Federal Government sought to secure from its Accord partner an agreement to discount the forthcoming national wage case (the September 1985 decision) for the price effects of the devaluation of the Australian dollar. The ACTU objected, claiming that such discounting would threaten the viability of the Accord. Eventually, however, in September 1985, the Accord partners negotiated a new agreement on wages, taxes and superannuation, known as the Accord Mark II, in attempting to respond to the pressures of international competition.

The Accord Mark II comprised two parts. The first was that the Federal Government would not argue for any discounting of the wage-indexation-based increases in the current case before the commission, and the ACTU would defer a claim for a productivity increase, to which it was entitled under the principles established by the commission in the September 1983 national wage case, for six months. The commission subsequently endorsed the first part of the Accord Mark II in the national wage case of November 1985. The second part of the

Table 2.1 Australian economic indicators, 1979–80 to 1992–93

Year	Price inflation (%)	Wage inflation (%)	Real wage growth (%)	Real GDP growth (%)	Employment growth (%)	Unemployment rate (%)	Change in real unit labour costs (%)
1979–80	10.1	9.9	–0.2	1.7	2.3	6.2	–0.8
1980–81	9.4	13.5	4.1	2.9	2.7	5.9	0.4
1981–82	10.4	13.7	3.3	2.1	1.2	6.1	1.9
1982–83	11.5	11.2	–0.3	–1.0	–1.7	8.9	–0.1
1983–84	7.9	8.5	0.6	5.1	0.9	9.5	–5.0
1984–85	5.8	6.9	1.1	5.2	3.0	8.5	–2.1
1985–86	8.4	5.9	–2.5	3.9	4.3	7.9	–0.9
1986–87	9.3	6.2	–3.1	2.5	2.7	8.3	–0.4
1987–88	7.3	6.0	–1.3	4.8	3.0	7.8	–3.1
1988–89	7.3	6.8	–0.5	4.1	4.1	6.6	–3.1
1989–90	8.0	6.6	–1.4	3.4	3.8	6.2	2.0
1990–91	5.3	5.9	0.6	–0.8	–0.4	8.4	2.0
1991–92	1.9	2.9	1.0	0.4	–1.6	10.4	0.6
1992–93	1.0	0.7	–0.3	2.5	0.2	11.0	0.0

Source: Department of the Treasury, *Economic Round Up*, AGPS, Canberra, various issues.

Accord Mark II was that in the 1986 national wage case the Accord partners would agree to discount the wage indexation increase for the price effects of the devaluation of the Australian dollar to a maximum of two per cent, income tax cuts would take effect from 1 September 1986, and the productivity case would be converted into a claim for extending and improving superannuation for the Australian workforce to a three per cent wage equivalent.[10]

Before proceeding further it might be useful to discuss the position of some groups on the non-labour side of politics concerning industrial relations in the context of the international economic problems of the mid 1980s. The position of the Business Council of Australia, the H. R. Nicholls Society and the federal Coalition's industrial relations policy will be briefly examined.

The Business Council of Australia was formed in 1983 when the Business Roundtable and the Australian Industries Development Association merged after the National Economic Summit Conference.

Its membership comprises about eighty of Australia's largest companies. In the years 1984–86 a series of articles appeared in its regular publication, *Business Council Bulletin*, criticising excessive government regulation and extolling the virtues of competition and markets.[11] In a presidential address to the BCA's second annual general meeting R.J. White quoted the Business Roundtable of the USA concerning the links between the health of society and the existence of strong and responsible business enterprises. In addition, he bemoaned the preoccupation of Australians

> with the comforts of suburban life, a lack of real appreciation of the linkages between business achievement and their own living standards and, most worrying of all, a relatively dismissive attitude to the outward orientation, to the internationalisation that both business and government have come to see as priorities, and which the more educated leadership of the trade union movement sees as either inevitable or in the public interest.[12]

As far as the Accord and industrial relations were concerned, the BCA advocated, in the short run, a toughening up of the centralised system to reduce the extent of increases in wages and other concessions. Rather than six-monthly indexation it advocated an annual national wage case in which wages were linked to movements in national productivity.[13] In the longer run, however, consistent with its deregulatory pro-market stance, the Business Council wanted to develop an enterprise-based industrial relations system. In its March 1985 *Bulletin* it was claimed that

> substantial individual, organisational and national benefits can result from employees at all levels becoming more closely involved in their work and decisions that affect them, and from the consequent greater interest in and commitment to their work . . . Employee participation based on the individual or group at the enterprise level . . . must form the cornerstone of any long-term strategy to utilise more fully the creative talents of, and provide greater personal involvement to, the individuals who collectively form the Australian workforce.[14]

The May–June 1985 *Bulletin* states:

> Businessmen have come to hope . . . that any major reform of the industrial relations system would restore the primacy of the relationship of manager and employee at the enterprise level, that it would be directed

at improving competitiveness, restore the balance of power and move the system more to capacity to pay and other specific needs at an industry or enterprise level. More importantly we are hoping that there will be national leadership aimed at changing attitudes, restoring the freedom of individuals, and encouraging cooperation rather than conflict[15] and the reality that manager and employee have predominately common interests.[16]

In its *Bulletin* of December 1985–January 1986 the BCA claimed that:

A strong and developing body of opinion in the business community suggests that the economy would be better served by a gradual shift towards a more decentralised wage determination process which is also *responsive* to the widely differing and fluctuating economic capacities, prospects and other specific needs of *particular* industries and enterprises. This is especially so in the current era of fluctuating exchange rates, intensified domestic and international competition and rapidly changing market opportunities and conditions . . . It is recognised, however, that such a transition, if it is to be successful, will involve a slow, step-by-step process.[17]

Finally, BCA executive director Geoff Allan attacked the coercive power of trade unions and referred to an unpublished Roy Morgan survey that apparently revealed little support for trade unions. In advocating a more enterprise-based approach he said:

The challenge for unions is to move away from an outmoded role and rhetoric of class war[18] and conflict and find a cooperative role at the enterprise level in the mutual search by manager and operator for competitive performance which means survival and prosperity and personal fulfilment at work. Management clearly sees the need to shift to smaller, more flexible, decentralised, and more autonomous units of economic activity. If unions cannot adapt to also reflect that enterprise level decentralisation, and find a means of facilitating it rather than blocking it, I believe that not only will unions risk losing their political legitimacy, but after this fine current flourish of unprecedented power, they could become an industrial anachronism.[19]

The H. R. Nicholls Society was formed in early 1986 in reaction to the quasi-corporatist Accords negotiated between the ALP and the ACTU. The society and its members have been in the vanguard of trenchant criticism of the role of industrial tribunals—its inaugural conference and subsequent publication was entitled *Arbitration in Contempt*—and advocates the use of individual contracts between employers and employees and the common law to regulate employment relationships and to punish unions or individuals who employ strike action.[20] A number of leading lights of the Coalition have been prominent in the affairs of the society and have delivered speeches at its various functions.[21] The H. R. Nicholls Society has acted as a ginger group within the Coalition for discussing ideas and policies concerned with labour market deregulation and reductions in trade union power.

On 11 May 1986 the Coalition deputy leader and shadow spokesman on employment and industrial relations, Neil Brown, released a new industrial relations policy on behalf of the Coalition. The policy encouraged the commission to pursue a flexible approach in making awards and 'to have regard to the needs and wishes of individual enterprises and their employees'.[22] The policy also encouraged the use of voluntary agreements as a means to opt out of the orbit of industrial tribunals.[23] Such voluntary agreements would commence 'with small business employing 50 or fewer employees' and 'will be extended progressively as circumstances justify'. Employers and employees could enter into such agreements subject to a proviso that they 'must provide for at least the relevant award rate of pay for ordinary weekly hours of work for the particular classification of the employee [contained in awards] . . . calculated as an hourly rate'. While unions need not be involved in the negotiation of such agreements, the policy supported the certification of industrial agreements under the auspices of the *Conciliation and Arbitration Act* 1904. To the extent that disputes arose during the life of agreements, regulations would be introduced to the act for *private* conciliation and arbitration. The Coalition wished to ensure that the commission would not 'have jurisdiction over those industrial matters that are covered by a voluntary agreement whilst [it] is current'.[24]

During the hearing of the 1986 national wage case there was a continual stream of bad news about the economy. Feelings of doom and gloom were such that Treasurer Paul Keating, on 14 May, on talkback radio expressed the fear that Australia was in danger of becoming a 'banana republic'.

Two days later a meeting of the Advisory Committee on Prices and Incomes was held in Melbourne. This body had been formed in

October 1983 comprising representatives of Commonwealth and State Governments, unions (the ACTU) and business (the Confederation of Australian Industry, BCA and the Australian Council of Professions) to proffer advice about the implementation of wages and incomes policies endorsed at the April 1983 National Economic Summit Conference. During the meeting there was discussion of Australia's international economic plight and the rigidity, or inability, of the Accord to respond to such problems.[25] Keating and the employment and industrial relations minister, Ralph Willis, were able to use this discord to obtain agreement from union and business representatives for an economic summit in two weeks to rechart the course of the Australian economy. Keating, it seems, hoped to renegotiate the Accord Mark II with respect to both the promised tax cuts and the current national wage case before the commission. The ACTU, for its part, was prepared to discuss delaying tax cuts in exchange for employers agreeing to initiate more investment.

During this period there were reports of a group of 'economic rationalist' ministers 'who had been arguing for many months that the government needed to take special steps to produce a more flexible wages system for export-oriented and import competing industries'.[26] It was also reported that 'senior ACTU officials had been privately arguing the need for a major overhaul in thinking about methods of wage fixing and union attitudes to wages in the new and harsher environment brought on, in part, by the floating of the currency'.[27]

The politics of the proposed summit, mini-summit or adjourned Advisory Committee on Prices and Incomes meeting were complicated by a clash between Keating and Prime Minister Bob Hawke (who at the time of the 16 May meeting was visiting China and Japan) concerning economic policy. Hawke quickly wrested control of the proposed summit from Keating. The summit was scheduled for 5 June but Hawke doubted whether much could be achieved until after the commission had handed down its decision in the current national wage case. While the ACTU was prepared to countenance a delay to the promised tax cuts it was not prepared to renegotiate other parts of the Accord Mark II; if nothing else it (and certainly its affiliates) did not want to prejudice its current case before the commission. For their part employer representatives said investment decisions could not be determined centrally as such decisions were made by individual firms and enterprises in response to calculations of their particular needs. To shore up ACTU support for a delay in tax cuts the Federal Government developed initiatives to encourage investment and to strengthen the role of the Prices Surveillance Authority, another institution created as a result of the 1983 summit, to monitor prices.

On 30 May Hawke announced that he would make a major statement concerning the economy. Hawke also announced on 2 June that the proposed summit would be delayed until after the national wage case—a decision welcomed by both unions and employers. Following the commission's eventual decision on 26 June it was decided that there was no need to hold a summit meeting.

In a statement accompanying his nationally televised speech on 11 June Hawke said that the Federal Government supported the current applications before the commission, with the qualification that improvements to superannuation should be 'as limited as possible in 1986'. The promised 1 September tax cuts negotiated in the Accord Mark II might be deferred to 1 December, and it might be necessary to argue for future wage discounting at the next national wage case. In a press conference Hawke indicated that such a discount could be as high as three per cent.[28] Hawke's statement was formally submitted to the commission, who in turn invited written responses from the parties. On 26 June 1986 the commission handed down its decision, which endorsed the wages and superannuation[29] components of the Accord Mark II.

Following the commission's decision there was a continuing stream of bad news about the economy. The Federal Government pressured the ACTU to renegotiate the Accord and to agree to delay hearing the next national wage case and to a further round of discounting. The ACTU, or certainly its leaders, seemed to realise that there was little chance of obtaining future wage rises from the commission, given current economic conditions, without the support of its Accord partner. In July and August there were signs that ACTU leaders doubted whether full wage indexation was achievable.[30]

At Robe River in the Pilbara mining area of Western Australia a butterfly flapped its wings and produced a mighty storm that engulfed Australian industrial relations. During August and September a new management team at Peko Wallsend became involved in a major industrial dispute with its workforce and their unions over 284 restrictive work practices and a reassertion of managerial prerogatives.[31] The Robe River dispute, as well as earlier disputes at Dollar Sweets, Mudginberri and the South East Queensland Electricity Board involving the Bjelke-Petersen Government, were associated with an attempt by the New Right to take on and destroy trade unions and escape the regulatory net of industrial tribunals. In this period the media discovered the H. R. Nicholls Society (see above) and gave much publicity to its goals and objectives.

In early September it appears that the Federal Government was under pressure from within its own ranks, and the ACTU, to concede that there was a need for greater labour market flexibility, which would involve a rejigging of the Accord. The ACTU was prepared to countenance greater flexibility in wages and conditions on an industry-by-industry basis as had been achieved in industry plans[32] developed in the steel and heavy engineering industries.[33] For their part, employers wanted changes to work practices to enhance efficiency.

On 5 September 1986 the Economic Planning Advisory Council, a body comprising government, union, business and other groups, which was formed to continue the processes of consultation established at the 1983 summit,[34] met in Canberra. At that meeting BCA representatives Bryan Kelman (of CSR) and Alan Coates (of AMP) circulated a paper on restrictive work practices. The paper argued that the removal of such practices would enhance the efficiency of Australian industry and reduce problems associated with competing on international markets.[35] The Federal Government agreed to help business and unions to examine outmoded work and management practices. A work practices summit of representatives of the ACTU, CAI and BCA was scheduled for 24 September.

Prime Minister Hawke opened the summit by stressing the 'need to look carefully now at the way in which work is organised and managed so as to remove barriers to making the best use of our resources'. Hawke saw the function of the summit as providing leadership and direction on how to resolve management and work practices that vary across industries, enterprises and plants. He hoped the meeting would give 'greater emphasis' to enhancing the efficiency of Australian industry in order to 'meet the remorseless challenge of an increasingly competitive international environment'.[36] After delivering the speech Hawke left the meeting, which was chaired by Ralph Willis.

The participants in the summit produced an agreed statement that acknowledged the need to pursue a cooperative approach in removing restrictive work and management practices in order to enhance productivity and efficiency. The statement specified that

> discussions on work practices do not involve consideration of broad award conditions having general application, such as rates of pay, standard hours of work, leave loading and so on, even though specific areas that may require attention may have their basis in an award provision.

Areas identified that could enhance productivity were education and training to improve the skills of management and the workforce, removal of demarcation barriers, introduction of new technology concomitant with 'appropriate consultation and information sharing', dispute resolution procedures and employee participation. The statement said that: 'The parties are strongly of the view that the resolution of these issues is most effectively carried out at the plant and enterprise level'.[37]

Following the work practices summit Hawke signalled the end of wage indexation, which had underpinned the original Accord, and flagged the introduction of a two-tiered system of wage determination and industrial relations regulation. The first tier would comprise an across-the-board wage increase, and the second tier would be based on a new principle designed to change work practices and organisations so as to enhance efficiency and productivity. At the next national wage case all of the parties agreed that wage indexation was no longer sustainable and argued for the establishment of a two-tiered system. There were differences, however, between the parties concerning how such a system should operate. The commission formally brought wage indexation to an end on 23 December 1986 and deferred any decision concerning the two-tiered system until the parties had had a chance to confer.

In March 1987 the commission announced its two-tiered decision, which was described as the Accord Mark III. The first tier comprised traditional national wage cases, which would operate in two parts. The first part comprised a $10 per week increase and the second a hearing to start in October 1987, which 'shall not exceed the equivalent of a 1.5 per cent increase in wages and salaries'. The second tier comprised increases, up to a maximum of four per cent, determined on a decentralised industry-by-industry, or award-by-award, basis. Grounds for such increases would be based on work value streamlining, the removal of anomalies and inequities (two principles included in the commission's September 1983 national wage case) and a new restructuring and efficiency principle. The commission stated that 'it is primarily at the enterprise level that the objectives of this principle will be achieved'.[38]

INDUSTRIAL RELATIONS STRUCTURE AND ECONOMIC PERFORMANCE

The movement of Australian industrial relations away from centralisation and the embracing of the two-tiered system, which occurred in 1986 and 1987, raises consideration of the relationship between the structure of an industrial relations system and economic performance. Both the Accord Mark I (and before it wage indexation circa 1975–81) and the two-tiered system (and enterprise bargaining—see below) were championed on the basis of claims about their ability to bring about economic recovery, notwithstanding their different positions along a spectrum of centralisation and decentralisation. This interest in the relative effectiveness of centralised and decentralised systems of industrial relations and economic performance has its intellectual antecedents in claims made about the ability of wages and incomes policies and/or neo-corporatist societies to be able to resolve the macroeconomic problem of reducing levels of inflation without the harmful side effect of exacerbating unemployment. For example, economists who examined the operation of the Accord to the end of the 1980s have claimed it has been beneficial in helping to contain wages and enhancing employment growth.[39]

In 1989 Calmfors and Driffill published a seminal paper that, after examining seventeen Organisation for Economic Cooperation and Development member countries, concluded that both centralised and decentralised industrial relations systems were associated with superior macroeconomic performances—the so-called hump-shaped hypothesis. They maintained that economies with industrial relations structures somewhere between centralised or decentralised, or in transition from one to the other, performed relatively poorly. Their paper served to deflate corporatists.

Calmfors and Driffill defined centralisation '*as the extent of inter-union and inter-employer co-operation in wage bargaining with the other side*. The focus is . . . on the extent to which coalitions are formed among unions and employers respectively'.[40] There are two dimensions of Calmfors and Driffill's definition of centralisation: the first being the level at which bargaining occurs and, second, the degree of cooperation. What is meant by the term *cooperation*?

For economists all exchanges involve the cooperation of those concerned, otherwise they would not have entered into such exchanges. Individuals purchase goods and services or offer themselves on the labour market because it is in their own interest to do so. Industrial relations scholars tend to have a less benign view of cooperation. What passes for cooperation might involve nothing more than the coercion of those with authority over those lacking such authority. Co-operation is purchased because those lacking authority see themselves as having little choice but to agree to the terms offered by those with whom fate has determined they interact. For example, American scholars Chamberlain and Kuhn have developed the term *conjunctive bargaining* to describe this colder, more hard-edged view of the world. They state:

> Conjunctive bargaining . . . does not arise because of one party's sympathetic regard for the other or because of its voluntary choice of the other as partner; it arises from the absolute requirement that some agreement—*any* agreement—be reached so that the operations on which both are dependent may continue . . . Coercion is the principal ingredient of conjunctive bargaining power. The resolution of divergent interests through conjunctive bargaining provides a basis for the operation of the enterprise—and nothing more. With whatever coercive powers are at its disposal each party has wrested the maximum advantage possible, without much regard for the effect of this on the other. The bargaining relationship comes into being because it is inescapable, and neither party grants more than is necessary.[41]

Or, in taking this notion out of the constraints of the enterprise, employer and business groups 'cooperated' with wage indexation from 1975 to 1981 and the Accords Mark I and II because, in the circumstances of those respective periods, they felt that they had little choice.

Calmfors and Driffill maintained that in decentralised firm-based systems unions had little power and would be unable to push up wages 'artificially' . To the extent that unions might have experienced some short-run success in pushing up wages resultant increases in the unemployment of members would serve to discipline future claims. By dismissing union power at this decentralised level Calmfors and Driffill obviate the need to apply their notion of cooperation or to consider any differences between different decentralised systems. While they acknowledge that concentrations of power in the product market enhance the power of firm-specific unions they essentially see unions in decentralised systems as being epiphenomenal.[42]

In centralised systems Calmfors and Driffill argue that unions will behave responsibly. Because of the importance, or encompassing nature, of the responsibilities they have assumed they are sensitive and atuned to the economy-wide effects of their actions. Calmfors and Driffill maintain that in centralised systems unions realise that if they push too hard for wages or other benefits there will be an opportunity cost in terms of increases in prices, unemployment and so on. It is conceivable, however, that responsible people can make mistakes. It could be suggested that the adoption of the two-tiered system constituted a tacit recognition by the Accord partners that it had erred in basing its model of cooperation on the indexation of wages. It is at the centralised, economy-wide level that Calmfors and Driffill apply their notion of cooperation in seeking to measure degrees of decentralisation in different industrial relations systems.

At the intermediate level, where wages are determined on industry, occupational or craft lines, Calmfors and Driffill claim that unions and employers are indifferent about the impact of the decisions they make concerning wages (and other employment conditions) on levels of employment and/or the economy more generally. For reasons that are not clear Calmfors and Driffill do not apply their notion of cooperation to an analysis of the coalition-building that occurs in sustaining such industry, occupational or craft determinations. While acknowledging the iron fist of coercion that might reside in the velvet glove of cooperation it is conceivable that more cooperation, over a wider and deeper range of issues, could occur at the sectoral, rather than the national or centralised, level. Moreover, it is conceivable that wage setters in Calmfors and Driffill's intermediate world could make conservative or low decisions, providing scope for those at the firm or enterprise level to make decisions that respond to factors—such as not increasing levels of unemployment—relevant to their respective, and different, needs. Australia, for example, has traditionally operated such a system in which overaward pay has supplemented the decisions of industrial tribunals.

At this stage, then, two criticisms can be offered of Calmfors and Driffill's analysis. First, the notions of cooperation and coalition formation contained in their definition of centralisation are inconsistently applied. They have only applied such notions at the national level. At the decentralised enterprise level cooperation was a theoretical irrelevance and was ignored in their examination of intermediate systems. Second, depending on the wage norm adopted in industrial, occupational or craft-based systems, it is conceivable that intermediate systems might not have the adverse consequences suggested by them.

Skosice has criticised Calmfors and Driffill over the independent variable—centralisation—they employed in their analysis. He also criticises their preoccupation with unions in examining wages and incomes policies and centralisation while they ignore the coordination functions of employer organisations. Skosice argues that the level of economy-wide coordination has greater utility in explaining economic performance than the degree of centralisation. He claims that Calmfors and Driffill's '"centralised" wage-setting case is simply the case where wage setting is coordinated across the economy. Their theory therefore implies nothing about *where wages are technically set*, only that wherever they are set the process is coordinated'.[43] Skosice also argues that it is unnecessary to worry about levels of coordination among the ranks of both unions and employers in trying to determine measures of centralisation as 'coordination . . . takes place through the stronger party . . . the degree of coordination is taken to be the degree of co-ordination of the stronger party'.[44] In Skosice's hands coordination involves the exercise of power and sidesteps the problems identified with cooperation contained in Calmfors and Driffill's definition of centralisation. By replacing centralisation with coordination Skosice reclassifies several countries—particularly Japan and Switzerland, and to a lesser extent West Germany and the Netherlands[45]—in attempting to demolish the hump-shaped hypothesis and resurrect the case for neo-corporatism as a tool of economic management.

Skosice's notion of coordination is a more powerful and robust theoretical construct than Calmfors and Driffill's notion of centralisation.

As Skosice maintains, a system that has elements of decentralisation can none the less be coordinated. For example, although the two-tiered system combined centralisation and decentralisation, the Australian Conciliation and Arbitration Commission's March 1987 decision provided both a vehicle for coordinating the split between the two tiers and contained rules that governed decision-making in the decentralised second tier. The managed decentralism that occurred under the structural efficiency principle (see chapter 3 below) is also consistent with Skosice's notion of coordination. In addition, Skosice's observation that 'coordination takes place through the stronger party' enables incorporation of that uniquely antipodean institution, industrial tribunals, into analysis of the Australian case. Coordination in Australia can occur through the commission notwithstanding, conceivably, the wishes of the parties, individually or collectively.

Examinations of the relationship between industrial relations structure, whether described as neo-corporatist, centralised or coordinated, and economic performance have been conducted on the basis that structure is the independent variable. Industrial relations structure is portrayed as being independent of the phenomenon—economic performance—it is trying to explain. Moreover Crouch (whose analysis is based on centralisation) has said that 'institutional variables [structures] are relatively static, slow-changing factors that should be expected to affect behaviour over a fairly long term'.[46] He has also said 'independent variables change only slowly'.[47] Tarantelli, who has linked economic performance to degrees of neo-corporatism, has said:

> The degree of neo-corporatism [independent variable] is assumed as structurally constant through time, or as a 'structured' average of the estimated value in the period of observation in each country. This is clearly a rough approximation . . . More research attention on short-run changes in the degree of neo-corporatism [independent variable] is needed.[48]

Booth, in one of the quotations that heads this chapter, suggests that industrial relations structure is not independent of economic performance; in fact, that economic performance produces changes in structure. It will be argued that the Australian experience is consistent with Booth's analysis of the British case.[49] Moreover, the history of Australian industrial relations fundamentally undermines two assumptions that underpin discussions of the relationship between structure and economic performance. Industrial relations structure is *not* static, and its behaviour is not independent of economic performance.

Since 1960 Australia has experienced six different phases of co-ordination. The first was in the period between 1960–61 and 1966–67 when Australia operated a wage determination system that made use of basic wage and margins cases. The basic wage was a vehicle of co-ordination whereby the Commonwealth Conciliation and Arbitration Commission awarded wage rises to all workers covered by federal awards and margins, or additional wages, were determined for work-ers in particular awards to take account of relevant circumstances to the workers or sectors concerned (although they often constituted rubber-stamping exercises by the commission of deals negotiated by the parties). During these years the commission awarded relatively con-servative basic wage case increases, and overaward pay—wage rises, in addition to margins cases, directly negotiated by the parties on a decen-tralised basis—become increasingly significant.[50] These years could be described as one of partial or intermediate (fifty per cent) coordination.

The next period was ushered in by the events of the *Metal Trades Work Value* cases of 1967 and 1968 in which unions and employers, in a response to a favourable economic environment, increasingly nego-tiated improvements to wages and working conditions. While the com-mission adjudicated national (rather than basic) wage and margins increases, the period between 1967–68 and 1974–75 was one in which it played a passive or minor role (see preface). Industrial relations and wage determination were regarded as being dominated by market, rather than institutional, forces. The period was one of limited (twenty per cent) coordination.

In April 1975 the Australian Conciliation and Arbitration Commis-sion introduced wage indexation in attempting to overcome the eco-nomic problems of the mid 1970s: substantial increases in the level of inflation and increasing unemployment. Other than for its national wage case wage indexation decisions, the commission sought to ensure that wage rises from other sources were kept to a minimum. The period between 1975–76 and 1980–81 was one of strong (one hundred per cent) coordination.

With the demise of wage indexation in July 1981 Australia entered into its fourth phase of coordination. The mining and resources boom of the early 1980s enabled different combinations of unions and employers to break away from the shackles of the commission's system of wage indexation. Between July 1981 and late 1982 the commission played a minor role in Australian industrial relations, and changes in wages and working conditions resulted from the interactions of the parties concerned. This fourth period can be described as one of zero, or no, coordination.

Australia entered into a second phase of strong, or comprehensive, coordination that began with the introduction of a wages freeze in December 1982 and continued through various versions of the Accord until 1991. The wages freeze was introduced on the basis of its ability to enhance economic recovery,[52] as were the different versions of the Accord. The commission was afforded a prominent role in coordinating the industrial relations system and wage determination.

In 1991 Australia moved to a system of industrial relations regulation called enterprise bargaining, which substantially downgraded the role of the Australian Industrial Relations Commission (see below). At the risk of being accused of repetition this new industrial relations structure was created in response to the poor performance of the economy. Since 1991 Australia has operated a mildly (ten per cent) coordinated industrial relations system.

Table 2.2 presents information on levels of coordination and economic performance in Australia between 1960–61 and 1992–93, with the qualification that the fourth period finished at the end, rather than the middle, of 1982. Reductions in the level of unemployment can be 'purchased' either by adding to inflation or by exacerbating external balance. The Okun, or 'misery' index, adds unemployment and inflation levels, while the Alternative index adds the unemployment rate to the current account deficit as a percentage of gross domestic product. They provide two different measures of economic performance.

The table provides a stark depiction of the deterioration in the Australian economy since 1960. Australia's most successful economic period was 1960–61 to 1966–67, which was associated with a regime of partial, or intermediate, coordination. Australia's economic success in these years, however, would hardly be linked to the structure of its industrial relations system. Rather, it would be explained in terms of the successful application of Keynesian economics during the 1950s and 1960s. Since 1966–67 there has been a deterioration in both the Okun and Alternative indices with the former improving somewhat since 1982–83 and the latter worsening after 1980–81. The table might provide support for a pendulum hypothesis whereby economic performance produces the adoption of a new variant of co-ordination. Crises, it seems, demand a change in industrial relations structure.

Two major lessons can be drawn from this analysis. First, and in contradiction to Crouch, industrial relations structure is not static. For Australia, at least, incorrect or inappropriate values have been made concerning discussions surrounding structure.[53] More generally, it appears that within this literature structure is something that has been glossed over rather than following Tarantelli's call for more rigorous investigation. The second, and more serious, problem is the non-independence of the 'independent' variable. Changes in economic performance, at least in the Australian case—and Booth has argued similarly for Britain—have resulted in or 'produced' changes in industrial relations structure.[54] If this analysis is correct we are still left with the problem of seeking to arrive at an understanding of the determinants of economic performance. Could the answer lie with fiscal, monetary and external (exchange rate) policies, issues traditionally of concern to economists?

Table 2.2 Levels of coordination and economic performance in Australia 1960–61 to 1992–93

Time period	Level of coordination		Okun index	Alternative index
1960–61 – 1966–67	Partial	(50%)	4.3	4.8
1967–68 – 1974–75	Limited	(20%)	8.9	3.9
1975–76 – 1980–81	Strong	(100%)	16.3	8.6
1981–82 – 1982–83	None	(0%)	18.5	12.5
1983–84 – 1990–91	Strong	(100%)	15.3	12.8
1991–92 – 1992–93	Mild	(10%)	12.3	14.2

Source: Norton, W. E. and Kennedy, P. J. (1985), *Australian Economic Statistics 1949–50 to 1984–85: I Tables*, Reserve Bank of Australia, Occasional Paper No. 8A, November; and Department of the Treasury, *Economic Round Up*, AGPS, Canberra (various issues).

CONCLUSION

In early 1983 the ALP and the ACTU negotiated the Accord (Mark I), which enshrined the use of a wages and incomes policy based on a system of wage indexation as providing the best means to enable Australia to overcome the problems of a stagflationary economy. Given the constitutional protection afforded to the Australian Conciliation and Arbitration Commission, implementation of the wages component of the Accord depended on endorsement by the commission. It was argued that the commission believed that wage indexation provided the best prospects to enable Australia to overcome the economic and industrial relations problems of the early 1980s. The Accord partners were able to gain political kudos for a policy that the commission wanted, and had the power, to implement.

Despite the economic growth that occurred in the years immediately after the Accord, the Australian economy experienced a number of external problems with deterioration in the balance of payments and the terms of trade, a decline in the value of the Australian dollar and increased international debt. As a result pressure was mounted to abandon the assumption of wage indexation that underpinned the Accord. In late 1985 the Federal Government and the ACTU negotiated the Accord Mark II. The ACTU was prepared to discount wage-indexation-based increases for price effects associated with the devaluation of the Australian dollar in the 1986 national wage case, in exchange for reductions in taxation and improvements to superannuation.

During the hearing of the 1986 national wage case the continued deterioration of the economy was dramatically encapsulated in Keating's statement of 14 May that Australia was in danger of becoming a 'banana republic'. The Accord came under pressure again, and there were calls for a more flexible and decentralised mode of industrial relations regulation. This chapter has examined various manoeuvrings between the Accord partners, the policy stances of the BCA, the H. R. Nicholls Society and the federal Coalition parties. In addition, the chapter examined the aborted Advisory Committee on Prices and Incomes summit, the work practices summit of September 1986 and the adoption of the two-tiered system of industrial relations regulation and wage determination (the Accord Mark III).

The chapter also considered the issue of the relationship between industrial relations structure and economic performance, focusing on Calmfors and Driffill's notion of centralisation and Skosice's notion of coordination. Coordination was seen as being a more powerful analytical construct than centralisation. Six different phases of coordination were distinguished for Australia since 1960. It was argued that the major problem with this literature was that structure was not static and, in the Australian case at least, was heavily dependent on economic performance, the behaviour of which it was purported to explain and predict.

Clipping the wings of the commission

We have noted how the Court has been attacked on two flanks: by the High Court's refusal to grant it the full status of a superior Court of Record and its erection of other legal obstacles. The Court has been made dependent upon the goodwill of the Parliament, its critic on the other flank . . . The general observation is that the High Court has driven the Arbitration Court into the hands of a critical Parliament which has been subject to political pressures and has reflected these influences in its dealings with the arbitration tribunal.

Perlman, M. (1954), Judges in Industry: A Study of Labour
Arbitration in Australia, *Melbourne University Press, p. 33.*

It [the April 1991 National Wage Case] is a sickening decision, but there is no reason for the trade union movement to eat the vomit.

Bill Kelty, *quoted in* Australian, *2 May 1991*

For more than two decades Australia has been beset by a series of economic problems: inflation, unemployment, low rates of productivity and economic growth, a widening in the distribution of income, declining terms of trade, deterioration in the balance of payments, a depreciating currency and increases in international indebtedness.

Associated with Australia's international economic problems of the mid 1980s there was a revival of what has been called economic rationalism, policies that were ostensibly opposed to direct government intervention and stressed the importance of markets, competition, microeconomic reform and deregulation.[1] Chapter 2 documented the turning away from the wage indexation and centralisation assumptions that had underpinned the original Accord in the period 1985–87. As the chapter revealed, the Australian Conciliation and Arbitration Commission was afforded a prominent role in the transformation that occurred in those years.

In the late 1980s and continuing into the 1990s the commission,[2] however, has been perceived as part of the problem rather than the solution to helping bring about economic growth and recovery—and this ignores critiques by the New Right and the conservative side of politics! Whereas the Accords Marks I, II and III afforded a prominent role for the commission, the Accord partners, and in particular the Australian Council of Trade Unions, mounted a series of attacks and critiques and found a means to downgrade the commission's role.

This chapter will examine the dimensions of the clash between the Accord partners and the commission. The first part of the chapter contains an account of High Court decisions that have substantially eroded, if not removed, the traditional constitutional protection hitherto afforded to the commission. The second and major part of the chapter will document the tensions between the Accord partners and the commission, culminating in legislation of July 1992 that served to downgrade the commission's role in wage determination and industrial relations regulation. This clipping of the wings of the commission[3] has been associated, or overlapped, with a move of Australian industrial relations towards enterprise bargaining. This chapter will refer to enterprise bargaining, but it will be examined in greater detail in chapter 4.

THE CONSTITUTION AND THE HIGH COURT

In chapter 2 it was argued that the Australian Constitution has traditionally limited the ability of the Commonwealth Government to become directly involved in industrial relations. The industrial relations power is described in section 51, paragraph XXXV:

> The Parliament shall, subject to this Constitution, have power to make laws for the peace, order and good government of the Commonwealth with respect to . . . Conciliation and Arbitration for the prevention and settlement of industrial disputes extending beyond the limits of any one state.

Because the industrial relations power is an indirect power the Commonwealth Government has to delegate powers of conciliation and arbitration to industrial tribunals. While the Commonwealth has been able to call on the use of other powers—such as trade and commerce (section 51, paragraph I), defence (section 51, paragraph VI), referral from the states (section 51, paragraph XXXVII)—it has been forced by the Constitution to work through industrial tribunals to give effect to its industrial relations objectives.

On a number of occasions the government of the day has found itself embroiled in conflict with the major federal tribunal concerning its various decisions. The most celebrated example is the acerbic exchanges that occurred between Henry Bournes Higgins and Prime Minister William Morris Hughes in the years immediately before and after the conclusion of World War I.[4] Australia was undoubtedly the only country in the world whose national government lacked a direct industrial relations power concerning the operation of the private sector.

A series of High Court decisions concerning the corporations, external affairs and taxation powers of the Commonwealth have fundamentally challenged this traditional view of the constitutional basis of Australian industrial relations and enabled the Commonwealth to assume direct industrial relations powers. The Commonwealth is not only empowered to downgrade and erode the power of the commission but also, via section 109 of the Constitution—'Where a law of a State is inconsistent with a law of the Commonwealth, the latter shall prevail, and the former shall, to the extent of the inconsistency, be invalid'—can override or reduce the legislative powers of the states, thereby enabling the erection of a national system of industrial relations regulation.

Under the corporations power (section 51, paragraph XX) the Commonwealth can make laws with respect to 'Foreign corporations, and trading or financial corporations found within the limits of the Commonwealth'. In the *Huddart Parker* case of 1909 the High Court found that the *Australian Industries Protection Act* 1906 was invalidly based on the corporations power.[5] This decision was mainly based on the doctrine of reserved powers (the need to protect states' rights). Chief Justice Griffith clearly indicated that, if it wasn't for this doctrine,

> The Commonwealth Parliament [could] make any laws it thinks fit with regard to the operation of the corporation, for example, may prescribe what officers and servants it shall employ, what shall be the hours and conditions of labour, what remuneration shall be paid to them, and may thus, in the case of such corporations, exercise complete control of the domestic trade carried on by them.[6]

The doctrine of reserved powers was overturned in the *Engineers'* case of 1920.[7] The corporations power, however, was not tested again until the *Concrete Pipes* case of 1971.[8] On that occasion the High Court ruled that parts of the *Trade Practices Act* 1965 were validly based on the corporations power. *Concrete Pipes* opened up the prospect that the corporations power could expand the scope of the Commonwealth's jurisdiction. Such a proposition has received support from a string of High Court decisions.[9] The major consensus that seems to have emerged from commentators, particularly given the High Court's more expansive or literal interpretation of powers available to the Commonwealth,[10] is that legislation dealing with the operation of any aspect of section 51, paragraph XX corporations would survive constitutional challenges.[11] However, it should be noted that only those corporations that fall within the purview of section 51, paragraph XX are tautologically subject to its reach. In other words, most small businesses would be outside the scope of Commonwealth legislation based on the corporations power.

Section 51, paragraph XXIX of the Constitution empowers the Commonwealth to enact laws with respect to external affairs. The major issue for the High Court in interpreting this power is whether it should be confined to what Australia does 'externally'—such as the setting up of overseas embassies or participation in international forums—or have application, via the ratification of international treaties, to Australia's 'internal' affairs. In the *Burgess* case of 1936, which examined sections of the *Air Navigation Act* 1920, Justices Evatt and McTiernan, in a minority judgement, adopted a broad interpretation of the external affairs power.[12] They maintained, for example, that if Australia was a signatory to an international agreement, the Commonwealth could properly legislate for the 'regulation of labour conditions'.[13] Evatt and McTiernan said:

> It would seem clear, therefore, that the legislative power of the Commonwealth over 'external affairs' certainly includes the power to execute within the Commonwealth treaties and conventions entered into with foreign powers . . . But it is not to be assumed that the legislative power over 'external affairs' is limited to the execution of treaties or conventions . . . the Parliament may well be deemed competent to legislate for the carrying out of 'recommendations' as well as the 'draft international conventions' resolved upon by the International Labour Organisation or of other international recommendations or requests upon other subject matters of concern to Australia as a member of the family of nations. This power is a great and important one.[14]

In the *Koowarta* case of 1982 the High Court adjudicated on an action against the refusal of the Queensland Government to enable a group of Aborigines to acquire land.[15] The High Court was required to determine whether the *Racial Discrimination Act* (1975), which sought to give effect to the Charter of the United Nations Universal Declaration of Human Rights and the Declaration to Eliminate All Forms of Racial Discrimination, was properly based on the external affairs power. A majority of the High Court (4–3) upheld the legislation. In the *Tasmanian Dam* case a majority of the High Court (4–3) found that legislation based on the United Nations Convention for the Protection of the World Cultural and National Heritage was a proper application of the external affairs power.[16] In so doing, the High Court (or rather a majority) had adopted the minority position of Evatt and McTiernan in *Burgess*. This expansive interpretation of the external affairs power has been confirmed in the *Richardson* case of 1988, the 1989 *Queensland* case (both environmental matters) and the 1991 *Polykhovich* case (to do with war crimes).[17]

The members of the High Court who have been in the minority have sought to resurrect the doctrine of reserved powers in expressing opposition to the external affairs power. They have been fearful that section 51, paragraph XXIX, has the potential to upset the federal balance and substantially erode legislative powers available to the States. In the *Tasmanian Dam* case Chief Justice Gibbs pointed out that the 'external affairs power differs from the other powers conferred by S.51 in its capacity for almost unlimited expansion'.[18] In *Richardson* Mr Justice Dawson observed that the external affairs power 'has the potential to obliterate the division of legislative power otherwise effected by S.51'.[19] In *Koowarta* Chief Justice Gibbs lamented:

> if S.51(XXIX) empowers the Parliament to legislate to give effect to every international agreement which the executive may choose to make, the Commonwealth would be able to acquire unlimited legislative power. The distribution of powers made by the Constitution could in time be completely obliterated; there would be no field of power which the Commonwealth could not invade, and the federal balance achieved by the Constitution could be entirely destroyed.[20]

The majority have rejected this line of reasoning drawing attention to the *Engineers'* case.[21] Moreover, Mr Justice Mason (the current Chief Justice of the High Court) said in *Koowarta*:

> The consequence of the expansion in external affairs is that in some instances the Commonwealth now legislates on matters not formerly within the scope of its specific powers, to the detriment of the exercise of State powers. But in the light of current experience there is little, if anything, to indicate that there is a likelihood of a substantial disturbance to the balance of powers as distributed by the Constitution. To the extent that there is such a disturbance, then it is a necessary disturbance, one essential to Australia's participation in world affairs.[22]

The taxation power (section 51, paragraph II) empowers the Commonwealth to enact laws concerning 'Taxation, but so as not to discriminate between States or parts of States'. This power enables the Commonwealth to impose taxes on employers or individuals to fulfil desired objectives, such as contributing to superannuation funds (under the *Superannuation Guarantee Act* 1992 and the *Superannuation Guarantee (Administration) Act* 1992) or impose levies on firms that do not meet minimum required levels of expenditure on training (under the

Training Guarantee Act 1990 and the *Training Guarantee (Administration) Act* 1990). In the *Northern Suburbs General Cemetery Reserves Trust* case 1992 the High Court ruled that legislation concerning the payment of a training levy was properly based on the taxation power.[23]

The corporations power increases the ability of the Commonwealth to enact laws with respect to the internal affairs and industrial relations activities of 'foreign' and 'trading or financial' corporations. Its major weakness, however, is its inability to cover the field—most small businesses would be beyond its reach. Stewart is of the opinion that the taxation power could be used by the Commonwealth to pursue industrial relations objectives. He has argued that:

> the Commonwealth could legislate to require employers (or indeed workers or unions) to observe a wide range or duties, on pain of paying additional tax. Indeed with a little ingenuity any form of industrial regulation could be implemented by the Commonwealth in this manner, with the only apparent drawback being the cost of establishing the administrative machinery necessary to monitor compliance and collect the tax or levy from recalcitrants.[24]

The external affairs power also has potential to increase the reach of the Commonwealth's industrial relations powers substantially. Via the ratification of United Nations conventions on human rights and discrimination and International Labour Organisation conventions the Commonwealth is now able to legislate directly on a wide range of industrial relations issues.[25] In so doing the Commonwealth may decide to operate in tandem with industrial tribunals. On the other hand, if the commission is perceived as being a hindrance or a problem, the Commonwealth could compel it to behave in a certain way or bypass it altogether. The important point to note is that since the mid 1980s the High Court has provided the Commonwealth with the ability to become directly involved in industrial relations and the means, if it so desires, to downgrade the role of the commission.

THE ACCORD AND THE COMMISSION

The ALP has been in power at the Commonwealth level since March 1983. The various Accords it has negotiated with the ACTU have been an important component of Labor's management of the economy. In conjunction with other arms of economic policy successive Labor governments have used their relationship with the ACTU to negotiate deals concerning wages, the labour market and industrial relations regulation in responding to the various problems of the Australian economy.

In the relationship between the Accord partners the Federal Government has pressured the ACTU, and in turn its affiliates, to modify demands concerning wages and other benefits, and to pursue a more flexible and decentralised system of industrial relations regulation. In doing so the government has entered into trade-offs with its Accord partner concerning wages, taxes, superannuation, family assistance, incentives to encourage investment, price monitoring and schemes to reduce unemployment. The government has employed these trade-offs in two ways. First, it has impressed on the ACTU that the commission is more likely to agree to the proposals of a jointly argued case than one in which the ACTU appears alone. Second, it has made tax cuts and other social wage concessions conditional on low or satisfactory changes in the global movement of wages.

It could be reasonable to summarise the government's strategy as being based on promise, promise, delay, delay. In developing policies to restructure and increase the international competitiveness of the Australian economy the ALP has sought to portray itself as caring and generous. Successive reworkings of the Accord have been heralded as demonstrating to the electorate and its traditional constituency how much better off they would be under Labor compared to the alternative policies of the federal Coalition. The various Accords have signalled wage increases, reductions in taxation and other social wage benefits that could be available in the future if only a Labor Government was returned to office. Having portrayed itself in this positive light the Federal Government sought to drag out the implementation process. The mounting of a national wage case has been delayed because of the need to wait for another round of economic indicators, or demands have been adjusted downwards in the light of continuing bad economic news.[26] In terms of what might be called the 'big picture' the evidence suggests that, while the ACTU (or, more correctly, shifting orbits of aggrieved affiliates) might have been able to negotiate concessions or delays, the government has tended to be the dominant partner in the Accord relationship.

The various industrial relations policies developed by the federal Coalition are integral to an understanding of the dynamics of the Accord.[27] The Coalition's more deregulatory policies, with their downgrading of the role of industrial tribunals and awards, have been portrayed by the Accord partners (and others) as an attack on unions and the wages and working conditions of workers. Fear of the Coalition and New Right policies have been used as a vehicle to maintain adherence to the Accord. While the Accord might not enable affiliates of the ACTU to gain as much as they hoped or expected, it has been argued that life would be so much worse under the Coalition. The strident deregulatory and anti-union policies of the Coalition have aided the Labor Government.

Once a new variation of the Accord has been stitched up the Accord partners have expected that it would be endorsed by the commission.[28] The commission, however, has displayed a predilection for independence. On a number of occasions it has handed down decisions that have upset the Accord partners. This in turn has produced increasingly virulent and intense criticisms and attacks from the Accord partners.

The two-tiered system ushered in by the Australian Conciliation and Arbitration Commission in the national wage case of March 1987 combined centralisation and decentralisation. The March 1987 decision awarded an across-the-board increase of $10 per week and signalled the hearing of a national wage case beginning in October 1987, which would not exceed a 1.5 per cent increase in wages and salaries. The second tier provided wage increases, up to a maximum of four per cent, on a decentralised basis for reforming work practices and the organisation of work under the auspices of the new restructuring and efficiency principle.

The processing of second-tier increases was relatively slow. It was estimated that by mid October 1987 11.4 per cent of wage and salary earners had received such increases.[29] By the end of May 1988 this figure had increased to fifty per cent.[30]

On a number of occasions unions complained about problems they experienced in processing second-tier increases. Their major criticism was that employers, in both the private and public sectors, insisted on offsets, or 'give-backs', to 'pay' for the four per cent available under the restructuring and efficiency principle. Those unions that had negotiated efficiency changes in the past, or whose members were employed in activities in which it was difficult to quantify efficiency and productivity, were faced with the dilemma of either not proceeding with a wage claim under the second tier or agreeing to reductions in or the removal of established working conditions. Rather than helping to enhance productivity and efficiency in a positive manner the second tier, for unions, appeared to be nothing more than an exercise in negative cost-cutting.

In addition, criticisms were directed at the failure or slowness of tribunal members in arbitrating second-tier increases in instances in which employers refused to negotiate[31] and inconsistencies in the decisions of federal and State tribunals.[32] Feelings of disquiet were such that John Halfpenny, Victorian secretary of the Amalgamated Metal Workers Union, suggested that there should be an investigation into the work practices of commission members to enhance their efficiency and productivity.[33]

The CAI criticised second-tier negotiations on the basis of being converted into a 'general round' for a four per cent increase; there had been too much concentration on removing restrictive work practices and an absence of genuine attempts to improve productivity; and unions were resistant to changing award conditions.[34] Notwithstanding these criticisms, the commission, in the December 1987 national wage case, said it was 'satisfied that a body of worthwhile changes [had] resulted from application of the [restructuring and efficiency] principle'.[35]

In October 1987 Australia found itself caught up in a worldwide stock market crash. The Federal Government considered revising its position or withdrawing support for the second part of the first-tier increase foreshadowed in the commission's March 1987 decision. It seems to have been worried, however, that any short-term benefits it might have gained from reneging on an earlier deal with its Accord partner would be dissipated in the longer run, reducing its ability to negotiate future wage deals. Moreover, the government was aware of the slow progress of second-tier increases. Treasurer Paul Keating said that the

decision to reject knee-jerk calls for the Government to reverse its submission was made with a view to the fact that, should the worst occur and the stock market collapse lead to a damaging slump in world demand, Australia would be best served by having in place an effective and flexible means of wage restraint.[36]

During the hearing of the national wage case Industrial Relations Minister Ralph Willis spoke of the need to enhance wage flexibility and revise award conditions to improve Australia's efficiency and international competitiveness. He advocated increased flexibility in wage increases paid to different groups of workers, more industry or enterprise-level bargaining, encouragement for skills enhancement, opening up of career paths and alteration of award conditions (such as starting and finishing times), consistent with centralised control of overall wage outcomes.[37] At a meeting of the ACTU executive in December Willis floated performance pay and profit-sharing as part of a future wages system; proposals that apparently fell on deaf ears.[38]

In the national wage case, in which the commission considered the second part of the first tier, the ACTU converted the 1.5 per cent increase, which was apparently available, to a flat amount of $7 per week; the government argued for $6.50; and employer groups argued that the case should be adjourned until May 1988 when the commission would review its principles. The commission decided to defer its decision and reconvene on 28 January 1988. While it said, 'Movements in share prices alone have nothing to do with the outcome of national wage cases and we would not alter the decision we would otherwise make in this case simply because of the decline in share market prices', it was concerned about Australia's international economic performance. The commission said:

> it is of critical importance that no step be taken now that may handicap Australia's ability to cope with the rapid adjustment in the world economy now taking place. Additional time is needed to allow an assessment to be made of possible adverse effects on the economy.[39]

The Accord partners condemned the decision. Ralph Willis said it would undermine the support of unions and wage and salary earners for the current wages system 'at a time when it was crucially important that we have a viable . . . system'. He claimed that the commission had 'somewhat misrepresented' the government's position in stating: 'All parties agreed that changes in world and domestic economic activity brought about by recent developments would bear hard on the Australian economy and would adversely affect the Budget forecasts'.[40] 'On the contrary', said Willis, 'the government argued that the current prospects for 1987–88 were not substantially changed from the assessments in the Budget papers'.[41]

Unions were more hostile in their criticisms. ACTU secretary Bill Kelty reportedly said the December 1987 decision was 'incredibly stupid', the bench had behaved like 'a bunch of clowns', its attitude to the lowly paid was 'almost hypocritical', the union movement's regard for the commission had reached a 'bottom point', and one 'would have to be a very brave person to suggest the commission will be given any significant role' in the next wage-fixing system.[42]

On 28 January 1988 the commission duly reopened the national wage case. After a short hearing it awarded an increase of $6 per week on 5 February. The commission concluded that since the stock market crash

> there has not occurred such a change in relevant indicators as would reflect serious and adverse consequences of the collapse in share prices . . . the serious consequences predicted by some observers in October have not eventuated . . . the ill effects have not been drastic or immediate.

The commission added:

> it appears that the economic uncertainty which is now apparent will remain for an indefinite period. To further adjourn these proceedings because of 'uncertainty' would appear to make an open-ended commitment which would be inconsistent with any rational wage policy. We believe it would be counter-productive and we are not prepared to delay an increase.[43]

As foreshadowed by Kelty in his criticisms of the December 1987 decision, on 24 February 1988 the ACTU announced details of a plan to obtain wage increases, which would bypass the commission initially at least. Affiliates would mount campaigns in key sectors or industries to win increases from employers via direct negotiations thus presenting the commission with a *fait accompli*.[44]

Besides obtaining second-tier increases for those unions or workers who had not so far achieved them, wage campaigns would be based on a guaranteed increase linked to the prospective rate of inflation—expected to be six per cent in the 1988–89 financial year[45]—plus additional increases based on award restructuring (multiskilling, career paths, award simplification) or supplementary payments for workers on low incomes, or examination of private/public sector relativities.[46]

In the months that followed the government pressured the ACTU concerning the size, timing and processing of its wages campaign. Keating sought to link wage increases to future tax cuts. In an Economic Statement delivered on 25 May 1988 he foreshadowed unspecified cuts in personal income tax in the 1989–90 financial year. He said:

> The personal tax cuts we have foreshadowed will provide Australia with a unique opportunity to bring our wages growth further into line with our trading partners. However, the size and timing of these cuts will depend upon the size and timing of future wage rises. That is, the Government is prepared to provide substantial tax cuts provided there is an acceptable wages outcome in 1988–89 and an appropriate wages/tax trade-off in 1989–90.[47]

The ACTU was unimpressed by tax cuts that beckoned more than thirteen months away. In May affiliates initiated their campaign for guaranteed wage increases—three per cent from 1 July and another three per cent from 1 December 1988—plus additional increases.[48] The response of employers was to seek the reconvening of a national wage case, a request to which the commission acceded.

During the hearing of the case, which began on 16 June, the Accord partners sought to reach an agreed position to present to the commission. Fears of a worsening economy spurred the government to pressure the ACTU to lower its demands. Cabinet wanted to limit wage increases in 1988–89 to 4.5 per cent. Moreover, the government wanted unions and employers to base wage movements on productivity changes. Unions unable to obtain wage increases via negotiations would be safeguarded by arbitrated safety net increases, in two instalments, during 1989.

To the ACTU this sounded like a rerun of the problems experienced under the two-tiered system. It signalled its intention to hold a national strike in July as a means to force the government to alter its position. Ultimately, the government revised its position and, during the national wage case, argued for a guaranteed increase of three per cent from 1 September 1988, plus 2.5 per cent six months later, as well as encouraging the enhancement of productivity via award restructuring exercises.[49] This agreement was subsequently referred to as the Accord Mark IV. Employers, generally speaking, sought to link wages to productivity increases.[50]

The commission handed down its decision on 12 August. It was prepared to grant a three per cent increase from 1 September 1988 and $10 six months later—a total increase of about 5.2 per cent—to unions provided they formally agreed to 'cooperate in a review (to be monitored by the Commission) of . . . award[s] to give effect to the structural efficiency principle'.[51] In contrast to its decision of December 1987 the commission expressed disquiet concerning the two-tiered system. It said:

> The proper application of the restructuring and efficiency principle called for a positive approach by trade unions, their members, and individual workers and by employer organizations, their members and individual employers. In the Commission's experience some were inadequate for the task. Many others made positive efforts: the best not only derived benefits which produced immediate efficiency and productivity improvements but also laid the foundation for future improvement. Despite the degree of success achieved we are not satisfied that the principle in its present form and as understood and accepted by many parties should be continued. Because of the general approach adopted to its application, some parties have exhausted the usefulness of the principle and it would seem impractical to expect others, who have not yet been capable of applying the principle successfully, to repeat the process.[52]

Notwithstanding this, however, the commission (as did the parties) wanted to continue to encourage greater productivity and efficiency. It said: 'we must take steps to ensure that work classifications and functions and the basic work patterns and arrangements in an industry meet the competitive requirements of that industry'. The commission indicated various areas in which awards could be altered to enhance structural efficiency. They were:

- establishing skill-related career paths which provide an incentive for workers to continue to participate in skill formation;
- eliminating impediments to multiskilling and broadening the range of tasks which a worker may be required to perform;
- creating appropriate relativities between different categories of workers within the award and at enterprise level;
- ensuring that working patterns and arrangements enhance flexibility and meet the competitive requirements of that industry;
- including properly fixed minimum rates for classifications in awards, related appropriately to one another, with any amounts in excess of

these properly fixed minimum rates being expressed as supplementary payments;

- updating and/or rationalising the list of respondents to awards;
- addressing any cases where award provisions discriminate against sections of the workforce.

The commission also said, 'It is not intended that this principle will be applied in a negative cost-cutting manner or to formalise illusory short-term benefits', and it expected 'that any resultant restructuring will be done primarily by consultation and at minimal cost'.[53]

Following the August 1988 decision the Accord partners began discussions on a new wages–tax trade-off—of what eventually became known as the Accord Mark V—according to Keating's May 1988 Economic Statement. Three key issues dominated negotiations: the size of tax cuts (and other social wage benefits), award restructuring (the major instrument for processing future wage increases), and increasing the pay of those on low incomes (minimum rate adjustments) via supplementary payments. Early in these negotiations there were hints that wage increases in 1989–90 would be traded off, or would be minimal, in exchange for substantial cuts in income tax in the order of $25–$30 per week.[54]

In a television interview in early September Kelty said: 'We will be negotiating with the government on what we perceive to be the biggest tax cuts in the history of this country. We are after nothing less . . . What we are concerned about is to ensure that real disposable incomes are in fact increased'. He added:

> We are doing nothing less than restructuring every award and every agreement in the conciliation and arbitration system to make them better, fairer, to provide career structures for workers, to ensure that wage rates relate to skill and training, and to ensure that those groups who are on low-paid minimum wage awards get better wage rates. We will completely change the award fixing system in this country.[55]

In the machinations between and within the Accord partners the government sought to talk down, delay or stagger the size of the tax cuts and the extent of future wage increases. It was estimated that a general tax cut of $30 per week would cost $9.5 billion in the 1989–90 financial year.[56] Throughout the trade union movement there was opposition to trading off wage increases in 1988–89 for tax cuts.[57]

Moreover, they objected to the proposition of participating in award restructuring exercises *gratis*—employers would have to pay for the privilege of award changes that enhanced efficiency and productivity.

In November 1988 Kelty released details of a new wages strategy for consideration by ACTU affiliates. Rather than the traditional reliance on general across-the-board national wage cases, future wage rises would be processed by award restructuring. Depending on the level of skill of workers concerned, there would be a benchmark figure of $20 to $30, paid in two halves (six months apart), which would flow from restructuring exercises. In addition, there would be supplementary payments for low-income earners.[58] A meeting of the ACTU executive in December subsequently endorsed Kelty's proposals.[59]

However, after this meeting several unions expressed feelings of disquiet towards award restructuring. George Campbell, national secretary of the AMWU, wanted a general wage rise linked to inflation in addition to award restructuring wage increases plus cuts in personal income tax. He was reported as saying:

> Kelty knows as well as the rest of us that award restructuring is not going to deliver substantial increases in the short term . . . You have to include a general wage rise. Anything less is not acceptable. To me it doesn't matter how you look at it, we are being sold a package which means restraint.[60]

In the new year these feelings of disquiet spread to other, mainly left-wing, unions.[61] The clamour of affiliates to link wages to prices was intensified following a 2.1 per cent increase in the December 1988 CPI. New South Wales Labor Council secretary Michael Easson advocated the payment of a special cost-of-living allowance for Sydney workers.[62]

Given this mounting pressure it was decided that a special unions conference should be held to reconsider the union movement's attitude to wage fixation and award restructuring. Before the conference Kelty and leftist unions negotiated a compromise position. While award restructuring was accorded 'the priority element in the [ACTU] wages strategy', it was agreed that during 1989–90 there would be an increase in real disposable incomes as measured by the CPI—'all workers must receive a wage increase during the second half of 1989'—and tax cuts of $20 per week. The essence of the deal, plus a commitment to supplementary payments for low-income workers, was subsequently endorsed by affiliates at the special unions conference[63] and was backed by the government.[64]

On 16 February 1989 a national wage case began to review the progress of the structural efficiency principle per a schedule the commission had determined in its August 1988 decision. A major part of the case was concerned with examining the principles of the ACTU's recently determined blueprint for award restructuring. During the hearing of the case the government pressured the ACTU to reduce the extent of its substantive claims or, at a minimum, agree to delays in implementation.

Treasurer Keating issued an Economic Statement on 12 April 1989 that detailed a package of tax and social security measures as well as a commitment to award restructuring. This statement has been referred to as the Accord Mark V. Tax cuts would be provided from 1 July 1989, plus a further reduction in the top marginal rate (more than $50,000) from 1 January 1990. It was estimated that the tax cuts would cost $4.9 billion and the social security package $710 million.[65] Keating announced that the ACTU had agreed to limit average earnings growth in 1989–90 to 6.5 per cent (it was actually 6.6 per cent). Keating added:

> the new wages system will be determined by Justice Maddern and his colleagues on the Industrial Relations Commission in the current proceedings and the Wage Case scheduled for May. We are envisaging the most far-reaching overhaul of industrial awards since Federation, and the Industrial Relations Commission has a vital role to play in establishing the new wage system and presiding over the orderly change to award structures. Award restructuring will bring substantial benefits for all parties—for employers, a more flexible, productive and highly trained workforce; and for employees, more interesting, varied and better-paid jobs.[66]

The commission handed down its decision concerning the structural efficiency principle on 25 May 1989. It concluded:

> progress is uneven and varies from industry to industry and enterprise to enterprise . . . negotiations are proceeding at different levels and . . . in some cases, progress is slow because of disagreement over the agenda and procedure. Preparedness to consider change also appears to vary widely. Progress in some areas is considerable but in the majority it is

minimal. Notwithstanding that, we are satisfied that the principle so framed in the August 1988 decision can and should facilitate negotiations over a wide range of issues and awards.[67]

The commission also said that 'the main thrust of the principle is aimed at changing those award structures which inhibit measures to improve efficiency in individual establishments'. The commission saw its role as providing 'a framework for change and [obtaining] the necessary commitment from unions . . . the measure of success of the structural efficiency principle will be the extent to which changes made at award levels are implemented at the plant and enterprise level'.[68]

Following this decision on principles a national wage case began to consider the substance of the Accord partners' proposals about award restructuring. With one important exception the commission was prepared to endorse the wages component of the Accord Mark V. Subject to the parties to an award satisfying the commission that they have 'cooperated positively in a fundamental review of that award and are implementing measures to improve the efficiency of industry and provide workers with access to more varied, fulfilling and better paid jobs', the commission would award wage increases of $10–$15 per week or three per cent, whichever is higher, depending on the skill of the workers concerned, plus an increase of the same order six months later.[69]

While not wishing to limit 'opportunities for innovation' the commission identified the issues that could be the object of award restructuring exercises. They were:

- averaging penalty rates and expressing them as flat amounts;
- compensating overtime with time off;
- flexibility in the arrangement of hours of work, for example:
  —wider daily span of ordinary hours
  —shift work, including 12 hour shifts
  —ordinary hours to be worked on any day of the week
  —job sharing;
- introducing greater flexibility in the taking of annual leave by agreement between employer and employee;
- rationalising the taking of annual leave to maximise production;
- reviewing the incidence of, and terms and conditions for, part-time employment and casual employment;
- reducing options for payment of wages other than by electronic funds transfer;

- extending options as to the period for which wages must be paid to include fortnightly and monthly payment;
- changes in manning consistent with improved work methods and the application of new technology and changes in award provisions which restrict the right of employees to manage their own business unless they are seeking from the employees something which is unjust or unreasonable;
- reviewing sick leave provisions with the aim of avoiding misuse; and
- developing appropriate consultative procedures to deal with the day to day matters of concern to employers and workers.[70]

The major difference between the commission and the Accord partners, particularly the ACTU, occurred over supplementary payments for low-income workers. The commission rejected or modified downwards, in some cases halved, the ACTU's claim, with the first instalment not being available until 1 January 1990.[71]

Despite the commission's apparent endorsement of the Accord Mark V the ACTU and individual affiliates were critical of the decision. There was disappointment concerning the range of issues the commission had placed on the award restructuring bargaining table.[72] The major criticism, however, was directed at the commission's decision on supplementary payments.[73]

During the hearing of the principles case Kelty indicated that another wage–tax trade-off, in all probability, would form the basis of a new Accord to be negotiated in 1990.[74] Following the commission's August 1989 decision there were hints that a three per cent top-up in superannuation (to six per cent) would assume a prominent place in discussions of an Accord Mark VI.[75]

In July 1989 the Business Council of Australia produced a report on enterprise bargaining (which will be extensively analysed in chapter 4). While it was not formally launched until December copies were floating around for those who might have an interest in such matters.[76] In November Keating saw the move to enterprise bargaining as inevitable. He maintained, however, that there would need to be a reform of union and award structures before adopting such a decentralised approach. He said:

it is the Accord process, along with the Industrial Relations Commission, that can bring this about. There is a consensus developing amongst employer groups and the ACTU to rationalise and restructure awards to create a framework which can handle greater wage flexibility without generally destabilising flow-ons and wage break-outs. The consensus model is a powerful and effective force for change. Confrontation and Draconian legislation will not change the structure of unions nor build an environment where employees can sit down with management to devise working conditions which are in everyone's best interests. The problem with the labour market is that it requires a proper award and union structure to be in place before greater market flexibility can be sensibly entertained.[77]

During negotiations over the Accord Mark VI ACTU leaders indicated their preparedness to bargain over profits and productivity at the enterprise level.[78] In February 1990 Kelty outlined the ACTU's attitude to enterprise bargaining. He pointed out that 'Enterprise bargaining is not new. Enterprise awards incorporating overaward payment are not new either'. He added that it was 'not an issue of making some fundamental shift towards enterprise bargaining, but rather the nature of what is to be the bargaining at an enterprise basis'. He also pointed out that the logic of award restructuring implied 'implementation at an enterprise level'. He also wanted to ensure that aggregate wage outcomes had 'regard to national economic objectives' and that there was 'general protection for workers through the conciliation and arbitration system'. He went on to say:

> The issue . . . is not whether or not there will be enterprise bargaining but what sort of enterprise bargaining, what sort of relationships. There are two options for enterprise bargaining. Mature arrangements between unions and employers looking at productivity, profit-sharing, the application of restructuring, the development of better relationships between unions and employers. That is good enterprise bargaining. Then there is enterprise bargaining where you bargain . . . for whatever you can get.[79] That is collective bargaining. Now the ACTU has never supported the view that it is the most desirable way for this country to regulate its industrial affairs by just free collective bargaining. What we have said is that the next step in terms of award restructuring must and should involve positive enterprise bargaining . . . We're not interested in direct offset bargaining, looking at the past. Restructuring is about creating a new work organisation, it's about changes which are not established on the basis of negative cost.[80]

The renegotiation of the Accord occurred during a period in which it transpired that the economy had deteriorated yet further and in the lead up to a (March) federal election. On 21 February the ACTU and Federal Government reached agreement on the Accord Mark VI—a wages–tax–superannuation trade-off combined with continuing support for award restructuring and the adoption of enterprise bargaining. The government agreed if re-elected to provide tax cuts from 1 January 1991 equal to tax indexation, at an estimated cost of $2.5 billion. For workers on average earnings this translated to a tax cut of about $7.50 per week. The aggregate wage target for 1990–91 was seven per cent comprising a national wage case claim based on the September 1990 CPI, $12 six months later, plus award restructuring and minimum rate adjustment increases. In addition, a three per cent top up to superannuation would be phased in from 1 May 1991 to 1 May 1993.[81] The ALP duly won the March 1990 federal election.

PAYING THE PAYMASTERS

Before proceeding to examine events associated with implementing the Accord Mark VI and the move towards enterprise bargaining it might be useful to examine an issue that has not been considered so far but is relevant to subsequent events.

The ALP and ACTU had negotiated and renegotiated the Accord in attempting to respond to and overcome Australia's various economic problems, consistent with broader social and equity considerations. From 1985 renegotiations of the Accord had translated into real wage cuts (see table 2.1), although such reductions had been tempered by tax, superannuation and social wage trade-offs. While unions had exercised wage restraint throughout the second half of the 1980s and into the 1990s, other groups sought and/or obtained substantial increases in their incomes. Early in its period of office the Federal Government had floated the Australian dollar and deregulated the financial system. This in turn led to a boom in the income of finance and money market operators with flow-on effects to other professional groups such as lawyers and business executives. As State and Federal Governments sought to increase the efficiency of public service departments and government business enterprises they found themselves competing with the private sector for managerial talent and on the treadmill of generous salary packages for 'fat cat' public servants. In turn, politicians and members of the judiciary felt the need for extra compensation to maintain their place in the aristocracy of the professions.

Whenever a group of top public service bureaucrats, politicians or the judiciary made an application for, or were about to receive, sizeable increases in compensation the ACTU would invariably place pressure on its Accord partner to reject, resist or reconsider such a request. The ACTU would argue that such increases had the potential to destroy the commitment of unions to the Accord. Generally speaking, the government would respond by reducing the amount, altering the time frame of such increases or finding some means to finesse through improved benefits.

Following the announcement of the Accord Mark VI Bill Kelty, in an address to the annual conference of the New South Wales Labor Council, attacked the hypocrisy of those who preached wage restraint for unions and workers yet took hefty pay increases for themselves. In particular he identified 'judges and members of parliament, and even arbitration commissioners [who] are lining up for increases significantly higher than workers'.[82]

Traditionally, the salaries of the president and deputy presidents of the commission had been the same as that of the chief judge and judges of the Federal Court of Australia, with commissioners receiving seventy per cent of the salary paid to deputy presidents.[83] In the first half of 1990 the Federal Government, apparently in response to pressure applied by the ACTU, decided to break this nexus to allow the salaries of presidential members of the commission to fall below those of their colleagues on the Federal Court. In May 1990 the government passed the *Remuneration and Allowances Act* 1990 to give effect to this intention. Members of the commission were far from pleased about this turn of events.[84] In his annual report to parliament commission president Mr Justice Barry Maddern complained bitterly about this decision. He said:

> Without giving the Commission an opportunity to express any views as to the short and longer term effects of its decision, the Government unilaterally altered the contract of employment of Presidential Members of the Commission . . . This action removed the nexus between the salaries of Judges of the Federal Court and Presidential members of the Commission . . . The Government has also announced that a review of the structure of the Commission will take place. Members of the

Commission have a number of objections to the actions of the Government including that, notwithstanding the fact that discussions were not held with the Commission, discussions were evidently held with a number of other organisations who appear before it. The members of the Commission have made it known to the Government that their concern at the downgrading of the Commission's standing and status lies with the effect on the public perception of the Commission's integrity and independence.[85]

These concerns about salaries, structure, integrity and independence were to be a source of much angst for the commission. On 7 November 1990 the minister for industrial relations, Senator Peter Cook, established a three-member committee comprising Gerry Gleeson, former head of the New South Wales Premier's Department (chair), Professor Alan Fels, head of the Prices Surveillance Authority, and a South Australian Supreme Court judge, Mr Justice Olsson, to inquire into the salaries and structure of the commission.

The government proposed changes to the commission's three-tiered structure of president, deputy president and commissioners. It wanted an extra three designations: vice-president, senior deputy president and senior commissioners. The government's rationale seems to have been that, if the Australian workforce should have the opportunity of being exposed to new career paths under award restructuring, a similar privilege should be afforded to members of the commission.

The Gleeson committee recommended adoption of the government's proposals concerning a vice-president and senior deputy president but not senior commissioners. On salaries it recommended that the president's be equated with that of the chief judge of the Federal Court, the vice-president receive a salary three per cent higher than that of a senior deputy president, senior deputy presidents receive the same salary as a judge of the Federal Court, deputy presidents receive 95 per cent of a senior deputy president, and commissioners 70 per cent of a deputy president.[86]

In May 1991 the government acted on these recommendations in the *Industrial Relations Legislative Amendment Act (No. 2) 1991* in creating the positions of vice-president and senior deputy presidents, although no one was appointed to these positions until 17 August 1992.[87]

In his annual report for 1990–91 Mr Justice Maddern again voiced concerns about the downgrading of salaries of members of the commission and findings of the Gleeson committee. He said:

> the Commission should be neither judge nor advocate in its own cause in relation to salaries and conditions of employment and the implementation of the Gleeson report will be seen as doing further damage to the public perception of the Commission's integrity and independence. In my view, the major recommendations contained in the Committee's report are also inconsistent with the proper administration of the Commission. I am therefore opposed to the major recommendations of that Committee in so far as they relate to both the method of fixing the remuneration of Deputy Presidents and the restructuring of the Commission.[88]

During the second half of 1991 the Remuneration Tribunal (a body responsible for determining the salaries of senior public servants, politicians, the judiciary and so on) heard submissions about the salaries of members of the commission. Mr Justice Maddern argued for restoration of the salary nexus between the commission and Federal Court and against the creation of a vice-president and senior deputy president. He said he did not know what work he would delegate to a vice-president and doubted whether it was possible to distinguish, legitimately or illegitimately, on work value grounds between deputy presidents on the basis of skill or responsibility.[89] The Remuneration Tribunal concluded that the breaking of the salary nexus between the commission and the Federal Court 'could not be justified' and that no 'acceptable reasons were provided for such a change'.[90]

The government rejected this recommendation,[91] to the dismay of the commission, or at least a majority of the commission—there was a report of a split among its ranks concerning salaries and appropriate responses to claims of the Accord partners,[92] and there were rumours that some members contemplated retirement. Interestingly, Mr Justice Mahoney and Louis Mangan announced their resignation from the Remuneration Tribunal. According to Industrial Relations Minister Peter Cook, they 'did not resign in protest' because the government 'disagreed with its decision on salaries of members of the Commission'.[93] In April 1992 deputy president Russell Peterson retired from the commission to take up a dual appointment in the New South Wales

Industrial Commission and the New South Wales Industrial Court, increasing his salary by $20,000.[94] Several days later commissioner Ken Turbet announced his resignation and bitterly criticised the Accord partners. He claimed: 'The process of the Accord is now no more than a meeting between the Prime Minister [who was now Paul Keating] and the secretary of the ACTU. Everybody else, the whole of the trade union movement and the commission is expected to toe the line.'[95]

ACCORD MARK VI

On 22 August 1990 the ACTU executive passed a resolution for affiliates to pursue claims, outlined in the February 1990 agreement, from employers in direct negotiations, thereby (initially) bypassing the commission. This was a repeat of a strategy employed in pursuit of the Accord Mark IV in 1988 (see above). The 22 August resolution said that, despite the Accord Mark VI having

> been in existence since February, employers generally continue to oppose any agreement with unions to give effect to that understanding. It is also noted that employers have continually attempted to use the wage-fixing system to attack award conditions. Further, this Executive is extremely concerned with a number of decisions of the Industrial Relations Tribunal and State Tribunals which have not been consistent and have undermined key elements of the centralised wage fixing system. Executive therefore endorses the Metal Unions and other claims for negotiations with employers designed to achieve implementation of the ACTU/Government agreement including wage increases based on profitability/productivity/market adjustments.[96]

A number of mainly right-wing unions questioned the wisdom of pursuing wage claims in the field, given a deteriorating economy and rapid increases in unemployment. Ivan Hodgson, national secretary of the Transport Workers' Union, and Peter Sams, assistant secretary of the New South Wales Labor Council, maintained that unions and workers in weak bargaining positions would find it difficult, if not impossible, to secure concessions from employers via direct negotiations. For them the 22 August resolution amounted to nothing more than a *de facto* wages freeze for hundreds of thousands of workers.[97]

Both Prime Minister Hawke and Treasurer Keating expressed support for the ACTU's proposed campaign, seeing it as an understandable response to employers rejecting the Accord Mark VI. Keating colourfully described the ACTU as wanting 'to take a few carcasses with it' when a national wage case eventually began.[98]

Employer groups responded to the ACTU's campaign by running to the commission for an order for unions to desist from such action and a national wage case to review wage fixation principles.

The hearings that occurred on 13 and 14 September are most notable for the contribution of ACTU secretary Bill Kelty. Kelty reiterated the union movement's support for award restructuring and the move towards enterprise bargaining as outlined in the Accord Mark VI. He criticised employers for dragging the chain on moving towards a more flexible industrial relations system. He stressed the importance of providing a proper base for the way forward and criticised the commission for its decision in August 1989 on minimum rate adjustments. He foresaw under a regime of enterprise bargaining that the commission would play a more limited role, returning to its traditional function of establishing minimum rates of pay.

He bemoaned those groups in society, including (if not especially) members of the commission, who had gained substantial increases in their incomes when the majority of the workforce had exercised restraint and experienced large cuts in real income. In addition, he criticised the commission and State tribunals for inconsistent decisions and the problems they posed for maintaining the commitment of unions and workers to the system. He explained the ACTU's decision to pursue claims in the field resulting from frustrations experienced under the two-tiered system and award restructuring. He said:

> What we are seeking to do is establish by agreement with employers
> . . . the differences which may exist, so that people can more properly
> understand the basis for . . . transition . . . [to a new] system . . . [we
> do not want] to enter into a process of arbitration without a very clear
> understanding with employers as to what [is] meant . . . by efficiency
> . . . [and] restructuring . . . Our mistake as a union movement [with
> the two-tiered system] was to commit ourselves in advance . . . with-
> out sitting down with employers as to working out how that system
> would work . . . Restructuring . . . is about changing the course of

attitudes in this country and if it takes a little longer to establish more clearly with employers the way they perceive efficiency and restructuring, so be it.[99]

In a brief decision on 17 September the commission pointed out to parties 'the obligation to avoid industrial action', that such action contravened the principles of the August 1989 national wage case and that any agreements reached would be tested against the commission's principles. The decision also said that the commission would be prepared to convene a private conference, chaired by Mr Justice Maddern, to review the current wage principles on 24 September, 'provided no industrial action is occurring or threatened at that time'.[100] While conferences took place several ACTU affiliates steadfastly proceeded with campaigns to secure Accord Mark VI wage rises via direct negotiations with employers.

In mid October Reserve Bank Governor Bernie Fraser suggested that the Federal Government should enter into a new wage–tax deal with the ACTU as a means to further reduce the level of inflation. He did not believe that monetary policy could achieve such reductions without 'heavy costs in terms of lost production and employment'.[101] Initially, both Keating and ACTU president Martin Ferguson dismissed Fraser's proposal.[102]

The Accord Mark VI envisaged increasing wages, initially, by an amount equal to the rise in the September 1990 CPI. At the time the Accord Mark VI was negotiated it was anticipated that this figure would be in the vicinity of two per cent. The actual figure was 0.7 per cent. Following this lower than expected figure Fraser's proposal concerning a new wage–tax deal suddenly appeared attractive. After a series of negotiations the Accord partners eventually agreed to a new wage–tax deal whereby the tax cuts due on 1 January 1991 would be topped up for a worker on average earnings by $2.95 per week, at an approximate cost of $430 million to the federal budget.[103] This agreement has been described as the Accord Mark VIa.

On 3 December 1990 a national wage case began to consider the Accord Mark VI, the adoption of enterprise bargaining and future wage fixation principles. The commission asked the parties to put their submissions in writing and indicated a number of issues that should be specifically considered.[104] Parties were provided with a chance to make oral submissions, and the commission 'reduced to writing a number of questions' to which the parties had to respond by early February 1991. Final oral submissions were heard in late February, and the commission handed down its decision on 16 April 1991.

Early in the decision reference is made to the imbroglio over the salaries of commission members, the Gleeson report and public perception of the commission's independence and integrity. The commission was at pains to point out that its decision in this case was not influenced by these events. It said:

> The commission has a duty to consider properly the merits of submissions put to it. It has performed that duty and will continue to do so. It has not been—nor will it be—influenced by the source of submissions made to it.[105]

The Accord partners, and most employer groups,[106] regarded enterprise bargaining as an inevitable consequence of award restructuring and the structural efficiency principle contained in the August 1988 and August 1989 national wage cases. The commission's attitude to enterprise bargaining would hinge on its conclusions concerning the success or otherwise of the structural efficiency principle. It concluded that the principle had made little progress and 'has not yet been extensively implemented'.[107] The commission said:

> It is clear from the material before us that the results of restructuring to date have been uneven. In some areas substantial progress has been made, at least in terms of the framework at award level. In these areas, the stage is set for implementation of award changes at enterprise level. At the other end of the scale, there are areas where little progress has been made either in providing an appropriate framework at award level or in otherwise implementing the structural efficiency principle. In the case of the former, the efficacy of award variations have, generally, still to be tested properly at workplace level. In the case of the latter, more substantial change seems necessary at the award level before a concentrated effort can be made at the workplace level.[108]

Given its conclusion concerning the structural efficiency principle the commission felt disinclined, at this stage, to adopt an enterprise bargaining system. The commission wanted the parties to consider various issues raised in its decision in a future national wage case to be finalised after 1 November 1991 and maintained that the 'parties to industrial relations have still to develop the maturity necessary for the further shift to enterprise bargaining'.[109] It feared that enterprise bargaining would result in the development of an uncoordinated industrial relations system. For the commission enterprise bargaining had the potential to destroy the 'collective responsibility' it had been trying to nurture since the election of the Federal Labor Government in March 1983 (if not before in the wage indexation years of 1975–81). The questions that the commission had circulated to the parties earlier in February, and its April 1991 decision, reveal that the commission was worried that uncoordinated enterprise bargaining would involve Australia revisiting the industrial relations and economic problems of the late 1960s/early 1970s and the early 1980s.

In addition, the commission highlighted differences between the parties over the meaning of enterprise bargaining, problems with measuring productivity and profitability and their translation into wage increases, the lack of a 'receptive environment' for enterprise bargaining, the future role of national wage cases, and the problems of workers in weak bargaining positions such as women.

The Accord Mark VI sought to phase in increased superannuation contributions of three per cent by May 1993. Evidence was submitted concerning problems associated with superannuation—diversity of schemes, coverage, qualifying periods, exclusion of casuals and non-compliance—which the commission was asked to resolve. It decided to defer any decision on these matters—although it was prepared to resume 'on the application of any party to these proceedings'—and asked the Commonwealth Government to convene a national conference to consider various problems associated with the provision of superannuation.[110]

Finally, the commission rejected or modified the substantive wage application contained in the Accord Mark VI: the across-the-board $12 per week claim. The commission decided to make available a 2.5 per cent increase, on application, for those unions who demonstrated their commitment to the structural efficiency principle. It choose a percentage, rather than a flat, increase to avoid problems associated with the compression of relativities.[111]

The commission's decision seems to have caught the parties unaware. It was trenchantly criticised by the Accord partners. Keating said: 'I disagree with the decision and I disagree most strongly with the conservatism of the commission that has clung to the pre-eminent role of the national wage case awarding increases and postponed the introduction of a more flexible system of enterprise bargaining.'[112]

Kelty referred to the decision as a 'rotten egg', 'vomit' and 'wickedly unfair'.[113] He also said:

> The tragedy of the decision and the silliness of it is that despite the fact that nearly every representative said that there should be greater devolution, what they've in fact had is perhaps the most highly centralised wage system that's yet been produced. The only real issue is how they will try to contrive all the productivity and efficiencies . . . only Cuba and Australia would have such a highly regulated wages system. Well, Barry Maddern may see himself as some form of Fidel Castro, but the reality is that he lacks the authority and the political system in this country to enforce such a wages system.[114]

At a special unions conference on May Day the ACTU recommitted itself to pursuing the Accord Mark VI in direct negotiations with employers.[115] On 15 May the Federal Government issued guidelines for processing workplace bargaining, which were based on the spirit of the Accord Mark VI.[116] Affiliates found it difficult to extract concessions from employers in a recessed economy with increasing unemployment. In July Peter Sams, of the New South Wales Labour Council, criticised the ACTU (and hence Kelty) over the April decision and attitude to the commission as 'nauseating and absurd'. He was worried that attacks on the commission would play into the hands of the Coalition who wanted to do away with awards and industrial tribunals altogether. He also pointed out that the Labor Council and its affiliates had 'expended enormous amounts of money, time and resources in campaigning against Greiner's anti-union industrial "reforms" . . . A central focus of this opposition has been an effort to protect the independent role of the Industrial Commission against a renegade and uncaring government'.[117]

Affiliates who were unable to extract wage rises from employers found themselves attracted to the commission's April 1991 decision with its offer of a 2.5 per cent increase in exchange for a commitment to the structural efficiency principle. A small trickle, then a steady stream of pragmatic affiliates deserted the ACTU May Day resolution.[118] Kelty claimed that the commission had become 'a laughing stock of inconsistency' and had debauched its own guidelines in trying to entice

unions to accept its April 1991 decision.[119] Ian Spicer, executive director of the Confederation of Australian Industry, described the ACTU's
campaign as a failure, based on 'a huge miscalculation'.[120] At the end
of August Industrial Relations Minister Cook announced that the Federal Government was considering introducing legislative changes to
enable unions and employers to enter into fixed-term enterprise bargaining deals, thereby bypassing the commission.[121]

Also in August a national wage case began to consider issues
that the commission had raised concerning enterprise bargaining in its
April 1991 decision. The commission, in its decision of 30 October
1991, decided to endorse enterprise bargaining, if only begrudgingly.
It said:

> The submissions again revealed a diversity of opinions and a failure to
> confront practical problems. Despite this, the parties and interveners once
> more press us to move toward a more devolved system. Collectively,
> they have left to us the task of translating a general concept into work-
> able arrangements. There is little prospect, it would seem, that further
> postponement will lead to more fully developed proposals or to the res-
> olution of points of disagreement. Although the concerns expressed in
> our April decision have not been allayed, we are satisfied that a further
> and concerted effort should be made to improve the efficiency of enter-
> prises. In all the circumstances confronting us, we are prepared, on bal-
> ance, to determine an enterprise bargaining principle.[122]

It added that 'distribution of all of the benefits of productivity growth
at the enterprise level would lead to inequity and, ultimately, to a dis-
torted and unsustainable wage structure. Such a situation is compat-
ible with neither a flexible labour market nor industrial peace'. The
commission would approve enterprise bargaining agreements reached
by the parties that were consistent with the implementation of the
structural efficiency principle. It decided, however, to restrict its involvement to conciliation, refusing to avail itself of its arbitration powers in
the resolution of such exercises. The commission said its reasons for
this decision included

> the absence of satisfactory proposals from the parties and interveners as
> to how 'achieved productivity' should be measured and/or distributed;
> the potential for inequities in systems of enterprise bargaining based on
> 'achieved productivity'; the likelihood that arbitration will aggravate
> flow-on effects, with attendant industrial disputes; and the possibility

that an arbitration will be taken as erecting a standard for enterprise bargaining which may unnecessarily constrain outcomes in other cases.[123]

In December 1991 Paul Keating wrested the position of prime minister from Bob Hawke. In the weeks that followed Keating turned his mind to preparing a statement to counter the Coalition's *Fightback!* package with its advocacy of a goods and services tax, celebration of individualism and the market, advocacy of deregulation and associated attacks on government interference and the welfare state. His deliberations occurred at the time of a depressed economy, unemployment hovering between ten and eleven per cent, and a prediction that Labor was odds on to be defeated at the 1993 federal election.

During the preparation of the statement Accord-like discussions were held with the ACTU leadership. Issues canvassed included another wages–tax trade-off, a wages–jobs trade-off, legislated superannuation and changes to the *Industrial Relations Act* 1988 to encourage enterprise or, as it now seemed to be called, workplace bargaining. While the ACTU wanted to pursue an across-the-board wage increase linked to the inflation rate of Australia's major trading partners Keating counselled caution, seeking to delay such a case for as long as possible.[124]

On 26 February 1992 Keating released his *One Nation* statement. It held out the promise of tax cuts in July 1994 and January 1996 to counter the taxation proposals contained in *Fightback!* Legislation would be introduced that required employers to phase in increases in superannuation from three to nine per cent between 1992–93 and 2000–01. The statement expressed 'support for a continuing role for National Wage Cases'. It said: 'The Government will determine its attitude to the size and timing of National Wage increases in the light of keeping Australia's inflation rate comparable with those of our major trading partners'. The statement added: 'If wages growth were to become inconsistent with achieving inflation rates comparable with those of our major trading partners, the Government would need to reconsider the scheduled timing of increases in the prescribed minimum standard of superannuation'. Finally, *One Nation* pledged support for workplace bargaining and pledged legislative changes to encourage its usage.[125]

A national wage case was not held until June 1993 with a decision handed down in October. Moreover, it was not based on a general across-the-board increase linked to the inflation rate of Australia's major trading partners but rather a safety net increase of $8 per week for workers on low incomes.[126] Legislation was enacted to give effect to *One Nation*'s commitments concerning superannuation—*Superannuation Guarantee Charge Act* 1992 and *Superannuation Guarantee (Administration) Act* 1992—and the enhancement of workplace bargaining. Under revisions to the *Industrial Relations Act* 1988, section 134 requires the commission, subject to a 'no disadvantage' test, to certify workplace agreements negotiated by the parties.[127] This legislation, which took effect from 9 July 1992, enabled parties to negotiate such deals without the encumbrance of having to jump through the hoops of the commission's structural efficiency principle. The legislation has given effect to Kelty's desire to find a means to bypass the commission.

Mr Justice Maddern expressed concern about this legislation. In an annual report to parliament he said: 'The effect and significance of the legislation is unclear . . . the legislation read in conjunction with the Commission's October 1991 enterprise bargaining principle does mean that two sets of rules apply to consent arrangements. This . . . will, at least, create confusion'.[128] His criticisms in the annual report of the following year were more strident. He said:

> parties to a single enterprise agreement are not required to meet the tests of the enterprise bargaining principle (e.g. increased efficiency and productivity); they can also include in their agreement, without a public interest test, matters that, under the general provisions of the Act, must be subject to Full Bench scrutiny in the public interest. Indeed, an application for an award variation may be rejected by a single member and/or a Full Bench of the Commission and the subject matter of that application can be, and has been, incorporated in an agreement that is certified without scrutiny by the Commission by reference to public interest considerations. The agreement then has the status of an award and prevails over an existing award. This situation must have serious implications for the continuation of compulsory arbitration in the federal system of industrial relations.[129]

CONCLUSION

Isaac has written of how decisions of the federal tribunal provide 'employers, unions and governments with a convenient and socially useful whipping-boy . . . for certain unavoidable difficulties in wages and industrial relations'.[130] He has also described the federal tribunal as 'essentially a facilitator rather than a prime mover or an innovator, reactive rather than proactive, in the formulation and application of industrial principles'. He has sought to create the impression that the federal tribunal, and its various personnel, have no views of their own, no axes to grind. The tribunal, he claims, 'must try to frame principles that by and large conform to community values and expectations', and that its personnel 'have acted primarily, not as the originators of standards and principles, but as the interpreters of the signs of the times and facilitators of an approach which would serve these signs most effectively'.[131] A major problem with this analysis concerns how members of the federal tribunal interpret 'the signs of the times' when the parties that appear before them hold strongly divergent views concerning both goals to be achieved and methods of implementation. How should the tribunal proceed in choosing between the different positions of the parties? What straws in the wind should it clutch in determining what it is that the community expects? Is it conceivable that in making choices the tribunal makes decisions that reflect its own views concerning the best course of action that should be pursued?[132] William Jethro Brown, president of the Industrial Court of South Australia from 1916 to 1927, has pointed out how those who interpret community needs like to maintain the fiction that they do not make decisions. He has wryly noted:

> Lest they should innovate prematurely or capriciously, they have affected as a profession of faith that they cannot innovate at all . . . and, in so far as they have innovated, they have sought to conceal the fact from themselves as well as the public.[133]

An alternative interpretation is to see industrial tribunals as seeking to create 'a new province for law and order'. Like other interactors industrial tribunals and their personnel will develop their own solutions to the problems of their times. They will find themselves involved in an authority struggle (see chapter 1) with those with whom they interact in seeking to gain their acceptance of how to respond to the various problems of industrial relations.[134]

Mark Perlman in his analysis of the federal tribunal observed:

> Some [persons] of marked ability failed to function as effectively as might have been expected because they served during times of great social

conflict, or times which emphasized their weaker qualities. Often the very virtues which made an individual a great jurist become [their] greatest fault when [they] must handle sociological problems. In industrial relations the assumptions which the lawyer states are not necessarily internally consistent, since it is [their] tact, rather than [their] capacity for logical presentation, that often serves as [their] most convincing weapon.[135]

This literature casts an interesting light on the role of the commission during the period examined in this chapter. While the commission helped to 'facilitate' the development of the two-tiered system in its March 1987 decision, and the structural efficiency principle in August 1988, and to a lesser extent in August 1989, its decisions during this period were characterised by vacillation and uncertainty.[136] It was unsure how to respond to the stock market crash of October 1987 and the desire, of virtually all the major parties, in 1991 to move towards a system of enterprise bargaining. It set itself against community expectations because of fears of repeating mistakes of the late 1960s/early 1970s and early 1980s. In the process it lost a chance to be at the centre of developments to facilitate, if not be a prime mover in, directing enterprise bargaining in a way that would overcome dangers associated with an 'uncoordinated system'. In begrudgingly recognising the inevitability of enterprise bargaining in its October 1991 decision the commission refused to exercise its powers of arbitration in resolving such disputes—a decision that conceivably was inconsistent with its legislative and constitutional responsibilities.

The commission created a vacuum, which the Accord partners filled. They took advantage of High Court decisions, which had changed the constitutional basis of Australian industrial relations, to introduce legislation concerning superannuation and workplace agreements. The commission was an obstacle or problem that the Accord partners sought to overcome. The years 1987–92 witnessed the commission's role being marginalised. As Ludeke has noted, it is the Accord partners, rather than the commission in national wage cases, who determine the contours of wage movements and industrial relations regulation.[137] The years 1987–92 might ultimately be judged as one of the worst periods in the history of the federal tribunal. The commission not only contributed to a diminution in its own role but also, behind the banner of defending its independence and integrity, found itself embroiled in a struggle over the salaries that should be paid to its members.

ENTERPRISE BARGAINING

*More and more enterprises competing in global markets are build-
ing their production strategies around the concept that the real
capacity of a plant is limited only by its physical and engineering
limits.*

BCA (1989), Enterprise-based Bargaining Units: A Better Way of
Working, *Report to the Business Council of Australia by the Industrial
Relations Study Commission, Vol. 1, July, p. 67.*

. . . every worker should go to work each day expecting to be sacked.
*Larratt quoted in Thompson, H. (1992). 'The APPM dispute: The dinosaur
and turtles vs the ACTU',* Economic and Labour Relations Review,
December, p. 153.

Sheldon & Thornthwaite and O'Brien have claimed that the Business Council of Australia has been successful in capturing the debate concerning industrial relations reform generally and the move towards enterprise bargaining in particular.[1] In mounting their respective cases, however, they have ignored or downplayed developments that occurred in other orbits: the adoption of economic rationalist policies in Canberra;[2] the Accord partners embracing flexibility and restructuring to increase Australia's international competitiveness;[3] and their increasing antipathy, especially that of the Australian Council of Trade Unions, towards the Australian Industrial Relations Commission (see chapter 3).

Since the work practices summit of September 1986 and the two-tiered system contained in the national wage case of March 1987 identified the enterprise as the proper location at which efficiency changes would occur to enhance Australia's international competitiveness (chapter 2) the major parties, with the exception of the Metal Trades Industry Association and women's lobby groups, have been involved in a headlong rush to embrace enterprise bargaining.[4] They have competed with different and evolving models, trying to persuade each other that their own unique version constitutes the 'true path' that should be followed in moving towards enterprise bargaining. As ACTU secretary Bill Kelty said in February 1990, 'The issue . . . is not whether or not there will be enterprise bargaining but what sort of enterprise bargaining'.[5]

The proponents of enterprise bargaining attach different meanings to the term. The dimensions of these differences revolve around attitudes to the involvement or role of industrial tribunals and unions. Should enterprise bargains be processed through or apart from industrial tribunals? Should such deals be 'add-ons', in the tradition of over-award payments, or alternatives to awards? If it is decided that tribunals should play a role, should they be involved in the making of such agreements, should they vet or oversee deals negotiated by the parties to ensure that they are consistent with certain minimum standards or other 'public interest' tests, or should they be confined to resolving disputes via a grievance procedure? What should be the role of unions in enterprise bargaining? Some see unions as integral to the negotiation of enterprise deals. Others consider enterprise bargaining a Trojan horse for individual bargaining that enables employers to move away from unions (and tribunals) and attack the wages and working conditions of their employees.

Instead of providing a means that 'allows employers, workers and the community generally to share in the benefits of productivity and profitability gains achieved through restructuring'[6] enterprise bargaining might in fact encourage exercises in negative cost-cutting and propel Australia into a rash of recognition disputes like that experienced in the Australian Pulp and Paper Mill in Burnie, Tasmania, between March and June 1992.[7] The Metal Trades Industry Association's criticism of enterprise bargaining is that individual companies will find themselves at the mercy of large, powerful and well-organised unions.[8]

This chapter has three sections. A detailed analysis and critique of the Business Council of Australia's proposals concerning enterprise bargaining is provided in the first section. It is followed by an examination of legislative initiatives of the states to encourage enterprise bargaining. The final section examines initiatives at the federal level focusing on the Accord Mark VII and the *Industrial Relations Reform Act* 1993.

THE BUSINESS COUNCIL OF AUSTRALIA'S AGENDA FOR CHANGE

In the period 1984–86 the BCA made a series of statements concerning its desire to reform Australian industrial relations away from its traditional reliance on industrial tribunals and develop an enterprise-based system (see chapter 2). Consistent with this desire in March 1987 it issued a policy document entitled 'Towards an enterprise-based industrial relations system'. The document states:

> The Business Council, after a great deal of internal consultation, intensive work by a committee of Chief Executives, and discussion and decision making in meetings of the full council, has committed itself to pursue a major new direction for Australia's industrial relations system . . . The Council seeks a fundamental re-orientation of the system:
> - away from one largely focused outside the enterprise, adversarial in nature, and conducted by intermediaries positioned between management and other employees;
> - towards one which is centered on the enterprise, develops a high degree of mutual trust and interest, and strengthens the direct relationships between employers and employees.[9]

In a section concerned with implementation the document states that a 'clearer sense of direction must be set by management and this is accepted firmly as a chief executive responsibility requiring new levels of commitment'.[10] The BCA decided it would appoint a study commission

> to provide the Council with further advice . . . It will be asked to examine what legislative and institutional changes are required to enable our favoured system to be developed further. It will be asked to consider a program of institutional and legal changes which would facilitate a steady but manageable phasing in.

Particular issues the study commission was asked to consider were

- The institutional framework required for the development of enterprise agreements including the nature of Federal and State laws and their interaction.
- The role and nature of conciliation and arbitration in support of the enterprise oriented system.
- Means by which cohesive bargaining units can be developed at the enterprise level.
- Means to achieve enforceability of agreements including the role of sanctions and the phased implementation of the proposed enterprise system, especially legal and institutional changes that might be sought throughout the process.[11]

The terms of reference that guided the study commission, appointed in October 1987, essentially replicate the May 1987 policy document. The study commission has issued three reports. They are *Enterprise-based Bargaining Units: A Better Way of Working* in July 1989,[12] *Avoiding Industrial Action: A Better Way of Working* in 1991, and *Working Relations: A Fresh Start for Australian Enterprises* in 1993.[13] There is a degree of overlap and repetition between the three reports. The analysis that follows will mainly focus on the first report.

ENTERPRISE-BASED BARGAINING UNITS

It is clear from the study commission's terms of reference, the May 1987 policy document and earlier statements contained in its *Bulletin* that the BCA had decided that Australia needed to embrace a system of enterprise bargaining. As Frenkel and Peetz point out, the task assigned to the study commission was not to establish whether enterprise-based bargaining was appropriate to Australia, but rather to find ways of developing an enterprise-based system . . . Nonetheless, most of the research effort in the [first] report . . . is devoted to establishing the validity of the assumption that enterprise bargaining is appropriate to Australia.[14]

In preparing the first report the study commission commissioned research by the National Institute of Labour Studies and Malcolm Rimmer. The NILS produced two documents. The first involved a comparison between a small number of paired Australian and overseas (mainly American) companies. The second was an attitude survey of chief executive officers and site managers of BCA member companies. Rimmer presented historical data on the extent of enterprise and industry awards.[15]

Rimmer found that enterprise awards were a more significant feature of Australian industrial relations than has sometimes been realised and that their incidence was growing. Table 4.1 provides data on the incidence of private sector multi-employer and single-employer awards and public sector awards (which typically cover a single employer) in the respective federal and state jurisdictions in 1987. The table shows that there was a substantial number of private sector single-employer awards federally, in New South Wales, Queensland and Western Australia. However, it ignores industrial agreements in New South Wales and South Australia, the number of which at the end of the 1980s would probably have exceeded two thousand. Table 4.2 shows that there has been a marked increase in the number of federal, private sector single-employer awards between 1954 and 1987. Rimmer concluded that 'the power to make enterprise awards or agreements has been extensively used' and that 'Enterprise awards have now become relatively common'.[16]

Before presenting and examining the study commission's arguments and evidence for enterprise bargaining it might be useful to point out that the major criticism the study commission has encountered is that the evidence presented, a large proportion of which was derived from commissioned research by the NILS, does not support the conclusions derived.[17] It should be remembered that the BCA had already decided on the policy directions it wanted to pursue several years earlier. In response to criticisms of there being a contradiction between evidence

Table 4.1 Single-employer and multi-employer awards

	Private sector multi-employer awards	Private sector single-employer awards	Public sector awards and determinations
Federal	543	816	466
New South Wales	366	314	354
Victoria	174	21	38
Queensland	286	681	364
South Australia	122	8	78
Western Australia	213	120	247
Tasmania	75	2	63
Total	1779	1962	1610

Source: McDonald, T. and Rimmer, M. (1988), 'Award structure and the second tier', *Australian Bulletin of Labour*, June, pp. 469–91.

Table 4.2 Single-employer and multi-employer federal awards, 1954–87

	Private sector multi-employer	Private sector single-employer	Public sector	Total
1954	176	35	90	301
1974	320	256	155	731
1987	405	496	366	1267

Source: Rimmer, M. (1988), *Enterprise and Industry Awards*, Report Prepared for the Industrial Relations Study Commission of the Business Council of Australia, November.

(facts) and conclusions (theory), Hilmer and McLaughlin, on behalf of the study commission, claimed:

> Research in the social sciences, especially in new and under-researched areas, often requires an eclectic approach. Rather than seek to set up narrow experiments and observations that establish 'scientific' cause and effect, the eclectic approach draws on a wide range of sources, no one of which is compelling, but which together allow a reasonable inference to be drawn with respect to likely causes and effects.[18]

They footnote an article by Pettigrew apparently to support their position.[19]

An examination of Pettigrew's article provides scant support for their flexible, or fluid, approach to cause-and-effect statements. While Pettigrew draws on a range of data sources in studying organisational culture in a British boarding school, his analysis is consistent with an inductive approach employed in the social sciences. That is, Pettigrew's conclusions seem to follow logically from the evidence presented rather than being forced as a result of reasonable inferences. Hilmer and McLaughlin, in eschewing scientific cause-and-effect statements, seem to have abandoned research produced by the NILS on which the BCA's case for enterprise bargaining was based. Moreover, Hilmer and McLaughlin's inferential approach to cause-and-effect statements exposes them to the charge that their conclusions are based on mysticism and ideology rather than on the norms of traditional social-science-based research. The BCA, of course, had already decided or determined the conclusions for the study commission.

In its first report the study commission set itself the task of changing the structure of Australian unions away from their traditional craft and occupational focus, and the associated phenomena of several or many unions having representation rights in enterprises, to one of single-enterprise unions. The first report claimed: 'The biggest single industrial relations impediment to more efficient competitive Australian workplaces is the antiquated structure of our [sic] trade-union movement . . . Ideally what is needed is one bargaining unit at each workplace'.[20]

The study commission's first report is dominated by the idea that, in the context of the world of work, management is the font of all wisdom and knowledge. The function of workers is simply to respond to and carry out directives defined for them by management. In industrial relations writings this viewpoint is referred to as the unitarist perspective—that is, there is only one view concerning the *modus operandi* of the enterprise, which is determined by management. Management knows best.[21]

The unitarist perspective lays great stress on the notion of teamwork and cooperation. It refuses to acknowledge that its workforce might have different goals and aspirations from management or, more generally, that there could be a plurality of interests within the enterprise. Under the unitarist perspective tensions and problems that emerge have nothing to do with managerial decision-making; they are explained away as aberrations or the result of interference by external agents such as full-time trade union officials or government regulatory agencies.

The all-pervasive nature of the unitarist perspective can be illustrated by identifying two concepts or 'building blocks' used by the study commission in developing its case for reform. The first concept concerns its distinction between industrial relations and employee relations. 'Industrial relations' is seen as synonymous with the existence of industrial conflict and the apparent associated need for intervention and regulation by third parties. 'Employee relations', on the other hand, assumes a basic harmony of interests and little or no need for external regulation. The study commission maintains that 'we need to jettison the "industrial relations" mindset within our enterprises where it still rests on the outmoded assumption of conflict and move to "employee relations" in which industrial relations becomes a subsidiary part of relationships at work'.[22] It would be interesting to know what the study commission meant by 'work relations' and how it differs from both 'employee' and 'industrial relations'. The notion of 'employee relations' used by the study commission not only assumes away the existence of conflict but also seeks to abstract 'relationships at work' from other orbits relevant to the study of industrial relations (see chapter 1).

The second concept is the study commission's claim of the increased importance apparently afforded to the role of the individual at the workplace.[23] However, lurking within the report is a tension—rather an unresolved tension—between the needs of the individual and the collective needs of the enterprise. The study commission's recommendations to introduce single-union enterprise bargaining units are designed to enhance the ability of Australian firms to compete on international markets.[24] Elsewhere in the report the example of an American firm is quoted, with apparent favour, where 'management halved the workforce [and] cut wages by about 30 per cent for every employee at the site, including office personnel and managers'.[25] The quotation at the head of this chapter, with its attachment to technological determinism, should also be noted. Such strategies would seem to bode ill for the individual. The collective known as the enterprise is not interested in promoting individualism among its workforce; workers are only employed to the extent that they perform tasks required or expected of them by management or, to recall a quote from Hyman, 'Employ-ers require workers to the both dependable and disposable'.[26] The rationale of the study commission's concern with the individual is an ideological device to undermine the collectives that workers have tra-ditionally used to defend and advance their rights and interests at the workplace—namely, trade unions.

The study commission bases much of its case for reform on claims concerning increases in productivity that would flow from the intro-duction of single-union enterprises. The study commission presented OECD data about trends in labour productivity and total factor pro-ductivity and concluded that Australia's 'relative productivity has been declining for most of the past 25 years'.[27] Frenkel and Peetz point out that the data presented does not support this conclusion. While in the period 1960–73 Australian productivity grew at about two-thirds of that of other OECD countries, in 'the period 1974–1986 . . . Australian labour productivity grew at an average rate of only 0.1 points below the OECD average'.[28]

Frenkel and Peetz also criticise the study commission's interpret-ation of work by Haig concerning the comparative productivity of var-ious Australian industries with the UK, West Germany and the USA. The study commission claimed that 'our productivity in 1983 was sig-nificantly lower in all the major sectors except agriculture, primary production and building and construction . . . our productivity levels stood up reasonably well in most sectors relative to the United King-dom'.[29] Haig actually said: 'Australian manufacturing industries are relatively efficient by world standards', that 'the rate of productivity increase is relatively high', and that in the 1970s the productivity of Australian manufacturing

> was about 30 per cent higher than productivity in British industry, and about 7 per cent lower than the productivity of German industry. Since the mid-1970s productivity growth in Australian manufacturing indus-try has been as high [as] or higher than that of the average of Britain, Germany and the USA.[30]

Frenkel and Peetz ask:

> if unregulated enterprise bargaining is so superior, why should Australian productivity be better than that in the UK—which had experienced enterprise bargaining with weaker unions since the late 1970s—and

worse than West Germany, whose industrial relations system combines relatively centralised bargaining (mainly at industry and regional levels) with extensive enterprise consultation?[31]

Information about the pairing of eight Australian plants with similar overseas plants in terms of market size, products and technology is presented. The data was extracted from research performed for the study commission by the NILS. The study commission points to examples of overseas plants, particularly non-unionised American plants, with lower manning levels or greater workplace flexibility than Australian counterparts.[32] The NILS actually said:

> there is no meaningful difference in restrictive practices. Australians reported much higher job satisfaction, satisfaction with pay, commitment to their organisations, and workgroup cohesion, and slightly lower absenteeism . . . in none of the relevant case studies was it established that the American plants experienced productivity advantages traceable to greater efforts.[33]

The study commission based much of its case for reform on an attitude survey of site managers undertaken by the NILS. The introduction to the survey states: 'the principle aim of the research was to examine how the industrial relations system within Australia influences the productivity and competitiveness of organisations'.[34] It did neither.

No evidence or information was provided on productivity and profitability, and no attempt was made to link the performance of product and labour markets. The NILS researchers acknowledge that the data they gathered—which, after all, was an attitude survey—is only a proxy for performance, and they had not measured performance *per se*.[35]

A number of regression equations were developed from the attitude survey of site managers. The industrial relations, or independent variables, were such things as the number of unions, involvement of full-time union officials, closed shops, informal meetings, formal awards, company awards or agreements, both federal and state awards, use of piece rates, profit-sharing and so on. The performance, or dependent variables, included labour flexibility, shirking, restrictive work practices, number of stoppages and days lost. The equations achieved R^2 ranging from 0.307 to 0.528. Tests of significance were conducted for various independent variables. On the basis of such work it was concluded, for example, 'That union influence or power . . . is a powerful negative influence on labour flexibility and worker effort and a positive influence on restrictive work behaviour'.[36]

The NILS researchers themselves point out that 'regression analysis . . . does not distinguish between cause and effect . . . Unfortunately no unified, coherent and relevant theory of industrial relations exists, and so hypothesis selection is somewhat *ad hoc*, guided largely by our own *a priori* views and previous research'.[37] Given the *ad hoc* (even unscientific) nature of their theorising, it is conceivable that the NILS researchers have confused cause and effect. They hypothesise that the involvement of union officials results in poor workplace performance. It is equally, if not more, likely that the direction of causation is reversed. That is, problems at the workplace result in either managers or union members calling on full-time union officials to help resolve issues of concern. It is conceivable that all the NILS research has done is to confirm a tautology that in unionised workplaces industrial relations problems and full-time trade union officials are part and parcel of the same process.

If this is correct, we are still left with the question of the source of industrial relations problems. (This question, of course, has been answered in chapter 1 in terms of the desire of interactors to enhance their authority.) Frenkel and Peetz have pointed out that the R^2 obtained by the NILS researchers could have been improved if they had included variables concerning 'management strategy, organisation and style'.[38] In other words, it is conceivable that management, both in terms of the goals it sets and the methods it uses to achieve them, is a cause of industrial relations problems manifested at the workplace. Further research would undoubtedly yield highly reliable statistical tests linking the presence of senior management and workplace problems! Moreover, it should be again noted that the data that sustains these equations is based on an attitude survey of site managers. The NILS did not actually obtain any hard data on the productivity and profitability of different workplaces.

The study commission based much of its case for enterprise bargaining on claims made by chief executive officers of BCA companies concerning increased productivity. The study commission said:

Following extensive consultation with the chief executives of each of the workplaces included in the studies . . . a conservative estimate is that labour productivity in the workplaces concerned could be lifted by 20 to 25 per cent if labour could be deployed in an optimum way—if unnecessary demarcations could be eliminated, costly management and work practices removed.[39]

It should be remembered that BCA chief executives had decided several years earlier to embrace enterprise bargaining (see chapter 2). As Frenkel and Peetz point out:

the Business Council of Australia is both the source and object of the research. Council members set the research agenda, Council members answered the chief executive officer questionnaires and Council members selected the workplaces that took place in the site managers survey.[40]

In the context of knowing that the BCA and its chief executives are seeking to introduce reforms that they see as being advantageous to themselves, one should, and with all due respect to the chief executives concerned, attach as much credence to this statement on productivity as asking a group of Collingwood supporters who they thought would win an Australian Football League premiership.

The study commission claimed that Australia's industrial relations system and union activities act in 'subtle yet powerful ways' to stifle and thwart initiatives designed to enhance the productive performance of Australian enterprises.[41] However, evidence marshalled by the NILS fundamentally contradicts this view. Table 4.3 presents information from BCA companies on various workplace changes initiated by site managers, union resistance to such changes and changes discarded because of such resistance. The table shows, for example, that 89 per cent of companies sought to introduce new technology, 11 per cent of these attempts were resisted by unions, and one per cent discontinued because of such resistance. If we can make the arbitrary assumption that fifty per cent equals a pass mark, table 4.3 demonstrates that the industrial relations system and unions have been remarkably unsuccessful in resisting changes initiated by BCA site managers.

Such a conclusion is reinforced by the Australian Workplace Industrial Relations Survey conducted by the Commonwealth Department of Industrial Relations between October 1989 and May 1990. A survey of 891 managers found 'that Australian workplaces [had] experienced significant changes in the two to five years prior to the survey'. Fifty-seven per cent of managers said 'there was no change they could not make'. And, as revealed by table 4.4, 'attempts by management to become more efficient were hampered by management and organisational structure, management objectives and, in particular, financial or technical constraints, facing workplaces, rather than simply industrial relations considerations'.[42] Tables 4.3 and 4.4 would seem to cast serious doubt on the study commission's claim that 'complex, multi-union representation in most Australian workplaces hinders the process of continually adapting and improving work practices, particularly where many opportunities cross union and skill category lines'.[43]

Table 4.3 Workplace changes, union resistance and outcomes

	Yes initiated change %	Unions resisted change %	Change attempted but resistance precluded change %
Change workplace layout	83	9	1
New technology	89	11	1
Reduced overmanning	73	43	11
Changed system of overtime	39	57	23
Removed demarcation lines	57	64	24
Increased used of subcontractors	49	52	17
Increased use of part-time/ casual workers	46	45	13
Different working hours arrangements	60	41	18
Changed shiftwork arrangements	45	36	13
Improved job design	61	10	3
Measures to reduce absenteeism	46	33	11
Multiskilling	65	37	14
Increased employee training	80	3	1
Increased supervisor training	77	2	1
Enhanced roles for shop stewards	19	5	1
Other	3	45	9

Source: National Institute of Labour Studies (1989), *Employee and Industrial Relations in Australian Companies: A Survey of Management*, Report Prepared for the Industrial Relations Study Commission of the Business Council of Australia, March.

Table 4.4 Reasons why managers feel they cannot make efficiency changes at their workplace

	% of workplaces		
	Private	Public	All
Lack of money or resources	32	24	29
Management or organisation policy	14	32	20
Unions	14	14	14
Government rules and regulations	9	18	12
Awards	6	9	7
Other	28	15	24

Source: Callus et al. (1991), *Industrial Relations at work: The Australian Workplace Industrial Relations Survey*, AGPS, Canberra.

The study commission claimed that 'shared interests are more likely to blossom where employees bargain as one unit and with a workplace focus'.[44] Reference has already been made in chapter 1 to where the NILS paired analysis of multi-union Australian and non-union American firms discovered its 'curious anomaly in the data'. It found that 'Australian employees are more satisfied and committed to their organisations', the Australian industrial relations system provided 'an atmosphere where both high job satisfaction and commitment to organisations and peers flourish', and employees are protected from poor styles of supervision.[45]

One of the more interesting results of the NILS research was that site managers expressed more positive attitudes to the operation of the industrial relations system and trade unions in the context of the workplace than chief executives. The institute concluded that 'site managers appear reasonably content with the industrial relations system' and 'perceived a great deal of communication between unions and management, and between employers and managers, and have introduced participatory management programmes in most plants'. They also found that the majority of plant disputes were settled by plant managers via company-specific grievance procedures, and they successfully initiated 'changes in technology, plant lay-out, training, manning levels, job design and multi-skilling' (see table 4.3). On the other hand, chief executives 'are much more concerned that the industrial relations system is creating problems . . . [it] has created, or at least facilitated, hours limitations, restrictive practices and difficulties changing work assignments'.[46]

How should one interpret or respond to these contradictory perspectives from site managers and chief executives? It might seem reasonable to place greater weight on the perspectives of site managers, as they are closer to the 'coal face' than chief executives. The latter have too many responsibilities and other functions to perform, which might take them interstate and overseas, thereby reducing their familiarity with what happens in the various workplaces under their ultimate control. Both the NILS and the study commission, however, opted for an alternative explanation. They pointed to the regression equations from the site managers survey, which correlated the industrial relations system and trade unions with poor performance. It was argued that while 'plant managers are working within the system, often with great success, [they] have taken the system as given. The chief executives, on the other hand, see the system as changeable and in need of substantive change'.[47] To return to the unitarist perspective, it is not so much that management is right, rather senior management is right.

Frenkel and Peetz have provided a trenchant criticism of the study commission and the institute's method of resolving the contradiction between the site managers and chief executive responses. They argue that:

> like is not being compared with like. The *direct* questions asked of site managers show that non-industrial relations factors, such as skilled labour shortages, absenteeism, workplace layout and obsolete or unreliable equipment, are perceived as being more likely to have an adverse impact upon productivity than are industrial relations factors such as the number of unions. But the *econometric* tests used by the researchers to evaluate the impact of industrial relations factors did *not* include variables for most of these non-industrial relations factors. That is, there were no explanatory variables in their equations that measured workplace layout, or reliability of equipment, or the impact of labour shortage, so it would simply not be possible to deduce that the econometric tests showed that industrial relations factors were more important than non-industrial relations factors. It is important to note that the site managers did *not* say that industrial relations factors were 'no problem'; they just mentioned industrial relations factors as being *less* of a problem than a number of non-industrial relations factors.[47]

The study commission states that 'Employees have a democratic right to participate in the activities of and be represented by trade unions if they so choose'.[49] This 'democratic right', however, does not extend to workers being able to join unions of any type or organisational form; craft and occupational unions do not fit into the Business Council's future plans for Australia. The study commission wishes 'to speed up the reduction of the number of trade unions *in each workplace*, the ultimate goal being one per workplace with a workplace focus'.[50] There is also evidence to suggest that the study commission's ideal or ultimate goal for Australian unions is not one per workplace but rather union-free workplaces; or, alternatively, single-union workplaces are simply a stepping stone towards a 'final solution' for Australian trade unions. In a section entitled 'Steps towards enterprise focus' the study commission sees the creation of non-union workplaces as the final destination of its journey.[51] In a section entitled 'Some longer-term directions' it advocates the use of representative elections, as used in the USA, as a device to keep unions out of 'greenfield sites' and the creation of non-union workplaces.[52] O'Brien quotes a Business Council representative who said the council's policy was one of union avoidance rather than union busting.[53]

Through the creation of enterprise unions the BCA hopes to wrest workers away from what, for want of a better term, might be called 'fair dinkum' unions and, via the registration of enterprise agreements, break down the coverage of awards. By isolating workers and reducing the relevance and coverage of awards the BCA would be able to redistribute bargaining power substantially in favour of employers. In the USA, for example, companies have used threats of closure and a preparedness to move operations and finance elsewhere as a powerful device either to destroy unions or to reduce wages and salary conditions or both.[54]

AVOIDING INDUSTRIAL ACTION

In 1991 the study commission issued *Avoiding Industrial Action: A Better Way of Working*. It argues that 'Australia has a relatively poor record of industrial action, which reflects some fundamental flaws in the design of our [sic] industrial relations system. A disproportionate share of the action is short-term and avoidable'.[55] The study commission also maintains that the 'result has been costly to Australia in terms of lost output, market share and low commitment in the workplace'.[56] This claim concerning low workplace commitment by employees, of course, was contradicted by the paired research of Australian and overseas companies conducted by the NILS (see above).

Most Australian strikes are short. In the period 1980–90 between (approximately) 45 and 70 per cent were resolved in one day and between (approximately) 60 and 80 per cent in two days. Moreover, many Australian strikes are of a protest nature with approximately 60 per cent involving a resumption of work without negotiations (though for Business Council companies this figure was seven per cent).[57] It has generally been argued that part of the reason for Australia's pre-deliction for short sharp, 'protest' disputes is the lack of, or effective-ness of, grievance procedures. The implication is that workforces make use of 'protest' strikes to draw attention to unattended grievances.

The study commission advocates greater use of grievance proce-dures and improving their effectiveness in attempting to reduce the level of industrial disputation in Australia. In addition, it advocated the use of fixed-term awards. In so doing the study commission distin-guished between short- and long-term objectives. With respect to the short term, if parties were unable to reach agreement and a dispute occurred, the compliance provisions of the *Industrial Relations Act* 1988 would prevail (sections 178 and 180–7 sanctioned fines of $500 or $1000 for breaches plus cancellation and suspension of awards), plus actions under the common law and sections 45D and 45E of the *Trade Practices Act* 1974.

In the longer term the study commission was prepared to allow industrial action to be exempt from remedies under industrial law, and limited exemptions under the common law, but not sections 45D and 45E of the *Trade Practices Act* 1977. If agreement could not be reached within a specified period either party could ask the commission to exer-cise jurisdiction. Once this occurred any industrial action would be subject to a directional injunction process. In both the short and longer terms industrial action taken during the life of an award would be sub-ject to fines, imposed by the Federal Court of Australia, of not less than $1000 and not more than $10 000 per breach per day, as well as con-tempt of court remedies.[58] The fines proposed were a significant increase on those contained in the *Industrial Relations Act* 1988.

Criticisms can be directed at the study commission's claim that 'Australia has a relatively poor record of industrial action'. The statement is based on a comparison of Australia with other OECD countries in the periods 1978–82 and 1983–87. In the first period each Australian employee spent 0.600 of a day per year on strike, compared to 0.375 for other OECD countries. In the second period both Australia and other OECD countries were equal at 0.250 of a day per year.[59] Clearly the Australian level of disputation has declined and, between 1983 and 1987, was equal to that of other OECD countries.

Moreover, assuming that the length of the working year in these two periods was equal to 226 days,[60] between 1978 and 1982, on average, each Australian worker lost 0.265 per cent of the total time available for work in industrial disputes and, between 1983 and 1987, 0.111 per cent.

In addition, this 1991 report—and hence the BCA—do not appear to be concerned with other sources of lost production that impair the ability of Australian firms to compete on international markets. Losses to production from industrial disputes are relatively low compared to other sources of lost production.

For the late 1970s Crawford and Volard estimated that 5.5 per cent of total work absence was due to industrial disputes.[61] This compared with other sources of lost time from industrial accidents 6.3 per cent, other accidents 12.2 per cent, alcohol and drug abuse 17.8 per cent, 'the sickie' 18.9 per cent and other sickness and diseases 39.3 per cent. A study based on 1988 data estimated that the annual cost to the economy resulting from problems with alcohol and drug abuse exceeded $14.3 billion. These estimates, moreover, ignored the costs of absenteeism and reduced productivity resulting from such abuse.[62]

An examination of coroner-certified deaths in Australia between 1982 and 1984 found that 1544 work-related deaths occurred in the civilian labour force—an average of more than 500 per year.[63] A 1993 report by Worksafe Australia found that for the period between 1987–88 and 1989–90 at least 510 Australian workers died of occupational injury and disease each year. Moreover, the real number of fatalities was higher as there are many workers, such as those who are self-employed, who are not covered by workers' compensation. In addition, the workers' compensation system is a poor source of data on occupational disease. The Mesothelioma Register maintained by Worksafe Australia records at least 300 new cases of this fatal occupational disease each year. Worksafe Australia also estimated that for the period between 1987–88 and 1989–90 there were almost 200 000 new injury and disease cases each year involving five days or more off work. 'This means that every year about 1 worker in 30 suffers a compensable occupational injury or disease involving at least five days off work'.[64] An ILO study found that the rate of workplace deaths in Australia was 77 per million workers, compared with 37 per million in the USA, 24 in the UK, 22 in Sweden and 20 in Japan.[65] Worksafe Australia reported that for the period between 1987–88 and 1989–90 the figure for Australia had increased to 84 deaths per million workers.[66]

The Australian Workplace Industrial Relations Survey also provides additional data concerning sources of lost time from work. Both dismissals and voluntary labour turnover are seen as an indicator of poor worker–employer relationships and impose costs on firms (and individuals) in terms of losses expended in recruitment and training (what economists refer to as the fixed costs of employment). The workplace survey found an average dismissal rate of 4.5 per cent and a voluntary turnover rate of 19 per cent. Absenteeism can have detrimental effects on enterprises in increasing labour costs and lowering overall productivity and efficiency. The workplace survey reported an average absenteeism rate per week of 4.5 per cent.[67]

In concluding this examination of the study commission's second report attention will be directed to the phenomenon of Australia's predilection for short sharp strikes and the associated issue of grievance procedures. The study commission found that while 92.3 per cent of Business Council companies surveyed had grievance procedures in place, they were not overly used.[68] The more broadly based Australian Workplace Industrial Relations Survey found 49 per cent of workplaces, covering 67 per cent of employees, had instituted grievance procedures but rarely used them.[69]

Managers who responded to the workplace survey were asked how often such procedures were used to handle or resolve grievances. Callus et al. report:

> Forty per cent said rarely or never. Of the 63 per cent of workplaces that indicated the procedure was used, 37 per cent indicated it had not been used in the previous year. This is despite the fact that grievances occurred at most workplaces. Only 16 per cent of workplaces claimed that the

procedure was used for grievance handling all the time. This low level of regular use suggests that grievances may be dealt with effectively through more informal methods.[70]

Why is it that grievance procedures are used so infrequently? Or, alternatively, why does there appear to be an apparent lack of effort to prevent the occurrence of short strikes? The answer to these questions may be provided in four parts. First, as was pointed out above, industrial disputes involve a relatively small percentage of lost time. Second, and following on from this, disputes associated with workplace frustrations and the lack of, or usage of, grievance procedures must necessarily also account for a limited amount of lost time and hence output and production. Third, the resources necessary to maintain a grievance procedure, which is readily available to avoid or 'put out' short strikes, might be relatively costly in terms of time, personnel and resources. Fourth, the cost of maintaining a grievance procedure might be higher than the benefits of a reduction in the level of short strikes. Hence employers, companies and unions have decided on the basis of an intuitive cost–benefit analysis to avoid the use of grievance procedures despite their increasing inclusion in awards and agreements. On the basis of this analysis attempts either to impose grievance procedures or to make them more prominent, as proposed by the study commission,[71] might constitute little more than a direction from above, which results in a waste of resources and the time and energy of those who manage Australian workplaces. (It is also, incidentally, the antithesis of a philosophy based on deregulation.)

WORKING RELATIONS

Working Relations: A Fresh Start for Australian Enterprises, published in 1993, is the study commission's third report. Its analysis and recommendations traverse much of the same ground as the two earlier reports, is somewhat anti-climatic and will only be briefly examined here. The study commission claims that the 'rules for bargaining . . . have remained largely unchanged over the last decade'.[72] In making this statement the study commission seems to be unaware of the changes to Australian industrial relations—the increasing decentralisation and devolution—documented in chapters 2 and 3 (although, in contradiction, five pages later the study commission lists the major changes that did occur!).

The study commission criticises overaward bargaining because it 'is more likely to reflect mainly market considerations affecting wages'.[73] The major reason for such a criticism is that overaward bargaining has traditionally been an important source of flexibility in Australian industrial relations and constitutes a competitor to the BCA's quest for the adoption of stand-alone enterprise agreements.[74] Despite this, to criticise overaward bargaining because it 'reflect[s] mainly market considerations' seems at odds with the pro-market rhetoric associated with the BCA since its formation in 1983. To criticise behaviour on the basis of reflecting market considerations suggests that lurking within the Business Council's advocacy of enterprise bargaining is a dependency on non-, or extra-, market decisions that need to be made to enhance Australia's international competitiveness.

And it is not as if the study commission could have turned to the NILS to unravel mysteries of overaward bargaining. In 1992 Drago, Wooden and Sloan published *Productive Relations?*, a reworking of research previously conducted for the study commission in preparation of its first report. At one point we are told that awards are akin to laws, and at a particular company there was no overaward pay because of the strictures of the Accord. It is also stated that the award system precludes managers from making use of monetary incentives. Their survey of Business Council companies revealed that 67 per cent provided overaward pay, to an average level of 16.5 per cent.[75]

Finally, the study commission, in discussing the question of the representative rights of unions at workplaces, says:

> There will be no gains to enterprises in leaving employee representation arrangements to chance, allowing employee choice to be determined willy nilly . . . employees will have a choice of representation and the arrangements we propose will enable managers to influence that choice, just as they do with many other aspects of employees' work.[76]

In other words, non-members of a union—in this case management—have presumably as much, if not more, discretion than members (workers) to determine the shape or form of organisations that represent them in negotiations with employers.[77] In making such a statement the study commission seems to be unaware that it contravenes International Labour Organisation convention number 98, The Right to Organise and Collective Bargaining, ratified by Australia in February 1973. A section of convention number 98 states:

Workers and employers' organisations shall enjoy adequate protection against any acts of interference by each other or each other's agents or members in their establishment, functioning or administration. Acts which are designed to promote the establishment of workers' organisations under the control of employers shall be deemed to constitute acts of interference.[78]

The States and enterprise bargaining

Beginning with the September 1986 work practices summit and the March 1987 two-tiered system, Australian industrial relations has moved from an approach that emphasises the needs of the system to one that focuses on the needs of the enterprise.

In the initial moves towards a more decentralised system the commission, or industrial tribunals, was afforded a prominent role in processing enterprise bargains negotiated between unions and employers. Such bargains, of course, had to be consistent with the commission's structural efficiency principle. The enterprise bargaining model, which operated at the federal level between March 1987 and July 1992, was predicated on tribunal and union involvement. Given the existence of legislation in each of the states that virtually required their respective tribunals to follow the lead of the federal commission on major issues,[79] the States, via such legislation, invariably found themselves adopting the same model of enterprise bargaining pursued at the federal level.[80]

Chapter 3 has documented how the Accord partners became increasingly disenchanted with the AIRC. In July 1992 legislation came into force that enabled unions and employers in single bargaining units to enter into workplace agreements bypassing the commission. Under the *Industrial Relations Legislation Amendment Act* 1992 the commission was required to ratify workplace agreements unless it disadvantaged the workers concerned, the said workers had been consulted and the agreement contained a grievance procedure and had a definite period of operation. The commission could employ its traditional approach in resolving disputes, including public interest tests, which involved two or more workplaces. This second model of enterprise bargaining in single workplaces took industrial tribunals out of the processing of such deals. Unions were presumed to play a prominent role in negotiating workplace bargains.

The two Labor States of Queensland and South Australia introduced legislation that basically followed the lead of their federal colleagues. The Queensland *Industrial Relations Amendment Act* 1992 became operative on 7 December 1992, while the South Australian *Industrial Relations (Miscellaneous Provisions) Amendment Act* 1992 began operation on 1 February 1993. With the election of a Liberal government in South Australia in late 1993 it is likely that its legislation governing industrial relations and enterprise bargaining will be altered.

Before the July 1992 federal legislation New South Wales had already pioneered an alternative approach to enterprise bargaining. As with the July 1992 federal model, the New South Wales *Industrial Relations Act* 1991 provided an enterprise bargaining route as an alternative to awards.[81]

The New South Wales Industrial Relations Commission could register or process consent awards negotiated between unions and employers (although this had been a feature of previous legislation). The most distinctive feature of the legislation, however, was that the making of such agreements was not confined to negotiations between employers and unions/unionised work groups. Employers could enter into deals with non-unionised work groups.

The legislation requires that, in negotiating enterprise deals with non-unionised work groups, 65 per cent of the employees identified in the appropriate bargaining unit must agree, in a vote conducted by secret ballot, to be covered by the said agreement. The legislation specifies that enterprise bargains must contain three minimum conditions: a minimum hourly rate of pay equal to that which previously applied under an equivalent award, a minimum forty-hour week averaged over fifty-two weeks,[82] and a minimum of one week sick leave on full pay for each year of service. New South Wales unions feared that enterprise deals would enable employers to persuade or force non-unionised workers to accept employment on terms that would erode, if not substantially reduce, terms and conditions enshrined in awards. Signed copies of enterprise agreements have to be lodged with the commissioner for enterprise agreements. The function of the commissioner is to arrange a meeting of those who are party to such an agreement, ascertain that they understand their rights and obligations under the agreement, or awards, that govern their employment and then certify the said agreement.

The adoption of enterprise agreements in New South Wales following commencement of the Industrial Relations Act on 31 March 1992 has been somewhat slow, if not desultory. As of 31 December 1993 there were 441 registered (and varied) agreements covering 28 225 employees (by 28 February 1994 there were 497 agreements covering 40 488 employees).[83] Of these agreements 179 have been negotiated with the Independent Teachers Association, with 146 (about a third) representing deals negotiated in private schools. Only 16.9 per cent of enterprise bargains cover the total terms and conditions of employees, with 83.1 per cent being partial agreements, often only covering a single issue such as pay rates or sick leave. More than seventy per cent of enterprise agreements have resulted from negotiations between unions and employers, with 29 per cent between employers and groups of workers. Most enterprise agreements (65 per cent) have involved, or been negotiated, with work groups of fifty or fewer.[84]

Finally, a study conducted by the New South Wales Department of Industrial Relations, Employment, Training and Further Education found that female workers were less likely to participate in enterprise bargains than men and, to the extent that they did, received lower pay increases and surrendered more pay-related allowances and benefits for the increases gained.[85]

In Tasmania the *Industrial Relations Amendment (Enterprise Agreement and Workplace Freedom) Act* 1992, which began on 1 March 1993, emulated the New South Wales approach to enterprise bargaining. As with the New South Wales legislation, groups of workers were required to participate in secret ballots to demonstrate their acceptance of an enterprise agreement—although a 60 rather than 65 per cent majority is required; minimum terms and conditions (hourly pay and annual, sick and parental leave) have to be included, and there is a role for an enterprise commissioner. In distinction from New South Wales the Tasmanian legislation empowers the enterprise commissioner to investigate whether such agreements were made under duress, the minister (for industrial relations) can intervene in hearings evoking the public interest, and decisions of the enterprise commissioner can be appealed to a full bench of the Tasmanian Industrial Commission. The taking up of enterprise agreements in Tasmania has been relatively slow. At the beginning of February 1994 thirty-three agreements had been approved, with a further eleven waiting a hearing; and the over-whelming majority are confined to small workplaces.[86]

The election of the Kennett Coalition Government in Victoria in October 1992 witnessed the introduction of yet another variant of enter-prise bargaining. The Victorian *Employee Contracts Act* 1992, which began operation on 1 March 1993, allows groups of workers, who may be unionised and/or represented by union officials, to participate in the negotiation of collective employment agreements.[87] The act, however, abolishes awards and encourages the negotiation of individual employ-ment agreements. Individuals can be represented by union officials in negotiating such agreements. All Victorian awards came to an end on 1 March 1993, although their terms and conditions continue to oper-ate until the negotiation of a new collective or individual agreement. The Employment Contracts Act abolished the Victorian Industrial Relations Commission and replaced it with an Employment Relations Commission. This latter body can become involved in disputes and registering agreements (what the act refers to as awards) when all parties voluntarily agree to its participation. The act specifies that both collective and individual employment contracts should contain minimum terms similar to those contained in New South Wales and Tasmanian legislation.[88]

Victorian unions expressed strong opposition to the Kennett Gov-ernment's legislation, organising rallies and statewide strikes. They were concerned that the abolition of awards, in tandem with individual bar-gaining, would enable employers to use the threat of unemployment to force workers on to substandard employment contracts. In response, and in the context of a forthcoming federal election, the Keating Gov-ernment introduced legislation to enable workers who did not have access to a State tribunal that made use of compulsory arbitration to be covered by the federal commission. Since the passage of the Com-monwealth's *Industrial Relations Legislation Amendment Act (No. 2)* 1992, which began to operate on 21 January 1993, there has been an increas-ing exodus of Victorian workers to the federal system. It appears that the net result of the Kennett Government's experiment with enter-prise bargaining is to lose control of the regulation of industrial rela-tions in Victoria.

Another, more complicated model of enterprise bargaining was developed in Western Australia by the Court Liberal Government after it gained office in February 1993. A trio of legislation—the *Workplace Agreements Act* 1993, the *Minimum Conditions of Employment Act* 1993 and the *Industrial Relations Amendment Act* 1993, which came into force on 1 December 1993—combine a role for industrial tribunals with the negotiation of collective and individual agreements; unions are able to act as bargaining agents for both types of agreements.

The Western Australian legislation, as with the New South Wales model, provides two avenues for processing enterprise bargains. A distinction is made between industrial and workplace agreements. The former can be processed through the Western Australian Industrial Relations Commission in the traditional way, like a consent award. There are two types of workplace agreements: collective and individual. Neither fall under the jurisdiction of the Western Australian Industrial Relations Commission, being required to be registered with a commissioner for workplace agreements. The legislation has provision for the establishment of minimum rates of pay and various leave entitlements. However, Western Australia's approach to the determination of a minimum weekly wage, for a full-time employee, is distinctive. The Western Australian Industrial Relations Commission, in court session, is obliged to make a recommendation each year by 31 May concerning such a rate, which the minister may either accept or reject. Part-time workers will receive a minimum hourly rate one-fortieth of whatever the hourly rate is, with casuals receiving a 15 per cent loading on the hourly rate.

THE ACCORD MARK VII AND THE *INDUSTRIAL RELATIONS REFORM ACT* 1993

In a keynote speech to the International Industrial Relations Association's ninth world congress in Sydney on 31 August 1992 Prime Minister Paul Keating briefly outlined how Australia had developed its system(s) of industrial tribunals and provided an account of the Accord years (and their various successes!) and moves towards a more flexible system of industrial relations regulation. He said: 'Not only is the old system finished, but we are rapidly phasing out its replacement, and we have now begun to do things in a new way' and added: 'Bargaining is the [new] way'.

However, he made two important qualifications. First, Australia would not move to a regime of workplace bargaining unless the Federal Government had an agreement with the ACTU on wages to ensure that Australia's inflation rate was consistent with that of its trading partners. Australia, he said, 'could run into big trouble' without such an agreement.

> The union movement has the ability to control the timing and extent of claims. And we as a government have already said that our commitment to superannuation increases over the decade, and to a general minimum wage increase from time to time, would be reconsidered if wages growth started to outrun the level comparable with low inflation.[89]

Second, Keating envisaged 'an important role' for the Industrial Relations Commission in determining minimum award rates and in providing 'a safety net below which employees cannot fall'. He also said that the commission will

> have an important role in helping the parties to reach enterprise or industry agreements, in vetting single-enterprise agreements to make sure the employees have not been disadvantaged, and in vetting agreements which go beyond a single enterprise to make sure they are based on genuine productivity enhancements and relate to an industry rather than a craft or occupation.[90]

His speech then became 'a little partisan' while he extolled the virtues of Labor's cooperative approach to industrial relations in contrast to the 'industrial warfare' being preached by the Coalition—a federal election was in the offing.

In October 1992 the federal Coalition released *Jobsback!*, a blueprint of industrial relations reforms it would introduce if elected. *Jobsback!* is very similar to the enterprise bargaining model developed by the Victorian Kennett Government. It advocates the abolition of awards, an end to compulsory arbitration and the use of workplace agreements, negotiated between an employer and an individual or groups of workers. Where an award had expired and the parties concerned had not reached a new agreement *Jobsback!* specified that legislation would continue the terms of the old award. *Jobsback!* specifies a number of minimum terms and conditions that must be stipulated in workplace agreements: a minimum hourly rate linked to a relevant award, a minimum hourly rate of $3 or $3.50 for youths depending on age, four weeks annual leave, two weeks non-cumulative sick leave and unpaid maternity leave after twelve months continuous service. *Jobsback!* foreshadowed the creation of the office of the employee advocate who would investigate claims, provide advice or fund actions for workers covered by workplace agreements 'who have legitimate claims for unpaid wages or other entitlements, or who may have been unfairly dismissed or treated by their employers'.[91]

The ALP and the ACTU reached agreement on a new Accord—the Accord Mark VII—on 19 February 1993, three weeks before the federal election.[92] The Accord Mark VII, developed in response to *Jobsback!*, reconfirms the Accord partners' longstanding commitment to workplace bargaining and extols the virtues of awards and the important role to be performed by industrial tribunals.[93] In addition, and at a time when unemployment levels exceeded eleven per cent, the Accord Mark VII pledged the Federal Government to increasing employment by a minimum of 500 000 net additional jobs in three years. The Accord Mark VII is subtitled 'Putting jobs first'; the availability of its various entitlements is conditional on the prior achievement of acceptable levels of employment growth.[94]

Consistent with Keating's International Industrial Relations Association speech in August 1992 the Accord Mark VII said that 'in future the role of Industrial Tribunals should be increasingly focused on safety net provisions, test case standards, conciliation and dispute settlement'. While the Accord partners anticipated that most of the workforce would eventually be covered by workplace agreements, industrial tribunals were perceived as retaining 'a key function' in 'oversighting the operation and maintenance of the award system', assisting parties in conciliation where requested and ensuring that 'certified agreements do not disadvantage employees and other requirements spelt out in the legislation have been met'.[95]

In addition, the Accord Mark VII said that a Labor government would introduce legislation under ILO conventions to guarantee workers' award rights, regardless of the State or Territory they lived in, to minimum wages, equal pay for work of equal value by men and women, protection against unfair dismissal and unpaid parental leave. The Accord Mark VII outlined 'safety net' increases available for those unions that had entered into 'good faith bargaining' at the enterprise level but had been unable to obtain increases. An $8 per week increase would be available after 1 July 1993 as well as two further adjustments of between $5 and $10 per week from 1 July 1994 and 1 July 1995 respectively.

It has passed into folklore that *Jobsback!*, particularly its attack on awards, was an important ingredient in the subsequent defeat of the Coalition in the 13 March 1993 federal election.

Following Labor's electoral victory some unions expected that the first $8 safety net increase contained in the Accord Mark VII would be made available sooner rather than later and would cover a largeish proportion of the workforce. ACTU president Martin Ferguson sought to hose down such expectations. He urged affiliates to embrace workplace bargaining and stated that job creation was a major priority for the ACTU.[96] Under the Accord Mark VII safety net increases depend on attaining satisfactory levels of job creation. In addition, it appears that the ACTU leadership had decided to delay pursuing the first safety net increase until the last quarter of 1993 as part of a strategy to force affiliates to pursue workplace deals.[97]

There were two attempts by affiliates to persuade the ACTU to change its mind on the timing of the first safety net case. The first occurred in May when the Textile, Clothing and Footwear, Public Sector and Liquor, Hospitality and Miscellaneous Workers Unions complained about difficulties they had experienced in negotiating workplace deals with employers. However, in the absence of a national wage case to clear the way for safety net increases, they were unable to pursue such claims on behalf of members.[98] Other unions, such as the Automotive, Metal and Engineering Union, believed that a safety net case would prejudice its negotiations with employers. The ACTU decided to defer any claim for at least two months so as not to interfere with the processing of workplace deals and to wait for further signs of employment growth.[99]

This decision spawned a second round of criticisms of the ACTU. A group of ten, mainly right-wing unions, which coalesced around the New South Wales Labor Council, became increasingly vociferous in their criticisms. They canvassed the idea of mounting a New South Wales State wage case for the safety net increase in attempting to force the hand of the ACTU. In June the Labor Council passed a motion requesting the ACTU to review its policy on the $8 safety net increase.

The ACTU resisted this call, hinting that it would initiate a case in July. The New South Wales unions continued their campaign at the annual conference of the State branch of the Labor Party. The conference called on the Federal Government and the ACTU to pursue a safety net increase per the Accord Mark VII. As the end of June approached the ACTU indicated that it would mount such a case.[100]

In July the AIRC convened a national wage case. Beside adjudicating on the safety net increase the commission considered issues associated with the confusion flowing from the two paths to enterprise bargaining—its approach according to the October 1991 national wage case versus that of the Accord partners contained in the July 1992 legislation—and the resolution of superannuation disputes. The commission's decision, handed down on 25 October, retraces events associated with the emergence of the two paths and why it adopted the stance that it did. In doing so, however, it implicitly acknowledged that it might have erred in October 1991 (if not in April 1991) in not availing itself of arbitral powers in resolving enterprise bargaining disputes. The commission altered its principles to exercise such arbitral powers. Its involvement, however, was contingent on the negotiation of such deals being conducted in accordance with the implementation of the structural efficiency principle. It said:

> The Commission is aware of enterprise bargaining disputes which have occurred since October 1991 where conciliation has failed to achieve agreement on all or some issues. Too often this has meant that worthwhile efficiency improvements have had to be put aside, with consequential loss of extra income to both employers and employees and longer term reduction in competitiveness. Because of this, the Commission considers that it should be prepared to arbitrate in such disputes. It will arbitrate any outstanding matter in dispute and will determine it on the merits of the competing claims. This course is consistent with its responsibilities under the Act and should not only make it possible for more improvements in efficiency and productivity to be achieved but the availability of arbitration as a final resort should of itself, on past experience, enhance the prospects of success in conciliation.[101]

The commission again called on the Commonwealth Government to convene a conference to resolve matters associated with superannuation and 'a rational and sensible framework for retirement incomes'. Besides revisiting issues it had raised in its April 1991 decision, and examining Commonwealth legislation since then, the commission pointed to jurisdictional limitations on its activities 'particularly as regards non-unionists'.[102]

It was prepared to grant an $8 per week safety net increase from 1 December 1993 for workers who had been unable to obtain increases via enterprise bargaining and were not receiving overaward pay. In so deciding, however, the commission invited the parties to provide written submissions by 5 November concerning the level of safety net increase (another example of indecision?). After receiving submissions the commission, on 15 November, reaffirmed the granting of an $8 safety net increase.[103]

On 21 April 1993 Paul Keating delivered a speech to the Institute of Directors in Melbourne. It was his first major speech following his electoral victory in March and was heralded as setting the scene for the next three years of Labor's rule. The speech provides an account of the successes of Labor in enhancing Australia's international competitiveness. Keating said he regarded the 13 March election result 'as a mandate for an Australian social democratic agenda—for strong economic policy married to programs which produce not just social justice but social cohesion and strength'.[104] The final part of his speech was devoted to the links between industrial relations reform and economic progress. Keating said: 'there is no economic reform more central than to complete the construction of a system of industrial relations which will enhance productivity, protect the weak, and distribute fairly the rewards of cooperation in the workplace'. He then covered much of the same ground contained in his August 1992 International Industrial Relations Association speech and precepts contained in the Accord Mark VII. In extolling the virtues of workplace bargaining he appeared to suggest that it would replace awards. He said: 'We need to find a way of extending the coverage of agreements from being add-ons to awards, as they sometimes are today, to being full substitutes for awards'. In addition, he observed, 'there are lots of employees who for one reason or another don't have a union to represent them'.[105]

Some commentators interpreted this speech to mean that Labor was to embark on deregulation of the labour market.[106] Opposition leader John Hewson accused Keating of stealing the Coalition's industrial relations policies.[107] Keating's speech irritated unions that had campaigned and contributed funds to re-elect a Labor government on the basis of its support for the award system. After a flurry of activity the prime minister's office, and that of the minister for industrial relations, Laurie Brereton, repledged their support to awards and the Accord Mark VII; Keating's comment that workplace deals would replace awards had just been an unfortunate turn of phrase.[108]

Following Keating's speech the Federal Government took steps to introduce legislation to give effect to its program of industrial relations reform. In a number of speeches, media releases and interviews Brereton made it clear that he wanted to extend the ability to make enterprise deals to non-unionised workers—who comprised about 70 per cent of the private sector workforce.[109] For unions this sounded like the New South Wales approach to enterprise bargaining, with the potential for employers dealing with workers in poor bargaining positions to reduce wages and working conditions and thereby attack the awards of unionised workers. Despite representations from the ACTU, and being hissed and booed at the ACTU's biennial conference held in Sydney on 1 September 1993,[110] Brereton, or more correctly the Federal Government, steadfastly held to the desire to extend workplace bargaining to non-unionised workers. After a series of negotiations with unions, employer groups and other interested parties on a wide range of issues the *Industrial Relations Reform Act* 1993 was finalised in December, although it did not become operative until 30 March 1994.

The *Industrial Relations Reform Act* 1993 embodies significant changes to the operation of Australian industrial relations. The act draws on not only the industrial relations but also the corporations and external affairs powers of the Australian Constitution (see chapter 3). For example, one of the new objects of the *Industrial Relations Act* 1988 is to ensure 'that labour standards meet Australia's international obligations' (s. 3(b)(ii)).

The act substantially revises the institutional structure of federal-level industrial relations. A specialist industrial court—the Industrial Relations Court of Australia—was created to administer judicial functions associated with the operation of the *Industrial Relations Act* 1988. In addition, responsibility for secondary boycotts under sections 45D and 45E of the *Trade Practices Act* 1974 has been transferred to the jurisdiction of this new court. A specialist federal industrial court is not a new phenomenon for Australia. The Commonwealth Court of

Conciliation and Arbitration combined judicial and arbitral functions from 1904 to 1956. The *Boilermakers'* case[111] brought about a separation of functions and the creation of an Industrial Court, which operated between 1956 and 1977 before it was integrated with the Federal Court of Australia by the Fraser Government.

The *Industrial Relations Reform Act* 1993 has created two divisions, or streams, within the AIRC: an award and a bargaining division. The award division continues traditional functions performed by the commission under the *Industrial Relations Act* 1988. The functions of the bargaining division are to certify agreements negotiated by employers and unions, and to facilitate bargaining between employers and unionised or non-unionised work groups. According to the 1993 legislation the commission is required to ratify certified agreements negotiated at a single workplace, subject to a no disadvantage test of the terms and conditions of the employees concerned. Agreements covering multi-workplaces are subject to a public interest, as well as a no disadvantage, test.

Employers and work groups, unionised or non-unionised, can enter into enterprise flexibility agreements concerning wages and working conditions, which are presented to the bargaining division for ratification. The bargaining division can hear submissions from unions concerning such agreements and ratify deals subject to no disadvantage and public interest tests. This ability of the bargaining division to provide agreements negotiated by employers and non-unionised work groups with a quasi-award status seems to fly in the face of Henry Bournes Higgins' observation that 'the system of arbitration . . . is based on unionism. Indeed, without unions, it is hard to conceive how arbitration could be worked'.[112]

A potential problem associated with enterprise flexibility agreements involving non-unionised groups of workers should be noted. It is unlikely that such workers would be as skilled in what the Webbs called 'the higgling of the market' as those who employ them. As Sidney and Beatrice Webb observed at the turn of the century, bargaining 'forms a large part of the daily life of the entrepreneur . . . The manual worker, on the contrary, has the very smallest experience of, and particularly no training in, what is essentially one of the arts of the capitalist employer'.[113]

Notwithstanding the existence of no disadvantage and public interest tests, non-unionised workers—particularly those lacking skills and bargaining power, such as women, non-English-speaking immigrants and the young—might find it difficult to resist the entreaties of their employers to give up protections and conditions previously contained in awards.

The *Industrial Relations Reform Act* 1993 recognises, or enshrines, certain minimum entitlements for employees, which are based on various ILO conventions. These entitlements include minimum wages, equal remuneration for work of equal value, protection against unfair dismissal, parental leave and workers being able to attend to family responsibilities. Via section 109 of the Australian Constitution such entitlements would flow to workers in State jurisdictions, to the extent that there was an inconsistency between State and federal laws. In determining minimum wages the Reform Act requires the commission to examine

> so far as possible and appropriate in relation to Australian practice and conditions, to:
> (a) the needs of workers and their families, taking into account the general level of wages in Australia, the cost of living, social security benefits and the relative living standards of other social groups; and
> (b) economic factors, including the requirements of economic development, levels of productivity and the desirability of attaining and maintaining a high level of employment.[114]

This clause concerning minimum wage entitlements, coupled with regular claims for safety net increases according to the Accord Mark VII, has the potential to enable the commission to determine what might become regarded as a basic wage for workers, something Australia previously experimented with between 1907 and 1967.[115]

The *Industrial Relations Reform Act* 1993 also empowers the commission to review awards every three years (s. 150A(i)) to 'ensure, so far as it can, that the[y] . . . provide for secure relevant and consistent wages and conditions of employment' (s. 90 AA(2)(a)). This is designed to maintain the relevance of awards, regularly updating them for various changes negotiated in certified and enterprise flexibility agreements.

Finally, the act provides unions (and employers) with a period of immunity from common law and secondary boycott actions associated with strikes (and lock-outs). Either party can notify the other of its intention to use industrial action during a designated bargaining period for three days. The commission can intervene and make use of its traditional arbitral functions if it believes that the parties are not acting in good faith, if there is little likelihood of an agreement being reached, or on the grounds of public interest, in seeking to resolve the dispute.

CONCLUSION

One of the more intriguing issues associated with analysing Australian industrial relations is the intensity of the conflict and differences that have divided most of the major parties as they have rushed to embrace enterprise or workplace bargaining. To the untutored it has been difficult to understand why or how there could be such differences over a goal or object that seemingly everyone wants to (or should?) pursue. The answer, of course, is that 'enterprise bargaining' has become a catch-all phrase that means all things to all people. While enterprise bargaining signifies a move to a more decentralised or devolved system of industrial relations it conceals a myriad of differences between protagonists as to how it should be implemented and the associated role or involvement of industrial tribunals and unions, if any, in the future course of Australian industrial relations.

The BCA's case for enterprise bargaining is a thinly veiled, if not transparent, attack on industrial tribunals and especially unions. Having already made a decision to adopt enterprise bargaining by the mid 1980s the Business Council found itself involved in the unscientific exercise of ignoring, massaging or attacking data collected on its behalf that did not fit into its predetermined conclusions. The chapter also highlighted how Commonwealth and State Governments have experimented with a variety of models of enterprise bargaining. Under the *Industrial Relations Reform Act* 1993 the Accord partners have agreed— if in the case of the ACTU reluctantly—to extend enterprise bargaining to non-unionised workers. And the non-Labor States have differed over whether enterprise bargaining should be based on collectives (unionised or not) or individuals—compare New South Wales and Victoria.

Notwithstanding the incessant clamour for enterprise bargaining expressed by governments (and oppositions), the ACTU and various employer groups, its growth and spread has been relatively modest.

The taking up of enterprise bargaining in the States has been tardy. In New South Wales, for example, by the end of February 1994 about 40 000 workers were covered by such deals. At the federal level there are 1750 agreements covering some 800 000 employees, about twelve per cent of wage and salary earners.[116] Most of these agreements are add-ons rather than comprehensive stand-alone documents.[117] It also appears that women are less likely than men to have access to, or be in industries or occupations that are conducive to, the processing of enterprise deals.[118]

The following reasons might help to explain the relatively slow move towards enterprise bargaining.[119] First, those involved in industrial relations can still make use of the traditional channels provided by industrial tribunals to regulate their relationships. This in turn might suggest that, despite the rhetoric and heart-felt desires of those wanting to initiate change, tribunals perform an important, if unspectacular, function in helping to fulfil the needs of different groups of parties. Second, as the Australian Workplace Industrial Relations Survey revealed, site managers have had little difficulty in initiating workplace change, irrespective of developments at the formal level. In other words, workplace change does not appear to have been dependent on the prior rewriting of pieces of paper. Third, the enterprise bargaining legislation introduced by non-Labor States has been accompanied by industrial action and protests by unions in each of the States concerned. This, plus a recognition that unions could move to the federal jurisdiction, might have convinced many employers that they should tread warily in availing themselves of the advantages of enterprise bargaining. Moreover, as far as small business is concerned, it appears that the system of industrial relations plays a relatively minor role in problems experienced.[120] Finally, during the early 1990s the Australian economy was in recession. A slow-moving economy is usually associated with long wage rounds.

Two final comments concerning enterprise bargaining will be offered. First, the case for enterprise bargaining is based on a belief that the well-being of the economy would be enhanced by linking wages and other concessions to the productive performance of enterprises. Such a policy, however, might lead to a new set of economic problems. Machlup maintains that 'a policy that condones wage increases in industries which, because of increased productivity, can afford to pay increased wages without charging increased prices, is actually a policy that accepts a rising cost–price spiral without end'.[121] He had minor and major reasons for this conclusion. The minor reason was what he called the spill-over effect, or what we in Australia would call comparative wage justice, of the higher wages emanating from the higher productivity sectors concerned. The major reason was that a policy linking wages to productivity would result in technological unemployment in the sectors concerned. Other things being equal, firms with increasing wages would have an incentive to reduce employment and would be disinclined to employ additional labour. Linking wages to productivity would witness increased unemployment and/or exacerbate inflation if governments initiated expansionary policies to soak up the technologically unemployed. Machlup hoped benefits obtained in high productivity sectors would be translated into lower prices, helping to reduce inflation and enhance overall economic performance.

Second, enterprise bargaining has been seen to be consistent with or part of a move towards a more deregulated approach to industrial relations. It has in fact involved a *re*regulation of industrial relations; both Commonwealth and State Governments have enacted long and complex pieces of legislation to govern its operation.

5

WHAT IS TO BE DONE
WITH UNIONS?

....

The first and overriding responsibility of all trade unions is to the welfare of their own members. That is their primary commitment; not to a firm, not to an industry, not to the nation. A union collects its members' contributions and demands their loyalty specifically for the purpose of protecting their interests as they see them, not their alleged 'true' or 'best' interests as defined by others.

Flanders, A. *(1970),* Management and Unions: The Theory and Reform of Industrial Relations, *Faber & Faber, London, p. 40.*

Many union members fear that the union hierarchy, particularly the ACTU leadership, has lost touch with the ordinary concerns of ordinary workers.

Australian National Opinion Polls, quoted in Sydney Morning Herald, *1 April 1989*

....

In 1928 Selig Perlman published *A Theory of the Labor Movement*, one of the classic works of industrial relations scholarship. Among other things Perlman highlighted the struggle that occurs between unions and their 'natural' or 'home-grown' leaders, on the one hand, and intellectuals, on the other hand. For Perlman intellectuals emerge from outside the labour movement and seek to redirect unions to adopt programs of the intellectuals' making. Intellectuals believe they are more aware of the needs of unions than are unions themselves. Perlman saw intellectuals as being overcome by 'social mysticism', people who steadfastly refused to alter their thinking about unions despite 'Labor's repeated refusals to reach out for its appointed destiny'. When unions did not behave in the expected way, rather than admit any error in their theorising, intellectuals attack the facts of unionism: 'what has occurred is merely a temporary "delay" . . . [and] account for that delay by calling attention to the rise of a reactionary trade union bureaucracy'.[1]

A particular target for Perlman was V. I. Lenin's 1902 revolutionary polemic *What is to be Done?* Lenin observed what he regarded as the spontaneous emergence and actions of unions in their quest for improvements in wages and working conditions; what he referred to as economism. He attacked such spontaneity because it overwhelms the political consciousness, which he sees as being necessary to bring about the socialist transformation of society. Lenin criticised what he described as purely trade union struggles because workers 'would be fighting for themselves and for their children, and not for some future generations with some future socialism'. He claimed that 'the *spontaneous* development of the working-class movement leads to its subordination to bourgeois ideology'. According to Lenin, 'the task of Social-Democracy is *to combat spontaneity, to direct* the working-class movement from this spontaneous, trade unionist striving to come under the wing of the bourgeoisie, and to bring it under the wing of revolutionary Social-Democracy'.[2]

Perlman didn't confine his criticism of intellectuals to Leninist revolutionaries. He extended it to others who developed schemes or master plans or who professed to know what was best for unions. Australian unions have always been subjected to bountiful advice from intellectuals, or outsiders, concerning both their goals and methods of operation. Talkback radio commentators, writers of feature articles and newspaper editorials, various employers and employer groups, bankers, financial gurus, politicians, academics, members of industrial tribunals and the judiciary, and representatives of numerous community and interest groups continually deliver sermons about the appropriateness or otherwise of union behaviour.

At the risk of making a wickedly rash generalisation, it is as if these intellectuals are all busily plagiarising a tome entitled 'If only you would stop behaving like unions'.

In criticising and bemoaning the interference of intellectuals Perlman provides a defence, if not championing, of unionism *per se*. He is in effect arguing that unions—that is, the membership and their 'natural' or 'home-grown' leaders—should be the captains of their own destinies. It is up to each and every individual union to develop tactics and strategies in pursuit of the particular needs and interests of those who are members of the union. By inference, given that different unionised work groups experience different sets of problems and circumstances, unions will behave in different and variable ways. Such notions of variability and differences are consistent with the writings of other labour movement theorists. The Webbs, Hoxie and Tannenbaum, in different ways, have pointed to the pragmatism of unions, of how unions employ different methods in seeking the realisation of their goals (the Webbs), and evolve into various and different types as determined by the consciousness or needs of various and different groups of workers (Hoxie).[3]

Australia inherited or adapted the British model of craft or occupational unionism. Unions were formed on the basis of the skill, craft or occupation of the workers concerned. Workers, so it seemed, had a predilection for forming collective organisations with others doing the same sort of work rather than with workers in the same workplace or industry performing other or different types of work. This 'salt and pepper' unionism has meant that many Australian unions have traditionally had small pockets of members sprinkled over a large number of work sites. Or, contrariwise, most work sites, even those with a relatively small workforce, have in their midst workers who belong to a variety of different unions.

As noted in chapter 4, the Business Council of Australia has advocated the formation of enterprise unions (whereby workers at a particular enterprise belong to a single union); although the genuineness of this recommendation is somewhat clouded as it appears to be a stepping stone in a strategy to bring about the ultimate destruction of Australian unions.

One of the methods adopted by the Australian (or, as it was then called, the Australasian) Council of Trade Unions on its formation was 'the closer organisation of the workers by the transformation of the trade union movement from the craft to an industrial basis by the establishment of one union in each industry'.[4] For more than half a century the ACTU initiated little or no action to bring about such a rationalisation. This situation changed dramatically in the late 1980s. The ACTU has sought to restructure unions away from their traditional craft or occupational form to one based on either industry or general (conglomerate) unionism.

This chapter will examine various issues associated with this transformation. It is organised in four sections. Section one will examine problems associated with discerning the number of unionists and the level of unionisation in Australia. Unfortunately the Australian Bureau of Statistics publishes two data sets that provide substantially different estimates of the extent of unionisation. Section two will outline various policy initiatives of the ACTU, and legislative changes introduced by its Accord partner, concerning the rationalisation of the structure of Australian unions. The third section will present an evaluation of the success or otherwise of this program. The next section will attempt to assess the impact of union restructuring from the perspective of a representative marginal unionist—an individual belonging to a union who has doubts about maintaining his or her membership, or a non-unionist who is contemplating joining a union. This latter discussion will also incorporate consideration of various twists and turns in the Accord on the decision-making of the marginal unionist.

AUSTRALIAN UNIONS: HOW MANY MEMBERS?

The Australian Bureau of Statistics publishes two different data sets that provide markedly different estimates of the number of unionists and levels of unionisation in Australia. Table 5.1 provides estimates of the number of workers and percentage of the workforce unionised for different years in the period 1976–92. This table is based on a survey of Australian employees that, initially at least, was conducted infrequently and since 1986 every two years. If we examine the percentage of the workforce unionised table 5.1 shows a continuing or steady decline in levels of union density. In 1976 51.0 per cent of the workforce was unionised; by 1992 this figure had fallen to 39.6 per cent. Table 5.1 shows that the number of unionists has remained fairly constant. Slightly more than 2.5 million workers have been union members in the years when this survey has been conducted; 2.66 million members in 1990 was the highest estimate. Should the relative stability of the number of unionists be a cause for concern? Table 5.1 seems to indicate that both good and bad times have only a limited impact on the number of unionists. The corollary of this, of course, is that with an expanding workforce the percentage of the workforce belonging to unions has fallen.

Other ABS data casts doubt on the inferences that can be drawn concerning the fortunes of unions provided by table 5.1. Table 5.2 provides data on the number and percentage of the workforce unionised, both total and financial, for 1976 and the years 1980–93. The data contained in table 5.2 is based on information provided annually by individual unions. Table 5.2, in other words, is a census whereas table 5.1 is a survey. Table 5.2 records substantially higher numbers and rates of unionisation than table 5.1. Throughout most of the period covered by table 5.2 the percentage of the total workforce unionised has hovered around 54 or 55 per cent, with a fall to 51 per cent in 1993. The level of financial membership (for which data has only been provided since 1985) has been between five and seven percentage points below that of total membership. In addition, table 5.2 records both increases and decreases (1983 and 1991–93) in the number of unionists. The most marked differences between tables 5.1 and 5.2 concerning union membership occurred in 1988 and 1990—in both years the latter table recorded 760 000 more unionists. The exclusion of non-financial members in both years reduced the difference in both years to about 400 000 members.

The ABS points out that the two data sets make use of different methodologies—which helps to explain why they record different levels of union membership. Five reasons are provided for differences between the two data sets. The survey only records the trade union membership of a respondent's main job. In this way a person holding

Table 5.1 Surveys of Australian union membership 1976–92

	Year	Union membership (thousands)	Percentage of workforce unionised
November	1976	2512.7	51.0
March–May	1982	2567.6	49.0
August	1986	2593.9	45.6
	1988	2535.9	41.6
	1990	2659.6	40.5
	1992	2508.8	39.6

Source: Australian Bureau of Statistics, *Trade Union Members, Australia*, Canberra, Catalogue No. 6325.0

Table 5.2 Australian union membership, financial and total, 1976 and 1980–93

	Year	Financial		Total	
		Union membership (thousands)	Percentage of workforce unionised	Union membership (thousands)	Percentage of workforce unionised
December	1976	n.a.	n.a.	2800.6	55.0
	1980	n.a.	n.a.	2955.9	56.0
	1981	n.a.	n.a.	2994.1	56.0
	1982	n.a.	n.a.	3012.4	57.0
	1983	n.a.	n.a.	2985.2	55.0
	1984	n.a.	n.a.	3028.5	55.0
June	1985	2802.8	51.0	3154.2	57.0
	1986	2870.5	50.0	3186.2	55.0
	1987	2909.2	49.0	3240.1	55.0
	1988	2922.3	48.0	3290.5	54.0
	1989	2988.4	47.0	3410.3	54.0
	1990	3053.2	48.0	3422.2	54.0
	1991	3027.9	50.0	3382.6	56.0
	1992	2822.6	47.0	3135.1	53.0
	1993	2715.2	46.0	3000.1	51.0

Source: Australian Bureau of Statistics, *Trade Union Members, Australia*, Canberra, Catalogue No. 6323.0

a second job and belonging to a second union is eliminated. A person who changes jobs and belonged to a union in both will only have the membership of their union in the current job counted. Unemployed people who are union members are not included in the survey. People who elect to belong to more than one union are only counted once. Finally, unions might experience difficulties in maintaining their membership files and might include unfinancial members.[5]

The survey (table 5.1) consistently records a lower number and level of unionisation than the census (table 5.2). During the 1980s the survey revealed a substantial decline in levels of union density, which was not replicated in the census. In 1988 the difference between the two was thirteen percentage points—although, again, data concerning financial members reduced the extent of such differences. In the early 1990s both have revealed a fall in the percentage of the workforce unionised. The census shows that the number of unionists in Australia fell by more than 400 000 in the years 1990–93. However, it should be remembered that the early 1990s was a period of recession and increasing unemployment (see table 2.1).

AMALGAMATE, AMALGAMATE, AMALGAMATE

In May 1987 the ACTU released a discussion paper entitled *Future Strategies for the Trade Union Movement*. The document reveals that the ACTU leadership was concerned about the public image of unions, New Right attacks and the increasingly anti-union rhetoric and policies of the Coalition, at both State and federal levels. *Future Strategies* emphasised that the 'union movement throughout the industrialised world is very much on the defensive'.[6] The object of the discussion paper was to promote policies that will improve communication channels between unions and their members, provide more services more efficiently and enhance the ability of unions to recruit new members. Besides putting aside funds for publicity campaigns to enhance the image of unions,[7] the major policy recommendation in *Future Strategies* was for affiliates to embark on a massive program of amalgamations. *Future Strategies* suggested that Australian unions should rationalise themselves into seventeen industry or general (conglomerate) groupings. Such a program, it was argued, would enable unions to reap economies of scale thereby releasing resources to enhance the delivery of services to members and recruit new members and withstand attacks from unionism's enemies.

Australia Reconstructed, a document jointly produced by the Commonwealth Department of Trade and the ACTU, published in July 1987, reiterated the need for Australian unions to embrace amalgamation. *Australia Reconstructed* said that 'the Australian trade union movement should plan to have no more than twenty union organisations within two years'. It also said that in enhancing the progress of union rationalisation it would be necessary for 'some reallocation of coverage by agreement of unions and members between unions' coordinated by the ACTU, and there should be no registration of new unions other than those flowing from the amalgamation process.[8]

In developing its case for reform *Future Strategies* states:

> there are as many unions today as there were 80 years ago. There are only 40 fewer unions than there were in 1945. This suggests that the Australian union movement as a whole has yet come to terms with the rationalisation issue.[9]

It is not clear, however, that Australian unions have been as opposed to rationalisation as implied by this statement. First, notwithstanding the similarity in the number of unions in 1907, 1945 and 1986 (the latest data available to the author(s) of *Future Strategies*), they varied significantly in size and, by inference, in terms of their external and internal dynamics. The 323 unions of 1907 had an average of 620 members; in 1945 the average size of Australia's 362 unions was 3300 and, by 1986, 326 unions had an average of 9800 members.

Second, and more significantly, the relative stability in numbers obscures more or less continuous changes to the structure of unions. The emergence (and registration) of new unions is counterbalanced by union amalgamations and the disappearance of 'defunct' and/or deregistered unions. Griffin and Scarcebrook found that, between 1905 and 1986, 313 unions had been registered under the *Conciliation and Arbitration Act* 1904. A hundred and sixty-four organisations had lost their registration. Of these organisations 94 had merged with other unions, 16 had been deregistered for punitive reasons, and 54 had been deregistered for other reasons. Griffin and Scarcebrook found that amalgamations tended to occur between unions with common skills.[10] Rimmer also found that changes had occurred to the structure of New South Wales unions. Between 1920 and 1970 the number of manual unions had decreased from 155 to 81, while non-manual (white-collar) unions had increased from 34 to 63.[11] In other words, the rationalisation that had occurred among manual unions had been counterbalanced by the emergence of new non-manual, white-collar unions. Gill and Griffin also noted a similar trend for Queensland unions in the period 1961–78[12] (also see table 5.3 below).

Before 1972 amalgamations at the federal level only required agreement of the leadership of the organisations concerned—one union would file for deregistration and join another whose rules had been appropriately altered to process the enrolment of the new members concerned. In 1972 the *Conciliation and Arbitration Act* 1904 was altered to require 50 per cent of the members of both organisations concerned to vote and for majorities to be recorded in both unions to enable an amalgamation to take place. An exception was granted to large unions having to ballot their members if they wanted to amalgamate with a small union. If the membership of the small union(s) was less than five per cent of the large union, only a ballot of the small union(s) was required. The Australian Electoral Commission reported that six amalgamations took place under this legislation, and in all but one case the larger organisation was exempted from holding a ballot.[13] In 1983 legislative amendments reduced the proportion of members required to vote in an amalgamation ballot from 50 to 25 per cent. In addition, the proposed amalgamation had to be viewed by a designated presidential member of the Australian Conciliation and Arbitration Commission to be furthering the objects of the act and that there was a 'community of interests' between the unions concerned.

The ACTU 1987 biennial congress held in Melbourne endorsed the rationalisation and amalgamation proposals in *Future Strategies*—although the number of proposed union groups had increased from seventeen to twenty in accordance with *Australia Reconstructed*.[14] The *Industrial Relations Act* 1988 contained three provisions designed to enhance the process of union amalgamation. First, the 25 per cent membership voting requirement was deleted where a designated presidential member of the AIRC determined that there was a 'community of interest' between unions wanting to merge. A simple majority of votes cast would determine whether an amalgamation could occur. Second, the minimum size of registered unions was increased from 100 to 1000 members. Unions with fewer than 1000 members were given three years to increase their membership to 1000 or merge with other unions. If a union with fewer than 1000 members, after this three-year period, cannot satisfy the commission that there are special reasons why it should exist, its registration would be cancelled. A group of small unions—the Medical Scientists' Association of Victoria, the Woolclassers' Association of Victoria, the Ambulance Employees' Association of Victoria and the Association of Hospital Pharmacists of Victoria—who apparently spoke on behalf of ten other small unions, approached the Coalition's industrial relations spokesman, Senator Fred Chaney, and the Democrats urging them to oppose this amendment.[15] Third, in seeking to resolve demarcation disputes, section 118 granted a presidential member of the commission power to grant or exclude rights to perform work to the members of a particular union(s).

While affiliates at the ACTU 1987 congress might have endorsed the amalgamation proposals in *Future Strategies,* they hastened slowly to put them into effect. In 1988 and 1989 there were a total of eight amalgamations at the federal level.[16] In mid 1989 the ABS published its latest survey on the level of unionisation of the Australian workforce. It showed that union density had fallen to 41.6 per cent in 1988 (see table 5.1 above). This set off alarm bells among the leadership of the ACTU and simultaneously provided it with a stick to beat affiliates to pursue its rationalisation and amalgamation proposals with more speed and vigour.[17]

At the 1989 congress held in Sydney ACTU leaders renewed their call for affiliates to embrace union amalgamation. The future viability and survival of unions was linked to the acceptance of such a strategy.[18] Concern was also expressed about the problems unions experienced in recruiting women and younger workers. The ACTU executive circulated a motion that essentially restated the precepts of *Future Strategies,* with added emphasis on recruiting female and younger workers. As part of a strategy to enhance female membership delegates agreed that, by 1999, 50 per cent of executive positions should be held by women. At this congress, however, they only elected five women to a thirty-eight-member executive (and three of these positions were specifically reserved for women). By and large delegates at the 1989 congress accepted, or rather re-endorsed, the leadership's amalgama-tion strategy.[19] The only dissident voices came from Terry Johnson of the Electrical Trades Union and W. Smith of the Federated Clerks. They did not regard industry unionism as a panacea for Australian unions, amalgamation was imposing reform from above, and ballots should be held to determine transfers of members from one union to another. Their opposition was simply dismissed as two narrowly based unions refusing to confront the need to change.[20]

In mid 1990 the ACTU leadership developed a further set of guide-lines to help streamline and speed up the process of union rationali-sation. The objective of this exercise was to ensure that there would be no more than two or three unions in each industry or enterprise, operating as a single bargaining unit. A distinction was made between principal, significant and other unions. *Principal* (or *dominant*) *unions* were those with prime responsibility for representing workers and con-ducting negotiations with employers. Such unions would have full constitutional capacity to recruit and cover workers in the industry concerned. *Significant unions* were those with a significant membership base in the industry, who would be able to retain their constitutional rights and recruit potential members. However, they had to give a com-mitment to work in a single bargaining unit with principal unions. *Other unions* were those that already had an established membership base in an industry or enterprise. They would be able to maintain their presence only if their members insisted they didn't want to join another (principal) union. In the words of ACTU secretary Bill Kelty, this was 'the test of whether your members really love you'.[21]

A number of mainly right-wing unions, coalesced around the New South Wales Labor Council, expressed opposition to this proposed streamlining.[22] Besides complaining about lack of consultation their major concern was the potential recruitment scope of principal unions. They were fearful that principal unions would be enabled to poach members away from unions who already had membership coverage. In October 1990 meetings between leaders of the ACTU and dissidents reached an agreement that protected the representation rights of exist-ing unions.[23] The agreement, as ratified by the ACTU 1991 congress, supported the principle of significantly reducing the number of unions within each industry or enterprise. It said: 'Such unions may be occu-pationally based or industry based. As part of such a rationalisation of union coverage the members affected should be fully consulted and their existing and future rights and conditions properly protected'. Principal, significant and other unions were defined as follows:

> *A Principal union*—A Principal union shall have the capacity to recruit all employees in a given industry or, in certain cases, defined occupational category and shall recognise significant and other unions in the industry or occupational category and seek to reach agreement with them as to membership coverage and recruitment. Where an existing principal union has failed to service the needs of the workforce principal status is to be reviewed by the ACTU Executive.
>
> *A Significant union*—A Significant union is one which has:
> (i)   a substantial number of members in an industry or occupation
> (ii) agreed to be part of a single bargaining unit with the Principal union
> (iii) the capacity to maintain and recruit membership provided that, by agreement with the Principal union or unions, a Significant union may be able to recruit membership beyond its existing area of coverage with a view to maximising unionisation . . .
>
> *Other unions*—Other unions do not have a substantial number of members. They may be able to maintain membership on the following basis:
> (i)   they represent those employees who desire to have the union represent them
> (ii) they will not stand in the way of any employee wishing to join the Principal union
> (iii) they agree to be part of [a] single bargaining unit
> (iv) they service the membership
> (v)   the continuation of award coverage will be subject to periodic reviews.[24]

At the end of 1990 the Federal Government introduced legislation to enhance the processes of union amalgamation and rationalisation. The *Industrial Relations Legislation Amendment Act* 1990, which became operative on 1 February 1991, enhanced prospects for reforming the structure of Australian unions in the following ways. First, section 118 of the *Industrial Relations Act* 1988 was altered to increase the ability of the AIRC to award single-union coverage in resolving demarcation disputes. Second, the minimum size of unions was increased from 1000 to 10 000.[25] In evidence submitted to the ILO's Freedom of Association Committee it was estimated that, at the time this legislation was enacted, 92 of Australia's 149 federally registered unions had fewer than 10 000 members.[26] Unions with fewer than 1000 members, in accordance with the *Industrial Relations Act* 1988 (see above), were given until the period 1 March 1992 to 28 February 1993 either to increase their membership or to amalgamate before having to demonstrate to a designated presidential member of the commission that 'special circumstances' existed to justify maintenance of their registration. For unions with fewer than 10 000 (but more than 1000) members this period of grace was extended to 1 March 1993 to 28 February 1994. Third, the legislation encouraged recognition of federations of unions as a prelude to amalgamation. Fourth, ballot requirements for large unions were relaxed. Members of a large union were not required to participate in a ballot if the members of the organisation(s) it intended to amalgamate with had less than a quarter of the members of large unions. Fifth, financial assistance was made available to unions intending to amalgamate.

A number of clashes and disputes have occurred between different unions as they have sought to position themselves during this period of structural change. Those traditional rivals of the left and right, the Amalgamated Metal Workers Union and the Federated Ironworkers Association—and their respective amalgamated reincarnations, the Automotive Metals Engineering Union and the Australian Workers Union-Federation of Industrial Manufacturing and Engineering Employees—have continued their struggle for the hearts and minds of unionists. The Federated Ironworkers Association has also been involved in poaching wars with a number of other unions, such as the National Union of Workers (formerly the Storemen and Packers Union), the Electrical Trades Union and the Miscellaneous Workers Union. The clash with this last union involved coverage of members in the Northern Territory tourism industry. There was also a celebrated clash between the Federated Clerks Union and the Public Sector Union over members in the Australian Taxation Office. At a meeting of the ACTU's executive in March 1990 attempts were made to heal disputes between the Federated Clerks and Public Sector Unions over members in the Australian Taxation Office and between the Federated Ironworkers Association and Miscellaneous Workers Union in the Northern Territory.[27] The Federated Ironworkers Association also found itself in dispute with the Building Workers Industrial Union over members making shower screens in New South Wales. The former threatened the latter with secondary boycott action under sections 45D and 45E of the *Trade Practices Act* 1974 before the ACTU brokered a compromise.[28]

The ACTU 1991 congress, held in Melbourne, is noteworthy for the level of ill-feeling expressed concerning the ensuing rationalisation of the union movement. Forty delegates spoke in a debate either criticising the strategy or denouncing other unions over poaching raids of members. Nevertheless an overwhelming majority of delegates re-endorsed the need for unions to continue with the amalgamation and rationalisation process.[29]

In August 1993 ACTU president Martin Ferguson criticised affiliates because of their penchant for engaging in poaching raids rather than developing the necessary skills to recruit new members. He said: 'A significant number of unions have been penalised because they are adhering to ACTU policy on union coverage, in the face of legal action by other unions'. He also observed that many millions of dollars had been wasted over unnecessary litigation, which could have been better devoted to recruiting and servicing new members.[30]

The *Industrial Relations Legislation Amendment Act* 1990 increased the minimum size of federally registered unions to 10 000 with the qualification that smaller unions could continue their registration if 'special circumstances' were found to be present (see above). Unions with fewer than 10 000 members found a somewhat surprising white knight to champion their cause. In November 1990 the Confederation of Australian Industry[31] mounted a case before the ILO's Freedom of Association Committee. The CAI claimed that the 10 000 membership rule contravened the ILO's Conventions number 87—Freedom of Association and Protection of the Right to Organise—and number 98—Right to Organise and Collective Bargaining.

In November 1992 the committee ruled against the legislation. It said:

> This committee has always been wary of government pressure or favouritism, whether direct or indirect, which might influence the trade union membership of workers. While often difficult to prove that the government measure lies at the heart of the workers' choice, the fact remains that the treatment facing one union as compared with others risks jeopardising this important right of workers . . . the 10 000 members threshold does . . . influence unduly the workers' choice of

union to which they wish to belong . . . Workers, knowing that under 10 000 member unions will be called to justify their continued enjoyment of the benefits of federal registration, could be influenced in their choice of union. Organisations applying for registration, or already registered with fewer than 10 000 members, may have been forced to react for fear of being refused those benefits. The Committee is conscious of the support of the peak union body . . . for the amendments. If the current rationalisation philosophy is designed to ensure well-organised and well-resourced unions, the choice of a large size will be a natural reaction from the workers, seeking strength and maximum support; it need not be written into federal legislation.[32]

Following this decision Industrial Relations Minister Senator Peter Cook foreshadowed that the Federal Government would alter the act concerning the minimum size of unions.[33] This intention, however, did not protect two small unions from being involuntarily deregistered. In March 1993 the 109-strong Australian Federation of Catholic School Principals, and in June the thirty-five-member Arbitration Inspectors Association, were deregistered.[34] Representations on behalf of Industrial Relations Minister Laurie Brereton announcing impending amendments to legislation resulted in the commission adjourning hearings concerning the fate of other small unions.[35] The *Industrial Relations Reform Act* 1993 subsequently reduced the minimum size of federally registered unions to 100 members.

AN EVALUATION

At one level the ACTU has been successful in its quest to restructure the Australian union movement. Since 1987, and more particularly after the passage of the *Industrial Relations Legislation Amendment Act* 1990, federally registered unions have found themselves participating in a virtual orgy of mergers, accompanied by a substantial decrease in the number of unions.

Between 1988 and May 1993 the Australian Electoral Commission conducted sixty-two amalgamation ballots, of which only three were unsuccessful.[36] Forty-nine of these ballots occurred between 1991 and May 1993; only one was defeated.[37]

Tables 5.3 and 5.4 provide further evidence to support the success of the ACTU's amalgamation strategy. Table 5.3 presents information on the sources of change in the number of Australian unions from 1980 to 1993. Between 1980 and 1993 the number of unions declined from 325 to 188. In this period 67 new unions were created, 159 amalgamations occurred and 52 unions ceased to operate or were deregistered. Closer examination of the table reveals that most of this change occurred in the years 1991–93 after the passage of the *Industrial Relations Legislation Amendment Act* 1990. During the 1980s there was only a relatively minor change in the number of unions—from 325 in 1980 to 295 in 1990. By 1993 the number of unions had fallen dramatically to 188. The major reason for this fall was the 98 amalgamations that occurred in 1991, 1992 and 1993. In fact, 62 per cent of the amalgamations that have taken place since 1980 occurred in these years.[38]

Table 5.4 provides data on the number of federally and non-federally registered unions in Australia in the period 1980–93. Most

Table 5.3   Sources of change in the number of Australian unions, 1980–93

	Year	New unions	Amal-gama-tions	Ceased to operate/ deregistered	Number of unions
(December 1979)					(332)
December	1980	2	5	4	325
	1981	6	2	5	324
	1982	9	11	—	322
	1983	—	3	—	319
	1984	13	3	—	329
June	1985	4	2	8	323
	1986	10	6	1	326
	1987	—	8	2	316
	1988	—	6	2	308
	1989	—	7	2	299
	1990*	15	8	11	295
	1991*	3	19	4	275
	1992*	3	44	4	225
	1993*	2	35	6	188
Total		**67**	**159**	**52**	

Source: Australian Bureau of Statistics, *Trade Union Statistics Australia*, Canberra, Catalogue No. 6323.0
* Unpublished data, Australian Bureau of Statistics

non-federally registered unions would be registered at the state level, although there are a few small unions—such as the Australian Football League Players Association—that have not sought registration in any jurisdiction. Table 5.4 reveals that in the 1980s there were only small changes in the number of federally or non-federally registered unions. In the 1990s, however, there has been a marked decline in the number of unions, particularly at the federal level. By 1993 the number of federal unions had fallen to 66[39] from 134 in 1990, a decline of more than 50 per cent. The number of non-federal unions had fallen from 161 to 122, a more modest fall of 24 per cent.

In 1981 Gill and Griffin published an article in which they criticised what they described as the 'fetish' to restructure Australian unions on industry lines. Among other things they maintained that 'since unions negotiate with companies rather than industries, industry unions and awards offer the prospect that workers may win the industry battle but lose the company war'. They also said:

Table 5.4 Federally registered and non-federally registered unions, Australia, 1980–93

	Year	Federally registered unions	Non-federally registered unions	Total number of unions
December	1980	150	175	325
	1981	150	174	324
	1982	150	172	322
	1983	150	169	319
	1984	148	181	329
June	1985	149	174	323
	1986	146	180	326
	1987	144	172	316
	1988	146	162	308
	1989	140	159	299
	1990	134	161	295
	1991	125	150	275
	1992	94	133	227
	1993	66	122	188

Source: Australian Bureau of Statistics, *Trade Union Statistics Australia*, Canberra Catalogue No. 6323.0

The workload of a union within the existing award structure is . . . more likely to be affected by the number of awards and the number of classifications for which it is responsible than by the number of members. Thus, amalgamation without rationalisation of the number of awards would increase the concerns of union officials rather than spreading them over a wider membership; this would not occur where membership increased under existing awards and classifications. Taken together, these factors show that the increases in efficiency from increased size are not as certain as advocates of growth have presumed.[40]

Since the publication of this article unions have participated in second-tier negotiations, award restructuring under the auspices of the structural efficiency principle and embraced (their definition of) enterprise bargaining. Second-tier negotiations and award restructuring seem to have increased the intensity of the workload of union officials (and, as chapter 3 suggests, for little result), while enterprise bargaining will spread their work more thinly. The time, energy and resources that a union would need to devote to servicing and policing a relatively small number of awards[41] would seem to be less than those of a large number of potentially separate enterprise agreements.[42]

While the ACTU might have been successful in achieving many amalgamations it is not clear that amalgamation has produced the effects it was designed to achieve. Amalgamations and union rationalisation were championed on the basis of enabling unions to increase the quality of services provided to members and to enhance their ability to retain and recruit new members. While the ACTU has experimented with the provision of financial services—loans etc, which would seem to be a logical progression from its involvement with superannuation funds—there is no hard evidence that the quality of services provided by individual unions to members has been enhanced. Moreover, there is no evidence to suggest that the economies of scale flowing from amalgamations would release officials who would take on new functions on behalf of members.[43] Anecdotal evidence from talking to union officials and others who have contacts in the union world suggest that unions are laying off younger, junior officials. If anything, there seems to be an undercurrent of gloom and doom and feelings of disquiet concerning the amalgamation strategy.

Both measures of trade union membership compiled by the ABS reveal that in the 1990s there has been a decline in the number and percentage of the workforce unionised. This decline has occurred during a period in which individual employers and employer organisations have become increasingly aggressive and sophisticated in seeking to beat back unionism. The Coalition, at both the State and federal levels, has continually mounted attacks on unions. The election of Coalition governments in various States has been associated with the introduction of legislation designed to weaken the influence and power of unions. In addition, the economy has been recessed with growing and persistently high levels of unemployment, and restructuring has occurred away from those sectors with traditionally high levels of unionisation to those with relatively lower levels.[44]

Amalgamation and union rationalisation have involved unions in turning in on themselves at a time when wages and working conditions have been subjected to seemingly incessant attack by employers, fuelled by a never-ending stream of rhetoric supplied by the Coalition, at both State and federal levels, the New Right, the media and financial and other commentators. The bureaucratic and logistic problems associated with the merging of two or more organisations can be very costly in terms of personnel, time, energy and money—irrespective of the financial aid available under the *Industrial Relations Legislation Amendment Act* 1990. Also, there is no guarantee that once an amalgamation has been consummated that the separate organisations concerned will be able to cohabit harmoniously, let alone in a way that enables them to utilise resources more efficiently for the benefit of their joint members.

Amalgamations have the potential to create an illusion of bigness for unions at a time when their ability to retain or attract members is declining. Rather than attract new members a large union can increase its size by gobbling up members from smaller or other unions. It is interesting to recall Martin Ferguson's August 1993 criticism of affiliates for wasting millions of dollars on demarcation and poaching disputes.

At the 1993 ACTU congress—six years after the publication of *Future Strategies* and *Australia Reconstructed*—Mary Stuart delivered a report in which she maintained that Australian unions had failed to develop a 'recruitment culture'.[45] Her report states: 'Notwithstanding the fact that there remains a primary role for organisers to recruit, existing union organisers are often exclusively occupied with dealing with day-to-day servicing of members'. She recommended that 'union structures at all levels be reviewed to give effect to the priority objective of improved recruitment and retention strategy'. In addition, she said: 'The training and recruitment of union staff should be thoroughly reviewed and revamped'.[46] This report would seem to indicate that the 'enhanced recruitment' that underpinned the ACTU amalgamation strategy has not been realised. A commitment to recruitment, presumably, could be grafted on to any structure adopted by the union movement. Rather than expending resources on amalgamations to enhance recruitment, an alternative strategy could be to utilise such resources to attract and recruit new members, particularly in areas or sectors that have low rates of unionisation. To the extent that it might be necessary, such recruitment drives could be directed or coordinated by the ACTU.

Following its 1993 congress the ACTU announced that it would develop a training program for highly motivated people in their early twenties to become recruitment officers to help arrest the decline in union membership. The intention was to attract people who had a commitment to, rather than experience of, unionism.[47] It is not clear that this strategy will necessarily bear fruit. First, it might be more appropriate to select recruiters from among the ranks of workers on the shop floor. Such people could be identified by their respective unions and provided with extra training if and where necessary. The point is that a highly motivated recruiter who comes from the shop floor is more likely to understand the needs of workers and persuade them of the wisdom of joining a union than someone without such experience, other things being equal (obviously this comment doesn't apply to recruiters selected from the ranks of said unions). Second, how will ACTU recruiters be absorbed into the workings of unions and how will their work dovetail with those of other organisers and officials within the union? Could they be regarded as a 'foreign element' with a short-term or limited commitment to the interests of a particular union? Third, and related to the above question, what is the career path of an ACTU-trained recruiter? Could such highly motivated and talented people perceive their jobs as recruiters as being an initial step in establishing careers as labour *apparatchiks*?

THE MARGINAL UNIONIST

A marginal unionist is someone who is not sure about whether they should maintain their membership or is considering joining a union. The attitude of a representative marginal unionist towards unions will not be determined just by their reaction to union amalgamation. It will also be a function of their reaction to the Accord and its various incarnations.

A potential problem of union amalgamation for the marginal unionist is concerns associated with how their interests will be attended to in a larger union that appears to be more bureaucratic. This might be a matter of particular concern for members of small unions merging with larger bodies. As unions become larger and more amorphorous workers with what they regard as specific needs might wonder how their interests will be represented and attended to. Individuals contemplating joining a union might feel antipathetic to a larger organisation whose name is represented by an acronym. In short, for a marginal unionist largeness might translate into bureaucracy and faceless unapproachable leaders unable to attend to their particular needs and grievances.

Reduction in the minimum size of federally registered unions to 100 members, contained in the *Industrial Relations Reform Act* 1993, could be used to consider developing a 'small and new unions unit' under the auspices of the ACTU. Workers who are new to unionism and collective action could be provided with advice and logistic support as part of a longer-term strategy to ease them into a relationship and eventual merger with an established, larger and better-resourced organisation. Such a proposal implies that the key to the relationship between the health of unionism and structure is that the latter is fluid and forever evolving rather than seeking to conform with the dictates of a master plan. The ALP and its Accord partner, the ACTU, have both championed flexibility and adaptability as being key ingredients in helping to achieve economic growth and enhancing Australia's international competitiveness. The same precepts do not seem to apply when it comes to the issue of union structure.

To the extent that the Accord has been associated with real wage cuts (see table 2.1), marginal unionists might feel somewhat antipathetic towards unions. Since the Accord Mark II real wage rises have been traded off for increases in the social wage: tax cuts, superannuation and improvements in family assistance. The problem for marginal unionists is that social wage benefits flow to unionist and non-unionist alike. Moreover, they might be particularly bemused by business executives, professional groups, bankers and money market operators, politicians, senior public servants, judges and members of industrial tribunals—the very persons whom Bill Kelty has vehemently criticised for their greed—receiving the lion's share of the tax cuts that have been obtained in exchange for wage moderation.[48] Marginal unionists might also be bemused by ACTU calls alternatively to embrace the two-tiered system, award restructuring and enterprise bargaining. Second-tier negotiations and award restructuring[49] have been associated with unions negotiating give-backs (see chapter 3) and employers in large organisations downsizing their workforces in enhancing efficiency and productivity.

The ACTU has sought to push affiliates into the decentralised world of enterprise bargaining at a time when historically high levels of unemployment have reduced their bargaining power. In line with its Accord partner's desire to increase the international competitiveness of the Australian economy, the ACTU and the Australian union movement have adopted, if not embraced, the rhetoric of employers: restructuring, efficiency, wealth creation, penetrating markets, reducing budget deficits and reducing foreign debt. When unions and employers employ similar rhetoric marginal unionists might feel disinclined to join unions or maintain their union membership.

CONCLUSION

In 1987 the ACTU, in *Future Strategies* and *Australia Reconstructed*, initiated steps to transform Australian unions from their traditional craft/occupational basis to one of industry or general unions. Both documents advocated a substantial reduction in the number of unions. The case for union rationalisation was based on the reaping of economies of scale that enable larger, better-resourced unions to increase the quality of their services and arrest declines in union membership.

The ACTU's Accord partner, the Federal Government, in 1988 and again in 1990 introduced legislation to speed up the process of union amalgamation. Particularly since 1990 there has been a substantial decline in the ranks of Australian unions. Most of this decline has occurred among federally registered unions. The creation of large unions could have a major impact on the role and functions of State trades and labour councils. Large unions might not feel the need to maintain their affiliation and pay fees to such bodies, particularly if most of their members are covered by federal awards or enterprise agreements. This could be a particular problem for those councils whose internal decision-making processes have essentially been based on the domination of one faction by another. Enlarged unions belonging to the lesser or dominated faction might feel disinclined to maintain their affiliation. Against this, anti-union legislation developed by non-Labor State Governments could provide a rallying point helping to enhance the hegemony of State trades and labour councils.

While the ACTU might have won the amalgamation battle it is far from clear that it has won the recruitment and services war. Mary Stuart's report to the 1993 congress acknowledges that unions have been unsuccessful in recruiting new members. Nor is there any evidence to suggest that there has been a general lift in the quality and effectiveness of services provided to members. The costs associated with amalgamating and problems of cohabitation might have drained resources that could have been more usefully spent on recruitment and services enhancement. Smaller, more specialised unions might be better able to serve the needs of niche markets, particularly in attracting marginal unionists, than larger bureaucratic organisations.

The various Accords and the program of union rationalisation has been associated with the ACTU adopting the jargon and rhetoric of employers. In one of the quotations that heads this chapter Flanders has said: 'The first and overriding responsibility of all trade unions is to the welfare of their own members. That is their primary commitment, not to a firm, not to an industry, not to the nation'.[50] Alternatively, Flanders is postulating that if unions pursue the needs of other interests above those of their members, such people will feel disinclined to maintain their membership or join unions. For unions to be relevant to members they must not only protect and advance their welfare but also be seen to protect and advance their welfare. The ACTU, through its participation in the Accord and rationalising the structure of unions, has conflated the role of unions as representatives of unionists with the needs of enterprises, industries and the nation. This might constitute the major reason why unions have experienced difficulties in attracting marginal unionists to join, or remain members of, worker collectives.

EPILOGUE

In the debate about the manner and degree of regulation of industrial relations, the distinction between procedures and outcomes should be borne in mind. We should question whether, in order to produce a particular outcome, it is necessary to make drastic changes to the procedure. We should bear in mind that fashions change. In economics and politics, there are even fewer truisms than in most other fields of study. A new procedure, like the old one, might prove not to have all of the answers after all.

Gray, P. R. A. (1993), foreword in Ronfeldt, P. and McCallum, R., eds, A New Province for Legalism: Legal Issues and the Deregulation of Industrial Relations Research and Teaching, *Monograph No. 9,* University of Sydney, p. v.

. . . unions, employers and state agencies have myriad ways of affecting industrial relations and are not confined to any specific set of practices. One consequence of such reasoning is to widen the parameters of what is conventionally considered to be industrial relations and to emphasise the study of processes rather than institutions. More particularly, attempts to change the institutional form of industrial relations are just as much part of the general conflict as are attempts to change wages and conditions through those institutions. For example, the debates over arbitration and collective bargaining and over union structure should be seen as indirect methods of gaining sectional advantage by effecting control over production and distribution.

Guille, H. (1986), 'Domesticating unions with foreign ideas: Australian industrial relations 1940–80' in Bray, M. and Taylor, V., eds, Managing Labour? Essays in the Political Economy of Industrial Relations, McGraw-Hill, Sydney, p. 203.

It is commonly believed that Australia has developed a unique or at least distinctive approach to industrial relations. At an empirical level such uniqueness has been associated with the existence of state-sponsored industrial tribunals that regulate relationships between employers, workers and unions. Industrial tribunals were created by middle-class intellectuals in the decades either side of the turn of the twentieth century. In the oft-quoted words of Henry Bournes Higgins, they would usher in 'a new province for law and order'.

More conceptually, the creation and continuing existence of industrial tribunals rest on the supposition that the state, in the person of experts, can improve on the work of nature. It is believed that such experts can fashion solutions to the industrial problem, that they can make better and improve the operation of society. When this expectation has been challenged, when new problems or crises have emerged, changes have either have been proposed or implemented to alter the role of industrial tribunals or the ground rules of industrial relations.

Chapter 1 developed a general theory of Australian industrial relations. The major innovation of the theory was the notion of orbits of interaction. An *interactor* was defined as any individual, group or organisation involved in industrial relations. The definition included 'non-Australian', or overseas, interactors whose actions have an impact in Australia. Interactors interact in orbits of interaction, and orbits also interact with each other. Interactors have a presence in a number of different orbits. The composition of orbits is only limited by the imagination and ingenuity of interactors to find each other. Interactors will use their presence in a particular orbit or orbits in attempting to enhance their ability to prevail over other interactors in other or adjacent orbits. Less abstractly, interactors march backwards and forwards over industrial, legal, tribunal, political and other orbits, at both the State and federal levels, in seeking to dominate and outmanoeuvre each other.

Interactors are seen to be motivated by the desire to enhance their authority over those with whom they interact. Those with authority wish to maintain or extend their position, while those without authority or possessing limited authority wish to lift themselves up from their lowly position. These authority struggles provide the theory with its source of energy. The theory allows for both the creation of new and destruction of existing interactors. Industrial relations is perceived as an activity of unremitting, ceaseless struggle as interactors jostle with each other for their place in the sun. Within a particular orbit inter-actors constrain and are constrained by each other. Similarly, all orbits constrain and are constrained by each other. In seeking to understand a particular orbit it is necessary to understand its relationship with other orbits. To know the part it is necessary to know the whole; to know the whole it is necessary to know the parts. Orbits of inter-action are in a continual state of flux or evolution. They continually swirl around, overlap, intertwine and bump into each other, breaking up and combining in an increasing variety of new and different forms.

This theory was utilised to explain the major developments in Aus-tralian industrial relations in the late 1980s and the early 1990s—to the end of 1993 with the passage of the *Industrial Relations Reform Act* 1993. It has been a period of intense, hard-edged struggle. Various interactors have wanted to transform the operation of Australian indus-trial relations root and branch. Continual attacks have been mounted on the operation of industrial tribunals and what role, if any, they should perform in a 'new order'. In addition, attacks have been mounted against unions, and substantial changes have occurred to their struc-ture and operation.

The original Accord, and the subsequent election of the ALP in March 1983, championed centralisation as the best way to respond to the various industrial relations, economic and social problems of the early 1980s. In the mid to late 1980s Australia experienced a number of international economic problems, which placed pressure on the cen-tralisation assumptions contained in the original Accord. A centralised system of industrial relations regulation was perceived as being anti-pathetic to enhancing the ability of Australian industry and firms to compete in international markets. Beginning with the September 1986 work practices summit Australia has steadily moved from a centralised to a decentralised system of industrial relations regulation.

The Australian Conciliation and Arbitration Commission played a prominent role in implementing the wages and working conditions component of the early Accords. Whether they liked it or not, the Accord partners were forced to place the commission on a pedestal because of the traditional protection afforded to it by section 51, para-graph XXXV of the Australian Constitution. During the 1980s a num-ber of High Court decisions concerning the taxation, corporations and external affairs powers enabled the Commonwealth Government to regulate industrial relations directly, thereby bypassing and downgrading the commission's role. Chapter 3 examined various developments between the Accord partners as they sought to steer Australia towards decentralisation and their relationship with the commission. At various times the Accord partners felt that the commission was an obstacle blocking the path towards the changes they wanted to achieve. In the April 1991 national wage case the AIRC expressed reservations about and delayed the implementation of enterprise bargaining, much to the ire of the Accord partners, particularly the ACTU. In July 1992 amendments to the *Industrial Relations Act* 1988 marginalised the role of the commission by reducing its ability to be involved in the processing of enterprise deals.

The major issue to confront Australian industrial relations in the late 1980s and early 1990s was the struggle between interactors in attempting to shape and define the contours of a new decentralised system or systems. With some exceptions, virtually all interactors have been united in the belief that enterprise bargaining should be the cornerstone of a new approach. While they have seen enterprise bargaining as being the one and only true god they have found themselves worshipping in different churches and reading from the text of different bibles. Interactors have widely different definitions of enterprise bargaining. Such differences centre on the role that should be played by tribunals and unions, collective versus individual bargaining, the relationship between awards and agreements, and the role of safety nets.

Both State and Federal Governments have enacted legislation to encourage the use of different models of enterprise bargaining. At the State level we have seen the creation of a new interactor known as the commissioner for enterprise or workplace bargaining. The Kennett Government in Victoria abolished the Victorian Industrial Relations Commission and replaced it with an Employment Relations Commission. The *Industrial Relations Reform Act* 1993 has divided the work of the AIRC into award and bargaining divisions and has re-created a specialist federal Industrial Court. In addition, the act, with its notion of a minimum wage, seems to be advancing Australia towards a model developed by Henry Bournes Higgins in his famous *Harvester* judgment of 1907.

While the adoption of enterprise bargaining has been associated with Australia moving towards more decentralised industrial relations systems, it has not been accompanied by a reduction in the degree of regulation. Enterprise bargaining has been associated with the introduction of increasingly complex and detailed legislation.

The late 1980s and especially the early 1990s have been noteworthy for the magnitude of the changes that have occurred to Australian unions. The ACTU embarked on a major program of union amalgamation that has resulted in a substantial reduction in the number of unions, particularly small unions. The amalgamation strategy was based on the need to enhance the quality of services to members, increase the ability of unions to recruit new members and withstand attack from the New Right, the Coalition and aggressively anti-union employers. It is not clear, however, that union rationalisation has either increased the quality of services provided to members or increased the attractiveness of unions to marginal unionists.

The various models of enterprise bargaining developed by the States and the Commonwealth Government's *Industrial Relations Reforms Act* 1993 herald yet another new age for Australian industrial relations. Interactors, as always, will look for loopholes and explore avenues to manipulate these various pieces of legislation and others to their advantage. Justice Deirdre O'Connor became president of the AIRC following the death of Mr Justice Maddern in early 1994. The non-Labor State Governments announced their intention to mount a constitutional challenge to the *Industrial Relations Reform Act* 1993. The federal Coalition, despite its abandonment of *Fightback!*, still subscribes to the reform proposals contained in *Jobsback!* It is presumably only one or two elections away from having the chance to implement such policies. Similarly, when Labor governments assume office at the State level they will set about implementing new industrial relations legislation. Some interactors say Australia has not decentralised enough; others maintain that it has decentralised too much, that not enough protection has been afforded to the lowly paid and those lacking industrial or bargaining power or, alternatively, that too much protection has been provided. In industrial relations only two things are certain: struggle and death.

NOTES

ABBREVIATIONS

Throughout these notes the following abbreviations have been used:

ABL	*Australian Bulletin of Labour*
ABS	Australian Bureau of Statistics
ACTU	Australian Council of Trade Unions
AFR	*Australian Financial Review*
AIRC	Australian Industrial Relations Commission
AJLL	*Australian Journal of Labour Law*
BCA	Business Council of Australia
BCB	*Business Council Bulletin*
ILO	International Labour Organisation
JIR	*Journal of Industrial Relations*
NWC	National Wage Case
SMH	*Sydney Morning Herald*

PREFACE

1 Over the years the name of the major federal industrial relations tribunal has changed four times. From 1904 to 1956 it was called the Commonwealth Court of Conciliation and Arbitration; between 1956 and 1973, the Commonwealth Conciliation and Arbitration Commission; between 1973 and 1989, the Australian Conciliation and Arbitration Commission; and since 1989 the Australian Industrial Relations Commission.

2 NWC, 30 April 1975.

3 For an initial analysis of this decision see Dabscheck, B. (1975), 'The 1975 national wage case: Now we have an incomes policy', JIR, September, pp. 298–309.

4 Woodward, A. E. (1970), 'Industrial relations in the '70s', JIR, July, p. 116. See also Wootten, J. H. (1970), 'The role of the tribunals', JIR, July, pp. 130–44.

5 For further details of these events see Hutson, J. (1971), *Six Wage Concepts*, pp. 165–211; Isaac, J. E. (1971), 'Penal provisions under Commonwealth arbitration' in Isaac and Ford, eds, *Australian Labour Relations: Readings*, 2nd ed., pp. 451–64; and Dufty, N. F. (1972), *Industrial Relations in the Australian Metal Industries*, pp. 129–38.

6 Sir Richard Kirby, president of the Commonwealth Conciliation and Arbitration Commission, pointed out that 'the general increase in business which the Commission has experienced . . . could be seen as a refutation of the accusation that organisations are moving away from formal arbitration . . . [there seems to be] a continued trust in the ability of the Commission to deal satisfactorily with industrial disputes of all kinds' (CCAC Annual Report, 1970, p. 22). For further discussion of the commission's role in this period see Kirby, R. (1970), 'Conciliation and arbitration in Australia: Where the emphasis?' *Federal Law Review*, September, pp. 1–29 and Cupper, L. (1976), 'Legalism in the Australian Conciliation and Arbitration Commission: The gradual transition', JIR, December, pp. 337–64.

7 See Macintyre, S. and Mitchell, R., eds (1989), *Foundations of Arbitration: The Origins and Effects of State Compulsory Arbitration 1890–1914* and Rickard, J. (1976), *Class and Politics: New South Wales, Victoria and the Commonwealth 1890–1910*, for an examination of this period.

8 Macintyre, S. (1989), 'Neither capital nor labour: The politics of the establishment of arbitration' in Macintyre and Mitchell, op. cit.

9 For further information concerning Higgins see Higgins, H. B. (1915), 'A new province for law and order—I', *Harvard Law Review*, November, pp. 13–29; (1919), 'A new province for law and order—II', *Harvard Law Review*, January, pp. 184–217; (1920) 'A new province for law and order—III', *Harvard Law Review*, December, pp. 105–36; Lee, M. (1980), 'The Industrial Peace Act of 1920: A study of political interference in compulsory arbitration'; Callaghan, P. S. (1983), 'Idealism and arbitration in H. B. Higgins' new province for law and order', *Journal of Australian Studies*, November, pp. 56–66; McQueen, H. (1983), 'Higgins and arbitration' in Wheelwright and Buckley, eds, *Essays in the Political Economy of Australian Capitalism*, pp. 145–63; and Rickard, J. (1984), *H. B. Higgins: The Rebel as Judge*.

10 Leo XIII, *Rerum Novarum*, p. 33.

11 Webb, S. and B. (1902), *Industrial Democracy*, pp. 766–84.

12 Roe, M. (1984), *Nine Australian Progressives: Vitalism in Bourgeois Social Thought 1890–1960*. For further information on North American Progressivism see Mowry, G. E. (1946), *Theodore Roosevelt and the Progressive Movement* and (1958), *The Era of Theodore Roosevelt: 1900–1912*; Greer, T. H. (1949), *American Social Reform Movements: Their Pattern Since 1965*; Kolko, G. (1963), *The*

Triumph of Conservatism: A Reinterpretation of American History 1900–1916;
Lasch, C. (1966), *The New Radicalism in America*; Gould, L. L., ed. (1974), *The Progressive Era*; and Roe, op. cit.

13 Rickard, op. cit., pp. 173–4.

14 Austin, A. G. (1965), *The Webbs' Australian Diary 1898*; Rickard, op. cit., p. 88. Beatrice Webb described her meeting with Higgins in the following terms (Austin, op. cit., p. 76): 'In the evening Mr Higgins, a leading Melbourne lawyer and politician, came to dine with us. He is a bald-headed small-eyed man, of medium height; with a cultivated mind and a pleasant manner. He is not nearly so agile and astute as Isaacs [Isaac Isaacs, who served on the High Court 1906–31 and was the first Australian-born governor-general 1931–36]; but he is more anxious to find out the truth and act accordingly. His fault is a curious coldness and perhaps a lack of decision; he hesitates between complete opportunism and rigid adherence to theoretic principles; a hesitation which is emphasised by a slight stammer. He was rather pessimistic about Victorian politics: convinced of the honesty of the Government, but deploring the lack of intellectual leadership and the drifting of the policy according to the crude ideas of the majority of members, of the irresponsible advice of the "Age". "They take a good idea and they spoil it" is Mr Higgins' attitude towards many of the representatives of the community'.

15 See, for example, the introduction to Webb, op. cit., the discussion of arbitration and the national minimum wage, pp. xxi–lvi, 222–46 and 766–84.

16 Higgins, op. cit. The *Harvard Law Review* also published two articles by William Jethro Brown, president of the South Australian Industrial Court (1916–27). See Brown, W. J. (1919), 'Effect of an increase in the living wage by a court of industrial arbitration upon vested rights and duties under preexisting awards', *Harvard Law Review*, June, pp. 892–901 and (1922), 'Law, industry and post-war adjustments', *Harvard Law Review*, January, pp. 223–44. For details of Brown's career see Dabscheck, B. (1983), *Arbitrator at Work: Sir William Raymond Kelly and the Regulation of Australian Industrial Relations*, pp. 78–97 and Roe, op. cit., pp. 22–56.

17 Higgins (1915), pp. 13–14.

18 There is a marked difference between this approach to industrial relations regulation, whereby Higgins determined minimums, and that of the commission's 1975 experiment with wage indexation, which sought to control maximums. The point that needs to be realised is that the commission's approach to industrial relations regulation is forever evolving.

19 *Harvester* judgment, 2 CAR 1.

20 Higgins, 'A new province for law and order—II', p. 190. Consistent with this Macarthy, P. G. (1969), 'Justice Higgins and the *Harvester* judgment', *Australian Economic History Review*, March, pp. 17–38, claims (pp. 33–5) that Higgins' *Harvester* judgment was based on a calculation of what would

have emerged in collective bargaining between parties of equal strength. He saw himself forced to make a determination because the depression and strikes of the 1890s had reduced unions to virtual impotence as collective bargaining agents.

21 Higgins, 'A new province for law and order—I', p. 21.
22 The most famous exception was the 1929 unsuccessful attempt by the Bruce–Page Nationalist Government to repeal the *Conciliation and Arbitration Act* 1904. For details see Carboch, D. (1958), 'The fall of the Bruce–Page Government' in *Studies in Australian Politics*, pp. 121–282. Also see Bennett, L. (1989), 'The federal Conciliation and Arbitration Court in the late 1920s', *Labour History*, November, pp. 44–60.

CHAPTER 1 A GENERAL THEORY OF AUSTRALIAN INDUSTRIAL RELATIONS

1 To avoid misunderstanding a distinction is made here between industrial relations practitioners and scholars.
2 Howard, W. A. (1978), 'Doctrine, theory and teaching in industrial relations' in Turkington, ed., *Industrial Relations Teaching and Research in Australia and New Zealand*, pp. 25, 26.
3 Gurdon, M. A. (1978), 'Patterns of industrial relations research in Australia', JIR, December, p. 460.
4 Niland, J. (1981), 'Research and reform in industrial relations', JIR, December, p. 484. It might be useful to recall Baritz's stinging critique of those 'Many industrial social scientists [who] have put themselves on auction'. Baritz maintains that: 'A major characteristic of twentieth-century manipulation has been that it blinds the victim to the fact of manipulation. Because so many industrial social scientists have been willing to serve power instead of mind, they have been themselves a case study in manipulation by consent' (Baritz, L. (1974), *The Servants of Power: A History of the Use of Social Science in American Industry*, pp. 209–10).
5 Drago, R., et al. (1988), *The BCA–NILS Industrial Relations Study: An Overview of the Employee Survey*, pp. i, 33–4.
6 There can always be disputes about what is or is not a fact. For example, is an industrial dispute a strike or a lockout? Those with econometric skills sometimes consider whether pieces of statistical data should be included or excluded in attempting to produce better equations.
7 This, in turn, assumes that change of itself is somehow or other good. Individuals and groups evaluate change in terms of whether it benefits them.
8 With a little imagination normative statements can be manipulated to provide a basis for positive research.
9 Dunlop, J. T. (1958), *Industrial Relations Systems*, p. vii.
10 See Adams, R. J. (1993), ' "All aspects of people at work": Unity and division in the study of labor and labor management' in Adams and

Meltz, eds, *Industrial Relations Theory: Its Nature, Scope and Pedagogy*, pp. 119–60, for an examination of the evolution of the discipline of industrial relations.

11 Somers, G. G., ed. (1969a), *Essays in Industrial Relations Theory*, p. vii.

12 Somers, G. G. (1969b), 'Bargaining power and industrial relations theory' in Somers (ed.), op. cit., p. 39.

13 Hyman, R. (1980), 'Theory in industrial relations: Towards a materialist analysis' in Boreham and Dow, eds, *Work and Inequality: Ideology and Control in the Capitalist Labour Process*, p. 38.

14 Taylor, V. and Bray, M. (1986), 'Introduction: Directions in industrial relations research', in Bray and Taylor, eds, *Managing Labour? Essays in the Political Economy of Industrial Relations*, p. 1.

15 Blain, N. and Plowman, D. (1987), 'The Australian industrial relations literature 1970–86', JIR, June, p. 313.

16 Lansbury, R. D. and Westcott, M. (1992), 'Researching Australian industrial relations: Dawn or twilight of a golden age?', JIR, September, pp. 396–419.

17 Dunlop, op. cit., pp. vi, 380.

18 Ibid., p. 383.

19 Ibid., p. 13.

20 He states, for example, that the 'web of rules can be expected to change with variations in the three features of the context of the system'. Several lines later he qualifies his position somewhat by saying: 'Changes may originate within the organisations of the actors' (ibid., p. 27).

21 Shalev, M. (1980), 'Industrial relations theory and the comparative study of industrial relations and industrial conflict', *British Journal of Industrial Relations*, March, p. 26.

22 A similar statement can be made concerning industrial relations decisions handed down by courts.

23 Guille, H. (1984), 'Industrial relations theory: Painting by numbers', JIR, December, p. 494. He has also said, 'Unions, employers and state agencies have myriad ways of affecting the conduct of industrial relations, but they are not confined to "industrial relations" in their efforts to affect material standards' (p. 491). A holistic, or complete, account would seem to necessitate, following Guille, a combination of industrial relations with 'not industrial relations'.

24 Dunlop, op. cit., p. 385.

25 Ibid., p. 24.

26 Ibid., p. 92.

27 For previous examinations of these issues by the author see Dabscheck, B. (1980), 'The Australian system of industrial relations: An analytical model', JIR, June, pp. 196–218, and Dabschech, B. (1989), *Australian Industrial Relations in the 1980s*.

28 With respect to such issues as occupational health and safety, workers compensation, equal employment opportunity, affirmative action,

superannuation, apprenticeship, training and education, annual holidays and long-service leave.

29 Dunlop was quite dogmatic on this point. He said, 'Every industrial relations system involves three groups of actors' (op. cit., p. viii).

30 Seven, to be precise. One actor can dominate the other two; two actors can combine to dominate the third; or they could be locked in a tripartite Dunlopian embrace.

31 Kochan, T. A., McKersie, R. B. and Cappelli, P. (1984), 'Strategic choice and industrial relations theory', *Industrial Relations*, Winter, pp. 16–39; Kochan, T. A., Katz, H. C. and McKersie, R. B. (1986), *The Transformation of American Industrial Relations*.

32 For example, Dunlop said, 'Managers may liquidate the enterprise or work place or change the character of output to be more consonant with the product market or budget' (op. cit., p. 91).

33 For an alternative critique of the strategic choice model see Lewin, D. (1987), 'Industrial relations as a strategic variable' in Kleiner et al., eds, *Human Resources and the Performance of the Firm*, pp. 1–41.

34 Hills, S. M. (1993), 'Integrating industrial relations and the social sciences' in Adams and Meltz, op. cit., p. 184. But why confine it to the social sciences?

35 Adams, R. J. (1988), 'Desperately seeking industrial relations theory', pp. 8–9.

36 Cappelli, op. cit., p. 98.

37 Somers, G. G. (1969b), 'Bargaining power and industrial relations theory' in Somers, op. cit., p. 40.

38 See Blyton, P. and Turnbull, P., eds (1992), *Reassessing Human Resource Management*, for a critique of human resource management.

39 Voos, P. (1993), 'Designing an industrial relations theory curriculum for graduate students' in Adams and Meltz, op. cit., p. 18.

40 See Larouche, V. and Audet, M. (1993), 'Theorizing industrial relations: The dominance of logical positivism and the shift to strategic choice' in Adams and Metz, op. cit., pp. 255–82, for an examination of the different approaches employed by scholars to the study of industrial relations.

41 Dufty, N. F. and Fells, R. E. (1989), *Dynamics of Industrial Relations in Australia*, p. xii.

42 Hills, op. cit., pp. 184–5.

43 Hyman, op. cit., p. 42.

44 For further discussion of these issues see Dabscheck, B. (1989), *Australian Industrial Relations in the 1980s*, pp. 1–24.

45 Dunlop (op. cit., pp. 380–9) entitled his last chapter a 'general theory of industrial relations'. The theory developed here is radically different from his.

46 The term *orbit of interaction* needs to be distinguished from Ross's orbits of coercive comparison (op. cit., pp. 53–64). In his hands an orbit of coercive comparison involved unions basing claims for improvements in wages and working conditions on what had already been achieved by another, or other, unions.

47 Given a realisation that Australia has a Commonwealth, six State, two Territory and local government jurisdictions, the number of interactors within this firm orbit would be substantially increased.

48 For a brilliant account of how the decisions of common law judges shaped the activities of unions and the contours of industrial relations in the USA see Forbath, W. E. (1989), 'The shaping of the American labor movement', *Harvard Law Review*, April, pp. 1109–256. For examinations of the impact of the law in Britain and Australia see Wedderburn, Lord (1986), *The Worker and the Law*, and Creighton, W. B., Ford, W. J. and Mitchell, R. J. (1993), *Labour Law: Texts and Materials*, 2nd ed., respectively.

49 Which seems to be the ultimate point of the strategic choice model. Its proponents, however, have confined its application to enterprises/corporations unable to escape the straitjacket of traditional industrial relations scholarship.

50 Dahrendorf, R. (1959), *Class and Class Conflict in Industrial Society*, pp. 168, 169, 176.

51 Keenoy has said, 'Empirically, conflict behaviour may be indistinguishable from competitive behaviour. Do prospective employees compete with each other or come into conflict with each other for scarce jobs? Do managers compete with each other or come into conflict with each other for scarce promotions? Why is it that unions are invariably characterised as in conflict with employers while companies are invariably seen to compete with each other? Conflict would seem to be a euphemism for competition' (Keenoy, T. (1991), 'The roots of metaphor in the old and the new industrial relations', *British Journal of Industrial Relations*, June, p. 326).

52 A difference between Dahrendorf and the model developed here should be noted. Dahrendorf (op. cit., pp. 172, 173) states that 'the distribution of authority . . . is, in any given association [a shorthand term he uses which is equivalent to an orbit of interaction], the cause of the formation of two, and only two, conflict groups'. Proposition three rejects the notion that there can be only two struggling elements within an orbit. More than two, or any number of, interactors can be present in an orbit struggling over authority.

53 Hyman, R. (1987), 'Strategy or structure? Capital, labour and control', *Work, Employment and Society*, March, p. 43.

54 Dimmock and Sethi noted that the 'strategic choice' model, which its creators decided to leave encased in Dunlop's systems model, with its notion of a shared ideology, encountered problems when enterprises set about destroying unions, as they were employing such a 'strategy . . . to take sanctions against the industrial relations system itself . . . systems theory cannot interpret these results' (Dimmock, S. J. and Sethi, A. S. (1986), 'The role of ideology and power in systems theory: Some fundamental shortcomings', *Relations Industrielles*, No. 4, p. 744). This is not a problem for us. In destroying unions enterprises create new orbits in attempting to enhance their authority over the workforce in their employ.

55 *Boilermakers* case (1956), 94 CLR 254.

56 See note 51 above. George Orwell once said, 'The trouble with competitions is that someone wins them'. Orwell, S. and Angus, I., eds (1968), *The Collected Essays, Journalism and Letters of George Orwell*, Vol. 3, *As I Please 1943–45*, Secker & Warburg, London.

57 For a discussion of chaos theory and its place in the history of science see Appleyard, B. (1992), *Understanding the Present*.

CHAPTER 2 FROM CENTRALISATION TO . . .

1 Statement of Accord by the Australian Labor Party and the Australian Council of Trade Unions Regarding Economic Policy (1983), mimeo (i.e. Accord Mark I), p. 2.

2 Ibid.

3 Statement of Accord . . . (1983), p. 5.

4 Loveday, P. (1984), 'Corporatist trends in Australia', *Politics*, May, pp. 46–51; Schott, K. (1985), 'The consensus economy: An international overview', *Economic Papers*, June, pp. 1–22; Stewart, R. G. (1985), 'The politics of the Accord: Does corporatism explain it?' *Politics*, May, pp. 26–35; Gerritsen, R. (1986), 'The necessity of "corporatism": The case of the Hawke Labor Government', *Politics*, May, pp. 19–27; McEachern, D. (1986), 'Corporatism and business responses to the Hawke Government', *Politics*, May, pp. 45–54; Pemberton, J. and Davis, G. (1986), 'The rhetoric of consensus', *Politics*, May, pp. 55–62; Stilwell, F. (1968), *The Accord and Beyond: The Political Economy of the Labor Government*; Carney, S. (1988), *Australia in Accord: Politics and Industrial Relations under the Hawke Government*; Singleton, G. (1990), *The Accord and the Australian Labour Movement*.

5 Quoted in Perlman, M. (1954), *Judges in Industry: A Study of Labour Arbitration in Australia*, p. 32.

6 Dabscheck, B. (1989), *Australian Industrial Relations in the 1980s*, pp. 26–46.

7 *National Economic Summit Conference Documents and Proceedings* (1983), Vol. 2, *Record of Proceedings*, AGPS, Canberra, p. 194.

8 Burgmann, M. (1984), 'Australian trade unionism in 1983', JIR, March, pp. 91–8; Burgmann, M. (1985), 'Australian trade unionism in 1984', JIR, March, pp. 81–8; Mulvey, C. (1984), 'Wages policy and wage determination in 1983', JIR, March, pp. 112–19; Mulvey, C. (1985), 'Wages policy and wage determination in 1984', JIR, March, pp. 68–75.

9 NWC, 28 June 1986, p. 8.

10 Agreement Between the Government and the ACTU for the Discounting of Wages Indexation and Ongoing Wage Restraint (1985), 4 September, mimeo (i.e. Acccord Mark II).

11 BCB, June–July 1984, September 1984, November–December 1984, April 1985, May 1986. See also Allen, G. (1986), 'Management pressures for change and the industrial relations system' in Blandy and Niland, eds, *Alternatives to Arbitration*, pp. 334–50.

12 White, R. J., presidential address in BCB, October–November 1985, pp. 21–3.

13 BCB, May–June 1985, December 1985–January 1986, May 1986, July 1986, August 1986.
14 BCB, March 1985, p. 1.
15 This, of course, was an objective enshrined in the Accord.
16 BCB, May–June 1985, p. 12.
17 BCB, December 1985–January 1986, p. 10.
18 It is doubtful whether Australian unions have ever been involved in class war, let alone during the years of the Accord!
19 BCB, March 1986, p. 12.
20 For a presentation and critique of the views of the H. R. Nicholls Society see Dabscheck, *Australian Industrial Relations in the 1980s*, op. cit., pp. 113–14.
21 Stone, J. (1986a), introduction in H. R. Nicholls Society, *Arbitration in Contempt*, pp. 9–15; Stone, J. (1986b), introduction in H. R. Nicholls Society, *Trade Unions Reform*, pp. 3–5; Stone, J. (1987), presidential address in H. R. Nicholls Society, *The Light on the Hill*, pp. 13–15; Stone, J. (1989), 'Closing remarks' in H. R. Nicholls Society, *In Search of the Magic Pudding*, pp. 91–4; Stone, J. (1991), 'The wide-ranging politics of the Cook Bill' in H. R. Nicholls Society, *No Vacancies*, pp. 16–74; McLachlan, I. (1986), 'Farmers, Australia's cost structures and union power' in H. R. Nicholls Society, *Arbitration in Contempt*, pp. 69–90; McLachlan, I. (1989a), 'Terminating the Button rents on Australia's waterfront' in H. R. Nicholls Society, *The Legacy of 'The Hungry Mile'*, pp. 39–45; McLachlan, I. (1989b), 'The live sheep dispute: Some personal reminiscences' in H. R. Nicholls Society, *No Ticket, No Start—No More!*, pp. 55–8; Costello, P. (1986), 'Legal remedies against trade union conduct in Australia' in H. R. Nicholls Society, *Arbitration in Contempt*, pp. 131–55; Costello, P. (1989a), 'The Dollar Sweets story' in H. R. Nicholls Society, *In Search of the Magic Pudding*, pp. 27–32; Costello, P. (1989b), keynote address in H. R. Nicholls Society, *No Ticket, No Start—No More!*, pp. 1–6; Costello, P. (1990), 'Back to the waterfront: New IR Bill' in H. R. Nicholls Society, *Back to the Waterfront*, pp. 1–5; Costello, P. (1992), 'The Troubleshooters' case' in H. R. Nicholls Society, *For the Labourer is Worthy of His Hire*, pp. 85–92; Kemp, D. (1986), 'Trade unions and liberty' in H. R. Nicholls Society, *Trade Unions Reform*, pp. 15–23; Chaney, F. (1987), 'The Opposition's industrial relations reform in Australia' in H. R. Nicholls Society, *The Light on the Hill*, pp. 75–8; Chaney, F. (1988), 'Industrial relations: A managerial responsibility' in H. R. Nicholls Society, *Back to Basics*, pp. 27–32; Reith, P. (1989), 'The evolution of the Opposition's IR policy' in H. R. Nicholls Society, *No Ticket, No Start—No More!*, pp. 29–33; Greiner, N. (1990), opening address in H. R. Nicholls Society, *Public Interest or Vested Interest?*, pp. xi–xiv; Howard, J. W. (1990), guest of honour's address in ibid., pp. 47–50; Kemp, R. (1991), 'With particular reference to the Democrats' in H. R. Nicholls Society, *No Vacancies*, pp. 75–93.
22 Industrial Relations Policy (1986), Liberal Party of Australia, National Party of Australia, 11 May (mimeo), p. 4.

23 The Coalition had included such a clause in its 1984 policy. See *Policy on Industrial Relations* (1984), Liberal Party of Australia, National Party of Australia, 16 April (mimeo), p. 6.

24 Industrial Relations Policy (1986), pp. 3–4.

25 For an examination of events surrounding this meeting and subsequent developments see the *Australian*, AFR and SMH, 17 May–12 June 1986. See also Carney, op. cit., pp. 62–4 and Kelly, P. (1992), *The End of Certainty: The Story of the 1980s*, pp. 214–21.

26 *Australian*, 19 May 1986.

27 AFR, 29 May 1986.

28 See AFR, 12 June 1986, for the text of Hawke's speech and accompanying statement.

29 The commission's decision concerning superannuation was ambiguous, if not confused. For an analysis see Dabscheck, *Australian Industrial Relations in the 1980s*, pp. 100–7.

30 AFR, 11 July, 18 August and 22 August 1986; *Australian*, 11 July and 22 August 1986; and SMH, 11 July and 22 August 1986.

31 Smith, H. and Thompson, H. (1987), 'Industrial relations and the law: A case study of Robe River', *Australian Quarterly*, Spring and Summer, pp. 297–304; Copeman, A. C. (1987), 'The Robe River affair', JIR, December, pp. 539–43.

32 For an examination of industry policy see Ewer, P., Higgins, W. and Stevens, A. (1987), *Unions and the Future of Australian Manufacturing*; Ewer et al. (1991), *Politics and the Accord*; Costa, M. and Easson, M. (1991), *Australian Industry: What Policy?*; Capling, A. and Galligan, B. (1992), *Beyond the Protective State: The Political Economy of Australia's Manufacturing Industry Policy*; and Bell, S. (1993), *Australian Manufacturing and the State: The Politics of Industry Policy in the Post-war Era.*

33 AFR, 3 and 4 September 1986.

34 See Singleton, G. (1985), 'The Economic Planning Advisory Council: The reality of consensus', *Politics*, May, pp. 12–25, for an analysis of its operation.

35 Kelman, B. N. and Coates, A. W. (1986), *Restrictive Work Practices*. Submission to Economic Advisory Council of Australia on Behalf of Business Council of Australia, 6 September (mimeo).

36 Hawke, R. J. L. (1986). Remarks at the Opening of Meeting between Representatives of the ACTU, BCA and CAI on Work and Management Practices, Melbourne, 24 September (mimeo), pp. 2, 6.

37 The text of the Work Practices Summit is reproduced in the *Australian*, 25 September 1986.

38 NWC, 10 March 1987, p. 13.

39 Chapman, B. and Gruen, F. (1990), *An Analysis of the Australian Consensual Incomes Policy: The Prices and Incomes Accord*; Lewis, P. E. T. and Spiers, D. J. (1990), 'Six years of the Accord: An assessment', JIR, March, pp. 53–68.

40 Calmfors, L. and Driffill, J. (1988), 'Centralisation of wage bargaining', *Economic Policy*, April, p. 17.

41 Chamberlain, N. W. and Kuhn, J. W. (1965), *Collective Bargaining*, 2nd ed., pp. 425–6.

42 Calmfors and Driffill, op. cit., pp. 43–4.

43 Skosice, D. (1990), 'Wage determination: The changing role of institutions in advanced industrialised countries', *Oxford Review of Economic Policy*, Winter, p. 41. What does the term *coordination* mean? Economists maintain that markets provide the most efficient, and hence productive, method with which to coordinate the affairs of an economy. Monetarists argue that strict adherence to rules concerning alterations to the supply of money provide the best means for coordinating an economy. In short, a strong central bank is the key to understanding the success of an economy. If this analysis is correct the successes of the West German economy can be attributed to the coordination functions performed by the Bundesbank.

44 Skosice, op. cit., p. 54.

45 Dabscheck, *Australian Industrial Relations in the 1980s*, pp. 46–50, examined theoretical and statistical problems with classifying countries in terms of their degree of neo-corporatism. Also see Dell'Aringa, C. and Lodovici, M. S. (1992), 'Industrial relations and economic performance' in Treu, ed., *Participation in Public Policy-making: The Role of Trade Unions and Employers' Associations*, pp. 26–58, for a review of the literature on how societies are classified as either centralised or corporatist.

46 Crouch, C. (1985), 'Conditions for trade union wage restraint' in Lindberg and Maier, eds, *The Politics of Inflation and Economic Stagnation*, p. 127.

47 Crouch, C. (1990), 'Trade unions in the exposed sector: Their influence on neo-corporatist behaviour' in Brunetta and Dell'Aringa, eds, *Labour Relations and Economic Performance*, p. 171. In 'Conditions for trade union wage restraint' (1985) Crouch identified Australia as 'exhibit[ing] decentralised bargaining with weak confederations' (p. 117). He based this assertion on sources published in the period 1970–76. While his time of writing might have occurred before the centralised/coordinated days of the Accord he seems to be unaware of the wage indexation experiment between 1975 and 1981.

48 Tarantelli, E. (1986), 'The regulation of inflation and unemployment', *Industrial Relations*, Winter, p. 11.

49 Booth, A. (1982), 'Corporatism, capitalism and depression in twentieth-century Britain', *British Journal of Sociology*, June, pp. 200–23.

50 For an explanation of these years see Dabscheck, B. and Niland, J. (1981), *Industrial Relations in Australia*, pp. 318–21.

51 *Metal Trades Work Value* cases, 121 CAR 587, 122 CAR 169.

52 Dabscheck, *Australian Industrial Relations in the 1980s*, pp. 37–9.

53 In light of the discussion here it might be advisable for such writers as Dowrick (1993, *Wage Bargaining Systems and Productivity Growth in OECD Countries*) to reconsider the values of their 'independent' variables.

54 This might be a restatement of the policy on–policy off problem associated with traditional discussions of the effectiveness of wages and incomes policies. The achievements during 'policy on' were dissipated during periods of 'policy off'.

CHAPTER 3 CLIPPING THE WINGS OF THE COMMISSION

 1 Pusey, M. (1991), *Economic Rationalism in Canberra: A Nation-building State Changes Its Mind*; Carroll, J. and Manne, R., eds (1992), *Shutdown: The Failure of Economic Rationalism and How to Rescue Australia*; Forsyth, P., ed. (1992), *Microeconomic Reform in Australia*; Harcourt, G. C. (1992), 'Markets, madness and the middle way', *Australian Quarterly*, Autumn, pp. 1–17; Horne, D., ed. (1992), *The Trouble with Economic Rationalism*; Gruen, F. and Grattan, M. (1993), *Managing Government: Labor's Achievements and Failures*; King, S. and Lloyd, P., eds (1993), *Economic Rationalism: Dead End or Way Forward*; and Rees, S., Rodley, G. and Stilwell. F., eds (1993), *Beyond the Market: Alternatives to Economic Rationalism*. For a critical examination of economics see Thurow, L. C. (1983), *Dangerous Currents: The State of Economics*.
 2 Since March 1989 the commission has been called the Australian Industrial Relations Commission.
 3 Perlman, M., op. cit., refers to the High Court 'clipping the wings of the Arbitration Court' (p. 20).
 4 Higgins, H. B., 'A new province for law and order' II and III; Lee, op. cit.; Rickard, J., *H. B. Higgins: The Rebel as Judge*.
 5 *Huddart Parker* case (1909) 8 CLR 330.
 6 8 CLR 348.
 7 *Engineers'* case (1920) 28 CLR 129.
 8 *Concrete Pipes* case (1971) 124 CLR 468.
 9 *St George County Council*, 130 CLR 533; *Australian Industrial Court*, 136 CLR 235; *Kuring-gai Cooperative Building Society*, 22 ALR 621; *Adamson*, 143 CLR 190; *Actors Equity*, 150 CLR 169; *State Superannuation Board*, 150 CLR 282; *Fencott*, 125 CLR 570; *Tasmanian Dam*, 46 ALR 625.
10 In the 1983 *Social Welfare Union* case (153 CLR 297) the High Court adopted a broader definition of the words *industrial disputes* contained in section 51, paragraph XXXV, thereby reducing restrictions, or artificial barriers, on the issues or matters that could be adjudicated by the commission.
11 O'Donovan, J. (1977), 'Can the contract of employment be regulated through the corporations power?' *Australian Law Journal*, May, pp. 234–46; Smith, G. G. and McCallum, R. C. (1984), 'A legal framework for the establishment of institutional collective bargaining in Australia', JIR, March, pp. 3–24; Lindell, G. J. (1984), 'The corporations and races powers', *Federal Law Review* 14, pp. 219–52; Smith, G. F. (1985), 'The High Court and industrial relations in the 1980s', ABL, March, pp. 82–101; Spry, I. F. C. (1986), 'Constitutional aspects of deregulating the labour market' in H. R. Nicholls Society, *Arbitration in Contempt*, pp. 117–30; Spry, I. F. C. (1987),

'Constitutional aspects of deregulation', *Law Institute Journal*, May, pp. 471–3; McCallum, R. C., Pittard, M. J. and Smith, G. J. (1990), *Australian Labour Law: Cases and Materials*, 2nd ed., pp. 346 and 347; Craven, G. (1992), 'The Coalition and voluntary industrial agreements: Some constitutional aspects', *Economic and Labour Relations Review*, June, pp. 94–111; Solomon, D. (1992), *The Political Impact of the High Court*, pp. 52–63 and 107–19; Zines, L. (1992), *The High Court and the Constitution*, 3rd ed., pp. 70–93; Hulme, S. E. K. (1993), 'A constitutional basis for the Coalition's industrial relations policy', *Economic and Labour Relations Review*, June, pp. 62–76; and Stewart, A. (1993), 'Federal regulation and the use of powers other than the industrial power' in Ronfeldt and McCallum, eds, *A New Province for Legalism: Legal Issues and the Deregulation of Industrial Relations*, pp. 86–100.

12 *Burgess* case (1936) 55 CLR 608.

13 55 CLR 696.

14 55 CLR 687; see also 680–1.

15 *Koowarta* case (1982), 153 CLR 168.

16 *Tasmanian Dam* case (1983), 46 ALR 625.

17 *Richardson* case (1988), 164 CLR 261; *Queensland* case (1989) 167 CAR 232; *Polykhovich* case (1991), 172 CAR 501.

18 45 ALR 669.

19 164 CLR 321.

20 153 CLR 198.

21 28 CLR 129.

22 153 CLR 229.

23 *Northern Suburbs General Cemetery Reserves Trust* case (1992), 112 ALR 87.

24 Stewart, A., op. cit., p. 98.

25 Creighton, B. (1993a), 'Industrial regulation and Australia's international obligations' in Ronfeldt and McCallum, op. cit., pp. 101–31; Ludeke, J. T. (1993b), 'The external affairs power: Another province for law and order', JIR, September, pp. 453–67; Stewart, A., op. cit.

26 A similar strategy was employed by the Chifley Labor Government in the period 1945–59. See Sheridan, T. (1989), *Division of Labour: Industrial Relations in the Chifley Years 1945–49*.

27 *Liberal and National Industrial Relations Policy* (1988); *Industrial Relations: The Agenda for Reform* (1990); *Fightback! It's Your Australia* (1991); *Fightback! Fairness and Jobs* (1992); *Jobsback! The Federal Coalition's Industrial Relations Policy* (1992).

28 In chapter 2 it was argued that the Accord Mark I was designed to fit the desires or approach of the commission concerning industrial relations regulation.

29 Submission by the Commonwealth Government (1988), National Wage Case October 1987–January 1988, p. 63.

30 Submission by the Commonwealth Government (1989), National Wage Case June–July 1988, p. 65. For an examination of the subject matter and quality of second-tier increase see Submissions by the Commonwealth

Government (1988 and 1989); McDonald, T. and Rimmer, M. (1988), 'Award structure and the second tier', ABL, June, pp. 469–91; Rimmer, M. and Zappala, J. (1988), 'Labour market flexibility and the second tier', ABL, September, pp. 564–91; Frenkel, S. and Shaw, M. (1989), 'No tears for the second tier: Productivity bargaining in the Australian metal industry', ABL, March, pp. 90–114; and Reilly, S. (1989), 'An analysis of the factors influencing the second tier and its evolution', ABL, June, pp. 200–22.

31   The March 1987 decision had stipulated that, if the parties could not reach agreement on second-tier increase, 'the Commission will arbitrate in accordance with the relevant principle or principles, and, in such cases, the Commission will award no more than 2% to operate from a date no earlier than 1 September 1987 and no more than a further 2% to operate from a date no earlier than 1 July 1988' (NWC, 10 March 1987, p. 35).

32   SMH, 22, 28 July 1987, 19 September 1987; Davis, E. M. (1988), 'The 1987 ACTU Congress: Reconstructing Australia?' JIR, March, pp. 118–29; Gardner, M. (1988), 'Australian trade unionism in 1987', JIR, March, pp. 147–54; Petridis, A. (1988), 'Wages policy and wage determination in 1987', JIR, March, pp. 155–62. It is somewhat ironic in light of this to read the following extract in *Australia Reconstructed*, which the ACTU championed as a blueprint for the future: 'Wages outcomes must be linked with policies designed to rectify our current account difficulties. The best way of doing this is through consensus-based policies . . . A centralised system, like the new two-tiered system, is essential to ensure both appropriate aggregate outcomes and equitable and efficient flexibility at an industry and enterprise level' (Department of Trade (1987), *Australian Reconstructed— ACTU/TDC Mission to Western Europe: A Report by the Mission Members to the ACTU and the TDC*, p. xii).

33   SMH, 23 November 1987.

34   CAI, *Industrial Review*, August 1987; NWC, 17 December 1987.

35   NWC, 17 December 1987, p. 9.

36   SMH, 7 November 1987.

37   SMH, 2, 14 November 1987; *Australian*, 2, 14 November 1987; AFR, 2, 16 November 1987.

38   *Australian*, 11, 12, 17 December 1987.

39   NWC, 17 December 1987, p. 13.

40   NWC, 17 December 1987, p. 12.

41   *Australian*, 18 December 1987; AFR, 18 December 1987; SMH, 18 December 1987.

42   *Australian*, 19, 22, 24, 26 December 1987, 2 January 1988; AFR, 21, 30 December 1987; SMH, 22 December 1987.

43   NWC, 5 February 1988, p. 5.

44   There was even idle talk of the Federal Government, unions and employers negotiating a tripartite consensus on wages, thereby sidelining the commission (*Australian*, 9 February, 11 March 1988; AFR, 11 March 1988; SMH, 11 March 1988).

45 It was actually 7.3 per cent.

46 ACTU (1988), Report on Wages; *Australian*, 25 February 1988; AFR, 25 February 1988; SMH, 25 February 1988.

47 Keating, P. J. (1988), *Economic Statement*, p. 12.

48 ACTU (1989), *Executive Report*, Congress, p. 45.

49 For details of the twists and turns of these negotiations see the *Australian*, AFR and SMH between 17 June 1988 and 11 July 1988.

50 For a summary of the positions adopted by different employer groups see NWC, 12 August 1988, pp. 24–35.

51 Ibid., p. 10.

52 Ibid., p. 5.

53 Ibid., p. 6.

54 AFR, 25 and 26 August 1988; SMH, 26 August 1988.

55 *Australian*, 5 September 1988.

56 AFR, 9 September 1988.

57 *Australian*, 17 September 1988.

58 AFR, 22 November 1988; SMH, 22 November 1988.

59 ACTU (1989), *Executive Report*, pp. 49–50.

60 AFR, 5 December 1988.

61 *Australian*, 13 and 27 January 1989: SMH, 31 January 1989.

62 *Australian*, 1 and 2 February 1989: SMH, 1 and 2 February 1989.

63 ACTU (1989), *Executive Report*, pp. 51–3.

64 *Australian*, 11 February 1989; SMH, 11 February 1989.

65 Keating, P. J. (1989), *Economic Statement*, p. 4.

66 Ibid., p. 11.

67 NWC, 25 May 1989, p. 2.

68 Ibid., p. 4.

69 NWC, 7 August 1989, pp. 20–1.

70 Ibid., p. 10.

71 Ibid., pp. 11–14.

72 AFR, 8 August 1989.

73 AFR, 9 and 10 August 1989; SMH, 9 and 10 August 1989.

74 AFR, 24 April 1989.

75 AFR, 16 August, 2 October 1989; SMH, 16 and 28 August, 2 October 1989; *Australian*, 17 August, 2 October 1989.

76 BCA (1989), *Enterprise-based Bargaining Units: A Better Way of Working*.

77 AFR, 6 November 1989. Also see AFR, 25, 26 January 1990; *Australian*, 18 November 1989.

78 AFR, 30 January 1990.

79 Which sounds similar to the notion of conjunctive bargaining presented by Chamberlain and Kuhn in *Collective Bargaining* (1965); see chapter 2.

80 AFR, 14 February 1990.

81 Agreement Between the Federal Government and the ACTU, 21 February 1990 (i.e. Accord Mark VI); *Australian*, 22 February 1990; AFR, 22 February 1990; SMH, 22 February 1990.

82 SMH, 24 February 1990; *Australian*, 24 February 1990.

83 Gleeson Report (1991), pp. 20–1.

84 AFR, 1 May 1990; SMH, 4 June 1990; *Australian*, 5 June 1990.

85 AIRC (1989–90), Annual Report of the President, pp. 3–4.

86 Gleeson Report (1991), pp. 1–2.

87 AIRC (1992–93), Annual Report of the President, p. 1.

88 AIRC (1990–91), Annual Report of the President, p. 8.

89 Reports of his verbal submission are contained in *AFR*, 13 January 1992.

90 Remuneration Tribunal (1991–92), Annual Report, p. 5.

91 *Australian*, 16 March 1992; AFR, 16 March 1992.

92 SMH, 28 April 1992. See for example AIRC (1991–92), Annual Report, pp. 5–6.

93 *Australian*, 27 March 1992.

94 AFR, 23 April 1992; SMH, 23 April 1992.

95 SMH, 25 April 1992; *Australian*, 25 April 1992.

96 ACTU (1991a), *Executive Report*, Congress, p. 8.

97 *Australian*, 5 and 8 September 1990; SMH, 5 and 8 September 1990.

98 *Australian*, 29 August, 3 September 1990.

99 AIRC (1990a), Transcript of Proceedings, p. 53.

100 AIRC (1990b), Decision, Melbourne, 17 September, p. 3.

101 *Australian*, 16 and 27 October 1990; AFR, 16 October 1990; SMH, 16 October 1990.

102 AFR, 17 October 1990; *Australian*, 17 October 1990; SMH, 17 October 1990.

103 For details of these negotiations see the *Australian, AFR* and *SMH*, 9 November 1990 to 21 November 1990.

104 These are reproduced in NWC, 16 April 1991, pp. 3–5.

105 Ibid., p. 10.

106 The Metal Trades Industry Association was opposed to enterprise bargaining. See Evans A. C. (1990), Affidavit, MTIA.

107 NWC, 16 April 1991, p. 37.

108 Ibid., p. 22. This conclusion could be regarded as somewhat surprising. The Australian Workplace Industrial Relations Survey, conducted between October 1989 and May 1990, roughly the same period in which the national wage case occurred, found 'that Australians workplaces [had] experienced significant changes in the two to five years prior to the survey' (Callus, R. et al. (1991), *Industrial Relations at Work: The Australian Workplace Industrial Relations Survey*, p. 204). A possible way out of this conundrum is that whereas the Workplace Survey picked up changes occurring informally, the commission focused on the operation of the formal system.

109 NWC, 16 April 1991, pp. 63, 38.

110 Ibid., p. 61.

111 Ibid., p. 59.

112 SMH, 17 April 1991. Also see *Australian*, 1 May 1991.

113 *Australian*, 20 April 1991. At a swearing-in for former ACTU advocate Ian Watson, who had become a member of the commission, CAI

director-general Bryan Noakes offered to shake hands with Bill Kelty. Kelty refused, saying, 'We owe you nothing. It's war' (SMH, 14 May 1991).

114 AFR, 24 April 1991.

115 AFR, 2 May 1991.

116 Department of Industrial Relations (1991), 'Government guidelines for workplace bargaining'.

117 Sams, P. (1991), ACTU Wages Strategy: A Discussion Paper, p. 8. Also see criticisms of award restructuring in Costa, M. and Duffy, M. (1991), *Labor, Prosperity and the Nineties: Beyond the Bonsai Economy*, pp. 133–70.

118 *Australian*, 5, 25 June, 1, 8, 9 July 1991; AFR 11 July 1991; SMH, 11 July 1991.

119 AFR, 1 August 1991.

120 AFR, 19 July 1991.

121 SMH, 29 August 1991.

122 NWC, 30 October 1991, p. 3.

123 Ibid., p. 4.

124 For details of these negotiations see *Australian*, AFR and SMH, 21 December 1991 to 24 February 1992.

125 Keating, P. J. (1992a), *One Nation*, pp. 44–9.

126 NWC, 25 October 1993; see chapter 4 below.

127 The situation is a little more complicated than this with provisos and qualifications. See *Industrial Relations Legislation Amendment Act* 1992 and chapter 4.

128 AIRC (1991–92), Annual Report of the President, p. 4.

129 AIRC (1992–93), Annual Report of the President, p. 3.

130 Isaac, J. E. (1977), 'Wage determination and economic policy', *Australian Economic Review*, 3rd quarter, p. 24.

131 Isaac, J. E. (1989), 'The Arbitration Commission: Prime mover or facilitator', JIR, September, pp. 407–8.

132 This is not meant to imply that the various personnel of the tribunal have a common or uniform view on how it should proceed. In short, there can be disputes between tribunal members over the best course of action to be adopted. For examples of such clashes see d'Alpuget, B. (1977), *Mediator: A Biography of Sir Richard Kirby*; Dabscheck, *Arbitrator at Work*; and Kitay, J. and McCarthy, P. (1989), 'Justice Staples and the politics of Australian industrial arbitration', JIR, September, pp. 310–33.

133 Brown, W. J. (1906), *The Austinian Theory of Law*, p. 291.

134 Dabscheck, *Arbitrator at Work*, pp. 1–15.

135 Perlman, M., *Judges in Industry*, p. 39.

136 Its decision in the June 1986 national wage case concerning superannuation was also ambiguous and uncertain. See Dabscheck, *Australian Industrial Relations in the 1980s*, pp. 100–7.

137 Ludeke, J. T. (1993a), 'The government's new charter for industrial relations in Australia 1993–96', JIR, June, pp. 316–28.

CHAPTER 4 ENTERPRISE BARGAINING

1 Sheldon, P. and Thornthwaite, L. (1993), 'Ex parte Accord: The Business Council of Australia and industrial relations change', *International Journal of Business Studies*, October, pp. 37–55. O'Brien, J. (1994), 'McKinsey, Fred Hilmer and the BCA: The new management model of labour market reform'.

2 Pusey, op. cit.

3 It is interesting to recall Bill Kelty's September 1988 commitment to restructure every award in the country (*Australian*, 5 September 1988).

4 Evans, op. cit.; Boland, R., 'The alternative approaches to labour market reform' in Economic Planning and Advisory Council, *Issues in Enterprise Bargaining*, pp. 35–66; National Pay Equity Coalition (1993), Enterprise Bargaining and Women.

5 AFR, 14 February 1990.

6 Department of Industrial Relations, op. cit., p. 119.

7 Otlowski, M. (1992), 'The legal fallout from the APPM dispute', AJLL, December, pp. 287–94; Thompson, H. (1992), 'The APPM dispute: The dinosaur and turtles vs the ACTU', *Economic and Labour Relations Review*, December, pp. 148–64.

8 Evans, op. cit; Boland, op. cit.

9 BCA (1987), *Towards an Enterprise-based Industrial Relations System*, p. 1.

10 Ibid., p. 6.

11 Ibid., p. 8.

12 For those with an interest in things ironic the Business Council of Australia organised a conference to launch the report in late August/early September 1989. The conference was rescheduled to December because of problems associated with flying in attendees that resulted from the 1989 pilots' dispute. The pilots wanted to break away from the strictures of the Accord and enter into enterprise or collective agreements with their employers. For an analysis and list of bibliographic sources concerning the dispute see Burgess, J. and Sappey, R. (1992), *Corporatism in Action: The Australian Domestic Pilots' Dispute 1989*.

13 See also BCA (1993b), *Managing the Innovative Enterprise: Australian Companies Competing with the World's Best*.

14 Frenkel, S. and Peetz, D. (1990a), 'Enterprise bargaining: The BCA's report on industrial relations reform', JIR, March, pp. 69–99.

15 Drago et al. (1988), op. cit.; NILS (1989), *Employee and Industrial Relations in Australian Companies: A Survey of Management*; Rimmer, M. (1988), *Enterprise and Industry Awards*.

16 Rimmer, op. cit., pp. 1, 2, 4.

17 Frenkel and Peetz, op. cit.; Frenkel, S. and Peetz, D. (1990b), 'The BCA report: A rejoinder', JIR, September, pp. 419–30; Jamieson, S. (1990a), 'Enterprise bargaining: The approach of the Business Council of Australia', AJLL, May, pp. 77–82; Jamieson, S. (1990b), 'A rejoinder', AJLL, December, pp. 308–9.

18 Hilmer, F. G. and McLaughlin, P. (1990), 'The BCA report: A response to Frenkel and Peetz (1)', JIR, September, p. 407.

19 Pettigrew, A. M. (1979), 'On studying organizational cultures', *Administrative Science Quarterly*, December, pp. 570–81.

20 BCA, *Enterprise-based Bargaining Units*, p. 13.

21 For a classic exposition of the unitarist perspective see Fox, A. (1966), *Industrial Sociology and Industrial Relations*, and Fox, A. (1974), *Beyond Contract: Work, Power and Trust Relations*, pp. 248–55.

22 BCA, op. cit., p. 5.

23 Ibid., pp. 19–21.

24 Ibid., pp. 2–5.

25 Ibid., p. 71.

26 Hyman, op. cit., p. 43.

27 BCA, op. cit., p. 22.

28 Frenkel and Peetz, 'Enterprise bargaining: The BCA's report on industrial relations reform', pp. 78–9.

29 BCA, op. cit., p. 23.

30 Haig, B. D. (1986), *The Comparative Productivity of Australian Industry*, pp. i, 2.

31 Frenkel and Peetz, op. cit., p. 74.

32 BCA, op. cit., p. 78–82.

33 Drago et al., op. cit., p. 13. See also Drago, R., Wooden, M. and Sloan, J. (1992), *Productive Relations? Australian Industrial Relations and Workplace Performance*, pp. 101–71.

34 NILS, op. cit., p. 1.

35 Ibid., p. 39.

36 Ibid., pp. 39–40.

37 Ibid., p. 31.

38 Frenkel and Peetz, op. cit., p. 87.

39 BCA, op. cit., p. 25. Drago and Wooden point out: 'The 25 per cent claim *per se* does not appear in any of our research, but is instead based on the BCA's reading of the case studies, interviews with executives, and interpretation of macro-productivity studies' (1990, 'The BCA report: A response to Frenkel and Peetz (II)', JIR, September, 413n).

40 Frenkel and Peetz, 'The BCA report: A rejoinder', p. 427.

41 BCA, op. cit., pp. 59–71.

42 Callus et al., op. cit., pp. 204–5.

43 BCA, op. cit., p. 13.

44 Ibid., p. 110.

45 Drago et al. (1988), op. cit., pp. i, 33–4.

46 NILS, op. cit., pp. 46–7.

47 Ibid., p. 47. See also BCA, op. cit., p. 69. In Drago, Wooden and Sloan (op. cit., pp. 263–75) the NILS abandoned this approach, noting that the two groups had different approaches, being unprepared to make a judgement as to which might be right or wrong.

48 Frenkel and Peetz, op. cit., p. 428.

49 BCA, op. cit., p. 30.
50 Ibid., p. 84.
51 Ibid., pp. 94–6.
52 Ibid., pp. 102–4.
53 O'Brien, op. cit., p. 21.
54 Kochan, Katz and McKersie, op. cit.
55 BCA (1991), *Avoiding Industrial Action: A Better Way of Working*, p. 2.
56 Ibid., p. 39.
57 Ibid., p. 49.
58 Ibid., pp. 83–109.
59 Ibid., p. 40. It should also be noted that Australian data is more inclusive than that of comparable countries, which 'biases' the Australian data upwards. For a discussion of the different definitions countries use concerning strikes and data collection see Dabscheck, B. (1991), 'A decade of striking figures', *Economic and Labour Relations Review*, June, pp. 177–82.
60 Steinke, J. (1983), 'The long-term decline in the standard working year', JIR, December, pp. 415–30.
61 Crawford, B. and Volard, S. (1981), 'Work absence in industrialised societies: The Australian case', *Industrial Relations Journal*, May–June, p. 53.
62 Staples, P. (1991), 'Costs of drug abuse' (media release).
63 Harrison et al. (1989), 'Deaths as a result of work-related injury in Australia 1982–84', *Medical Journal of Australia*, February, pp. 118–25.
64 Worksafe Australian National Institute Report (1993), *Occupational Health and Safety Performance, Australia: Best Estimates*, p. 3.
65 Preiss, B. and Neery, J. (1990), *Review of Occupational Health and Safety in Australia*, p. 18.
66 Worksafe, op. cit., p. 3.
67 Callus et al., op. cit., pp. 53–61.
68 BCA, *Avoiding Industrial Action*, pp. 51–6.
69 Callus et al., op. cit., p. 130.
70 Ibid., p. 132.
71 BCA, op. cit., pp. 76–7.
72 BCA (1993a), *Working Relations: A Fresh Start for the Innovative Enterprise*, p. 47.
73 Ibid., p. 33.
74 The Business Council of Australia espouses competition but not for systems of industrial relations regulation.
75 Drago, Wooden and Sloan, op. cit., pp. 167, 162, 262, 216.
76 BCA, op. cit., p. 110.
77 On the basis of consistency the study commission would presumably have no objections to non-managers, non-board members or non-shareholders—say full-time trade union officials—making decisions concerning investment and employment, wages and salaries of workers and management executives.

78 Department of Employment and Industrial Relations (1985), *Review of Australian Law and Practice in Relation to Conventions Adopted by the International Labour Conference*, Convention No. 98.

79 For example, see section 57 of the New South Wales *Industrial Arbitration Act* 1940.

80 In December 1987 the Queensland Bjelke-Petersen Government had legislated for the introduction of voluntary employment agreements. Such agreements could be negotiated between an employer and unions(s) and an employer and 60 per cent of workers in a calling covered by an award or agreement. Both types of voluntary employment agreements were subject to public interest tests by the Queensland Industrial Conciliation and Arbitration Commission and had to contain minimum conditions specifying an hourly rate of pay according to the relevant award, public holidays, long-service leave of not less than thirteen weeks for each fifteen years of service, a 19 per cent loading for casuals and four weeks annual leave for weekly workers and five weeks for continuous shift workers. For details and commentary on the Queensland legislation see Stackpool, J. E. (1988), 'Industrial relations legislation in 1987', JIR, March, pp. 163–74; Hall, D. R. (1988), 'Deregulating the labour market in the pioneer state', AJLL, May, pp. 59–69; and Goodwin, M. and Maconachie, G. (1990), 'Voluntary employment agreements: Labour flexibility in Queensland', *Labour and Industry*, March, pp. 21–43.

81 The legislation was introduced following two green papers; see Niland, J., *Transforming Industrial Relations in New South Wales* (1989) Vol. 1 and (1990) Vol. 2. For commentaries see Rimmer, M. (1989), 'Transforming industrial relations in New South Wales: A green paper', AJLL, August, pp. 188–96; Shaw, J. W. and Walton, M. J. (1989), 'The Niland Report and labour law: A critical response', AJLL, August, pp. 197–205; O'Brien, J. M. (1990), 'Regulating decentralised industrial relations: The Niland prescription', JIR, December, pp. 544–59; Easson, M. and Shaw, J., eds (1990), *Transforming Industrial Relations*; Naughton, R. (1991), 'Transforming industrial relations in New South Wales: A Green Paper (Volume Two)', AJLL, March, pp. 89–91; Jamieson, S. (1992), 'Enterprise agreements in New South Wales: A new era?' AJLL, March, pp. 84–8; and Shaw, J. W. (1992), 'The Greiner Government's industrial relations laws: An experiment in deregulation', AJLL, August, pp. 158–70.

82 Given that the length of the standard working week was thirty-eight hours this constituted a *de facto* means of an extra two hours per week free of overtime loadings.

83 Information supplied by Enterprise Agreements Unit, NSW Department of Industrial Relations, Employment, Training and Further Education.

84 *Enterprise Focus*, Summer 1994, pp. 15–16.

85 NSW Department of Industrial Relations, Employment, Training and Further Education (1993), *Women and Enterprise Bargaining: A Review of NSW Enterprise Agreements*, p. 5.

86 Garnham, J. (1994), 'Workplace freedom and flexibility: Fact or fiction—The Tasmanian experience'.

87 The Victorian legislation was based on or borrowed from the New Zealand *Employment Contracts Act* 1991. For an analysis and bibliographical information concerning New Zealand industrial relations see Peetz et al. (1993), 'Workplace bargaining in New Zealand: Radical change at work' in Peetz, D., Preston, A. and Docherty, J., eds, *Workplace Bargaining in the International Context*, and Bray, M. and Haworth, N., eds (1993), *Economic Restructuring and Industrial Relations in Australia and New Zealand: A Comparative Analysis*.

88 By October 1993, 150 collective agreements had been lodged (Fox, C. and Teicher, J. (1994), 'Victoria's Employee Relations Act: The way of the future', p. 1). For commentaries on the Victorian legislation see Creighton, B. (1993b), 'Employment agreements and conditions of employment under the Employee Relations Act 1992 (Vic.)', AJLL, August, pp. 140–58; McCallum, R. C. (1993), 'The ascendancy of federal industrial law' in Ronfeldt and McCallum, eds, pp. 74–85; Naughton, R. (1993), 'The institutions established by the Employee Relations Act 1992', AJLL, August, pp. 121–39; Pittard, M. J. (1993), 'Industrial conflict and constraints: Sanctions on industrial action in Victoria', AJLL, August, pp. 159–82; and Fox and Teicher, op. cit. See also Arup, C. (1993), 'Workcover: Convergence or competition?' AJLL, August, pp. 183–204, and Johnstone, R., McKenzie, D. and Mitchell, R. (1993), 'The Industrial Relations Commission of Victoria 1982–92: A system under pressure', AJLL, August, pp. 97–120.

89 This is a reference to *One Nation* (Keating 1992a). See chapter 3.

90 Keating, 'A new charter for industrial relations in Australia', pp. 1, 6.

91 *Jobsback!* p. 25. For commentaries on *Jobsback!* see Dabscheck, B. (1993), 'The Coalition's plan to regulate industrial relations', *Economic and Labour Relations Review*, June, pp. 1–26, and Stegman, T. (1993), ' "Jobsback" and the future of wages policy', *Economic and Labour Relations Review*, June, pp. 50–61.

92 For details concerning negotiations of the Accord Mark VII see AFR, *Australian* and SMH, 25 January 1993 to 20 February 1993.

93 It also carried forward taxation and superannuation commitments contained in *One Nation* (Keating 1992a).

94 Accord Agreement 1993–96 (1993), 'Putting jobs first' (i.e. Accord Mark VII), p. 13.

95 Ibid., p. 5.

96 AFR, 15 March 1993.

97 *Australian*, 29 March, 3 April 1993.

98 *Australian*, 8 May 1993; SMH, 8 May 1993.

99 SMH, 11, 14 May 1993; *Australian*, 11, 14 May 1993; AFR, 14 May 1993.

100 For details of these events see AFR, *Australian* and SMH, 18 May 1993 to 26 June 1993.

101 NWC, 25 October 1993, p. 17.

102 Ibid., p. 30.

103 NWC, 15 November 1993.

104 Keating, P. J. (1993), speech to Institute of Directors luncheon, p. 4.

105 Ibid., pp. 10–12.

106 *Australian*, 22 April 1993; AFR, 22 April 1993.

107 SMH, 22 April 1993.

108 *Australian*, 23, 24 April 1993; SMH, 23, 24 April 1993; AFR, 23 April 1993.

109 Brereton, L. (1993a), address to the Industrial Relations and Wages Committee of the CBI; (1993b), 'The future: Awards and enterprise agreements'; (1993c), media release, 'Trades union promotions and publicity seminar on Australia's future'; (1993d), media release, ACTU Congress speech; (1993e), media release, 'Federal Government announces major industrial relations reform'; (1993f), interview transcript, *Sunday*, Nine Network; (1993g), media release, speech to Enterprise Bargaining Week.

110 Gahan, P. (1993), 'Solidarity forever? The 1993 ACTU Congress', JIR, December, pp. 607–25.

111 *Boilermakers* case (1956) 94 CLR 254.

112 Higgins, 'A new province for law and order—I', p. 23.

113 Webb, S. and B., op. cit., p. 658.

114 *Industrial Relations Reform Act* 1993 (Cwlth), section 170 AF.

115 For details of the operation of the basic wage see Dabscheck and Niland, op. cit., pp. 307–21.

116 *Australian*, 30 March 1994. For further examination of workplace agreements at the federal level see Department of Industrial Relations (1993), *Workplace Bargaining: The First 1000 Agreements*.

117 Department of Industrial Relations, op. cit., p. 6; Australian Chamber of Commerce and Industry (1994), *Report on Federal Enterprise Agreements in 1993*, p. 2.

118 Short, M., Preston, A. and Peetz, D. (1993), *The Spread and Impact of Workplace Bargaining: Evidence from the Workplace Bargaining Research Project*; MacDermott, K. (1993), 'Women's productivity: Productivity bargaining and service workers', JIR, December, pp. 538–53.

119 It might also be instructive to conduct a cost-benefit analysis concerning enterprise bargaining—to set against the benefits that have flowed from enterprise bargaining, other things being equal, the money spent on seminars, reports, time and energy in bringing the horse to water.

120 Isaac et al. (1993), *A Survey of Small Business and Industrial Relations*.

121 Machlup, F. (1969), 'Cost push and demand pull' in Ball and Doyle, eds, *Inflation*, p. 168.

CHAPTER 5 WHAT IS TO BE DONE WITH UNIONS?

1 Perlman, S. (1949) [1928], *A Theory of the Labor Movement*, p. 282.

2 Lenin, V. I. (1970) [1902], 'What is to be done?' in *On Trade Unions: A Collection of Articles and Speeches*, pp. 76, 80.

3 Webb, S. and B., op. cit.; Hoxie, R. F. (1924), *Trade Unionism in the United States*; Tannenbaum, F. A. (1952), *A Philosophy of Labor*.

4 See Hagan, J. (1981), *The History of the ACTU*, pp. 454–55, for a copy of the ACTU's original constitution. The 1991 consitution refers to the 'closer organisation of the workers by—The development of the Trade Union movement towards an industrial basis' and 'Amalgamation of unions where practicable to establish one union in each industry or sector'.

5 Since 1990 the survey (table 5.1) had excluded data for people aged 70 and older.

6 ACTU (1987), *Future Strategies for the Trade Union Movement*, p. 1.

7 The ACTU has run advertising campaigns in women's and youth magazines to enhance the profile of unions with two groups unions have historically found difficult to recruit. It is not clear that these were examples of money well spent.

8 *Australia Reconstructed* had a broader agenda than union amalgamation. For a brief survey of its proposals see Dabscheck, *Australian Industrial Relations in the 1980s*, pp. 146–50.

9 ACTU, *Future Strategies*, p. 13.

10 Griffin, G. and Scarcebrook, V. (1989), 'Trends in mergers of federally registered unions, 1904–86', JIR, June, pp. 258–61.

11 Rimmer, M. (1981), 'Long-run structural change in Australian trade unionism', JIR, September, pp. 323–43.

12 Gill, H. and Griffin, V. (1981), 'The fetish of order: Reform in Australian union structure', JIR, September, pp. 362–82.

13 Australian Electoral Commission (1993), *Amalgamations and Amalgamation Ballots*, p. 6.

14 Davis, E. M. (1988), 'The 1987 ACTU Congress: Reconstructing Australia', JIR, March, pp. 118–29.

15 AFR, 19 May 1988.

16 Australian Electoral Commission, op. cit., pp. 29–30.

17 The ABS annual census of unions revealed a density rate in 1988 for total members of 54 per cent and for financial members of 48 per cent (see table 5.2). Does this mean that the leadership of the ACTU has little confidence in the information supplied by union secretaries to the ABS?

18 Crean, S. (1989), presidential address, ACTU Congress; Kelty, B. (1989), keynote address, Rules and Finance, ACTU Congress; Berry, P. and Kitchener, G. (1989), *Can Unions Survive?*

19 A copy of the policy adopted is reproduced in Crean, S. and Rimmer, M. (1990), *Australian Unions: Adjustment to Change*, pp. 75–82.

20 Davis, E. M. (1990), 'The 1989 ACTU Congress: Seeking change within', JIR, March, pp. 101–3.

21 AFR, 9 July 1990.

22 As earlier chapters have revealed, the New South Wales Labor Council has been a focal point for dissident unions concerning ACTU policies on wages, award restructuring and enterprise bargaining.

23 AFR, 5, 11, 12, 15, 16 October 1990; SMH, 16 October 1990.
24 ACTU (1991b), *ACTU Policies and Strategies as Adopted at the 1991 ACTU Congress*, p. 122.
25 The Accord partners had wanted to increase the minimum size to 20 000 members (see ACTU (1991a), *Executive Report*, Congress, p. 15), but were blocked by the Democrats in the Senate.
26 ILO, Case no. 1559, November 1992, p. 48. Figures supplied by the ABS for June 1990 put the number of federally registered unions at 134. See table 5.4.
27 ACTU (1991a), *Executive Report*, pp. 24–5.
28 SMH, 30 May 1989, 27 October 1990; *Australian*, 30 May 1989; AFR, 1 June, 10 July, 18 August 1989.
29 AFR, 13 September 1991; *Australian*, 13 September 1991; Davis, E. M. (1992), 'The 1991 ACTU Congress: Together for tomorrow', JIR, March, pp. 87–101.
30 AFR, 6 August 1993.
31 On 31 August 1992 the Confederation of Australian Industry changed its name to the Australian Chamber of Commerce and Industry following a merger with the Australian Chamber of Commerce.
32 ILO, Case no. 1559, November 1992, pp. 62–3.
33 AFR, 13 November, 4 December 1992.
34 AFR, 3 June 1993; *Australian*, 3 June 1993.
35 AFR, 9 June 1993.
36 In 1991, in a proposed merger of four unions the membership of one union voted against amalgamation. The merger of the other three unions was consummated.
37 Australian Electoral Commission, op. cit.
38 It should also be noted that most of the amalgamations that occurred in the 1980s were at the state level.
39 Between the 1987 and 1993 ACTU congresses the number of affiliates declined from 162 to 72 (Davis, 'The 1987 ACTU Congress'; Gahan, P., op. cit.).
40 Gill and Griffin, op. cit., pp. 373, 370.
41 In saying this it is, of course, recognised that there can be overaward payments or arrangements and addendums to awards. Awards and the award system are more flexible than current discussions have implied.
42 Chapter 4 revealed that we should be wary of overstating the extent and impact of enterprise bargaining.
43 Costa and Duffy, op. cit., pp. 100–32, argue that amalgamations can result in diseconomies of scale and have criticised the ACTU's policies on union rationalisation. See Ellem, B. (1991), 'Solidarity in the nineties? The ACTU, Costa, Duffy and union amalgamation', *Economic and Labour Relations Review*, December, pp. 65–89, for a critique of their analysis.
44 Peetz ((1990), 'Declining union density', JIR, June, pp. 197–223 and (1992), 'Union membership and the Accord' in Crosby and Easson, eds,

What Should Unions Do? pp. 171–209) and Keynon and Lewis (1992, 'Trade union membership and the Accord', *Australian Economic Papers*, December, pp. 325–45) have conducted econometric studies on the level of unionisation at the end of the 1980s. Most of the data that sustains their analysis is based on the ABS survey of union members. Peetz concludes that half of the fall in unionisation is associated with compositional or structural changes in the economy. He said: 'up to half appears to reflect a declining propensity of employees to belong to unions' (Peetz, 'Declining union density', p. 209). Keynon and Lewis explain the decline in terms of a 'negative' reaction to the Accord.

45 Such a statement would not apply to the New South Wales Nurses' Association whose membership levels have steadily grown. See Staunton, P. (1992), 'Unions can survive: Marketing the nurses' union' in Crosby and Easson, op. cit., pp. 289–95, for an outline of how this union approaches the recruitment of members and servicing their needs.

46 Stuart, M. (1993), *United States Mission on Recruitment and Organisation: Summary Report*, pp. 11–12.

47 *Australian*, 6 December 1993.

48 Keynon and Lewis, op. cit., have also argued that the Accord has had a negative impact on union density.

49 Also see Bramble, T. (1989), 'Award restructuring and the Australian trade union movement: A critique', *Labour and Industry*, October, pp. 372–98, for a critique of award restructuring and its impact on unions and workers' wages and working conditions.

50 Flanders, A. (1970), *Management and Unions: The Theory and Reform of Industrial Relations*, p. 40.

BIBLIOGRAPHY

Accord Agreement 1993–96 (1993), *Putting Jobs First* (mimeo) (Accord Mark VII). February.

Accord Mark I *see* Statement of Accord . . . (1983).

Accord Mark II *see* Agreement Between the Government and the ACTU . . . (1985).

Accord Mark VI *see Agreement Between the Federal Government and the ACTU*, 21 February 1990 (mimeo).

Accord Mark VII *see* Accord Agreement 1993–96 (1993).

Adams, R. J. (1988), *Desperately Seeking Industrial Relations Theory*, Research and Working Paper Series, Faculty of Business, McMaster University, Ontario, Canada.

Adams, R. J. (1993), ' "All aspects of people at work": Unity and division in the study of labor and labor management', in Adams and Meltz, eds, pp. 119–60.

Adams, R. J. and Meltz, N. M., eds (1993), *Industrial Relations Theory: Its Nature, Scope and Pedagogy*, Scarecrow Press, Metuchen, NJ.

Agreement Between the Federal Government and the ACTU, 21 February 1990 (mimeo) (Accord Mark VI), in Department of Industrial Relations (1991a), *National Wage Case, December 1990–February 1991*, Vol. 2, *Exhibits Presented by the Commonwealth Government*, AGPS, Canberra, pp. 27–32.

Agreement Between the Government and the ACTU for the Discounting of Wages Indexation and Ongoing Wage Restraint (1985), 4 September (mimeo). (Accord Mark II).

Allen, G. (1986), 'Management pressures for change and the industrial relations system', in Blandy, R. and Niland, J., eds, *Alternatives to Arbitration*, Allen & Unwin, Sydney, pp. 334–50.

Appleyard, B. (1992), *Understanding the Present*, Picador, London.

Arup, C. (1993), 'Workcover: Convergence or competition?' *Australian Journal of Labour Law*, August, pp. 183–204.

Austin, A. G., ed. (1965), *The Webbs' Australian Diary 1898*, Pitman, London.

Australian Chamber of Commerce and Industry (1994), *Report on Federal Enterprise Agreements in 1993*, Melbourne, January.

Australian Council of Trade Unions (1987), *Future Strategies for the Trade Union Movement* (mimeo), May.

[Australian Council of Trade Unions] (1988), *Report on Wages*, 24 February (mimeo).

Australian Council of Trade Unions (1989), *Executive Report*, Congress, Sydney Town Hall, Sydney, 25–29 September.

Australian Council of Trade Unions (1991a), *Executive Report*, Congress, World Congress Centre, Melbourne, 9–13 September.

Australian Council of Trade Unions (1991b), *ACTU Policies and Strategies as Adopted at the 1991 ACTU Congress*, Melbourne, 9–13 September (mimeo).

Australian Electoral Commission (1993), *Amalgamations and Amalgamation Ballots*, AGPS, Canberra.

Australian Industrial Relations Commission Annual Reports, AGPS, Canberra.

Australian Industrial Relations Commission (1990a), Transcript of Proceedings 13–14 September, Commonwealth Reporting Service, Melbourne.

Australian Industrial Relations Commission (1990b), Application by the Confederation of Australian Industry and the Australian Chamber of Manufactures for relisting of the National Wage Case, August 1989, Print J4600, Melbourne, 17 September.

Baritz, L. (1974), *The Servants of Power: A History of the Use of Social Science in American Industry*, Greenwood Press, Westport, VA.

Bell, S. (1993), *Australian Manufacturing and the State: The Politics of Industry Policy in the Post-war Era*, Cambridge University Press, Melbourne.

Bennett, L. (1989), 'The Federal Conciliation and Arbitration Court in the late 1920s', *Labour History*, November, pp. 44–60.

Berry, P. and Kitchener, G. (1989), *Can Unions Survive?* Building Workers Industrial Union, Canberra.

Blain, N. and Plowman, D. (1987), 'The Australian industrial relations literature, 1970–86', *Journal of Industrial Relations*, June, pp. 295–320.

Blyton, P. and Turnbull, P., eds (1992), *Reassessing Human Resource Management*, Sage, London.

Boland, R. (1992), 'The alternative approaches to labour market reform', in Economic Planning and Advisory Council, *Issues in Enterprise Bargaining*, Background Paper No. 22, December, AGPS, Canberra, pp. 35–66.

Booth, A. (1982), 'Corporatism, capitalism and depression in twentieth-century Britain', *British Journal of Sociology*, June, pp. 200–23.

Bramble, T. (1989), 'Award restructuring and the Australian trade union movement: A critique', *Labour and Industry*, October, pp. 372–98.

Bray, M. and Taylor, V., eds (1986), *Managing Labour? Essays in the Political Economy of Industrial Relations*, McGraw-Hill, Sydney.

Bray, M. and Haworth, N., eds (1993), *Economic Restructuring and Industrial Relations in Australia and Zealand: A Comparative Analysis*, Monograph No. 8,

Australian Centre for Industrial Relations Research and Teaching, University of Sydney, March.

Brereton, L. (1993a), 'Address to the Industrial Relations and Wages Committee of the CBI', London, 16 June (mimeo).

Brereton, L. (1993b), 'The future: Awards and enterprise agreements', address to lunch hosted by Arch Bevis MP, Brisbane, 6 August (mimeo).

Brereton, L. (1993c), media release, 'Trade union promotions and publicity seminar on Australia's future', Melbourne, 20 August (mimeo).

Brereton, L. (1993d), media release, ACTU Congress speech, Sydney, 1 September (mimeo).

Brereton, L. (1993e), media release, 'Federal Government announces major industrial relations reform', 8 October (mimeo).

Brereton, L. (1993f), interview transcript, *Sunday*, Nine Network, 10 October (mimeo).

Brereton, L. (1993g), media release, speech to Enterprise Bargaining Week, Adelaide, 11 October (mimeo).

Brown, W. J. (1906), *The Austinian Theory of Law*, John Murray, London.

Brown, W. J. (1919), 'Effect of an increase in the living wage by a court of industrial arbitration upon vested rights and duties under preexisting awards', *Harvard Law Review*, June, pp. 892–901.

Brown, W. J. (1922), 'Law, industry and post-war adjustments', *Harvard Law Review*, January, pp. 223–44.

Burgess, J. and Sappey, R. (1992), *Corporatism in Action: The Australian Domestic Pilots' Dispute 1989*, Working Paper Series, No. 5, Employment Studies Centre, University of Newcastle, March.

Burgmann, M. (1984), 'Australian trade unionism in 1983', *Journal of Industrial Relations*, March, pp. 91–8.

Burgmann, M. (1985), 'Australian trade unionism in 1984', *Journal of Industrial Relations*, March, pp. 81–8.

Business Council of Australia (1987), *Towards an Enterprise-based Industrial Relations System*, 24 March (mimeo).

Business Council of Australia (1989), *Enterprise-based Bargaining Units: A Better Way of Working*, Report to the Business Council of Australia by the Industrial Relations Study Commission, Vol. 1, July.

Business Council of Australia (1991), *Avoiding Industrial Action: A Better Way of Working*, Employee Relations Study Commission, Allen & Unwin, Sydney.

Business Council of Australia (1993a), *Working Relations: A Fresh Start for Australian Enterprises*, Employee Relations Study Commission, Business Library, Melbourne.

Business Council of Australia (1993b), *Managing the Innovative Enterprise: Australian Companies Competing with the World's Best*, Innovation Study Commission, Business Library, Melbourne.

Callaghan, P. S. (1983), 'Idealism and arbitration in H.B. Higgins' new province for law and order', *Journal of Australian Studies*, November, pp. 56–66.

Callus, R., Moorehead, A., Cully, M. and Buchanan, J. (1991), *Industrial Relations at Work: The Australian Workplace Industrial Relations Survey*, AGPS, Canberra.

Calmfors, L. and Driffill, J. (1988), 'Centralisation of wage bargaining', *Economic Policy*, April, pp. 13–61.

Capling, A. and Galligan, B. (1992), *Beyond the Protective State: The Political Economy of Australia's Manufacturing Industry Policy*, Cambridge University Press, Melbourne.

Cappelli, P. (1985), 'Theory construction in IR and some implications for research', *Industrial Relations*, Winter, pp. 90–112.

Carboch, D. (1958), 'The fall of the Bruce–Page Government', in *Studies in Australian Politics*, Cheshire, Melbourne, pp. 121–282.

Carney, S. (1988), *Australia in Accord: Politics and Industrial Relations under the Hawke Government*, Sun Books, South Melbourne.

Carroll, J. and Manne, R., eds (1992), *Shutdown: The Failure of Economic Rationalism and How to Rescue Australia*, Text Publishing, Melbourne.

Chamberlain, N.W. and Kuhn, J. W. (1965), *Collective Bargaining* (2nd ed.), McGraw-Hill, New York.

Chaney, F. (1987), 'The opposition's industrial relations reform in Australia', in H. R. Nicholls Society, *The Light on the Hill*, pp. 75–8.

Chaney, F. (1988), 'Industrial relations: A management responsibility', in H. R. Nicholls Society, *Back to Basics*, pp. 27–32.

Chapman, B. and Gruen, F. (1990), *An Analysis of the Australian Consensual Incomes Policy: The Prices and Incomes Accord*, Discussion Paper No. 221, Centre for Economic Policy Research, Australian National University, January.

Commonwealth Conciliation and Arbitration Commission Annual Reports, Commonwealth Government Printer, Canberra (1950–73).

Copeman, A. C. (1987), 'The Robe River affair', *Journal of Industrial Relations*, December, pp. 539–43.

Costa, M. and Duffy, M. (1991), *Labor, Prosperity and the Nineties: Beyond the Bonsai Economy*, Federation Press, Sydney.

Costa, M. and Easson, M. (1991), *Australian Industry: What Policy?* Pluto Press, Sydney.

Costello, P. (1986), 'Legal remedies against trade union conduct in Australia', in *Arbitration in Contempt*, pp. 131–55.

Costello, P. (1989a), 'The Dollar Sweets story' in H. R. Nicholls Society, *In Search of the Magic Pudding*, pp. 27–32.

Costello, P. (1989b), keynote address in H. R. Nicholls Society, *No Ticket No Start—No More!* pp. 1–6.

Costello, P. (1990), 'Back to the waterfront: New IR bill' in H. R. Nicholls Society, *Back to the Waterfront*, pp. 1–5.

Costello, P. (1992), 'The Troubleshooters' case' in H. R. Nicholls Society, *For the Labourer is Worthy of His Hire*, pp. 85–92.

Craven, G. (1992), 'The Coalition and voluntary industrial agreements: Some constitutional aspects', *Economic and Labour Relations Review*, June, pp. 94–111.

Crawford, B. and Volard, S. (1981), 'Work absence in industrialised societies: The Australian case', *Industrial Relations Journal*, May–June, pp. 50–7.

Crean, S. (1989), *Presidential Address*, ACTU Congress, 1989, Sydney, 25 September (mimeo).

Crean, S. and Rimmer, M. (1990), *Australian Unions: Adjustment to Change*, National Key Centre in Industrial Relations, Monash University, October.

Creighton, B. (1993a), 'Industrial regulation and Australia's international obligations', in Ronfeldt and McCallum, eds, pp. 101–31.

Creighton, B. (1993b), 'Employment agreements and conditions of employment under the *Employee Relations Act* 1992 (Vic)', *Australian Journal of Labour Law*, August, pp. 140–58.

Creighton, W. B., Ford, W. J. and Mitchell, R. J. (1993), *Labour Law: Texts and Materials* (2nd ed.), Law Book Company, Sydney.

Crosby, M. and Easson, M., eds (1992), *What Should Unions Do?* Pluto Press, Sydney.

Crouch, C. (1985), 'Conditions for trade union wage restraint', in Lindberg, L. N. and Maier, C. S., eds, *The Politics of Inflation and Economic Stagnation: Theoretical Approaches and International Case Studies*, Brookings Institution, Washington, pp. 105–39.

Crouch, C. (1990), 'Trade unions in the exposed sector: Their influence on neo-corporatist behaviour', in Brunetta, R. and Dell'Aringa, C., eds, *Labour Relations and Economic Performance*, New York University Press, New York, pp. 68–91.

Cupper, L. (1976), 'Legalism in the Australian Conciliation and Arbitration Commission: The gradual transition', *Journal of Industrial Relations*, December, pp. 337–64.

d'Alpuget, B. (1977), *Mediator: A Biography of Sir Richard Kirby*, Melbourne University Press, Carlton.

Dabscheck, B. (1975), 'The 1975 national wage case: Now we have an incomes policy', *Journal of Industrial Relations*, September, pp. 298–309.

Dabscheck, B. (1980), 'The Australian system of industrial relations: An analytical model', *Journal of Industrial Relations*, June, pp. 196–218.

Dabscheck, B. (1983), *Arbitrator at Work: Sir William Raymond Kelly and the Regulation of Australian Industrial Relations*, Allen & Unwin, Sydney.

Dabscheck, B. (1989), *Australian Industrial Relations in the 1980s*, Oxford University Press, Melbourne.

Dabscheck, B. (1991), 'A decade of striking figures', *Economic and Labour Relations Review*, June, pp. 172–96.

Dabscheck, B. (1993), 'The Coalition's plan to regulate industrial relations', *Economic and Labour Relations Review*, June, pp. 1–26.

Dabscheck, B. and Niland, J. (1981), *Industrial Relations in Australia*, Allen & Unwin, Sydney.

Dahrendorf, R. (1959), *Class and Class Conflict in Industrial Society*, Routledge & Kegan Paul, London.

Davis, E. M. (1988), 'The 1987 ACTU Congress: Reconstructing Australia?' *Journal of Industrial Relations*, March, pp. 118–29.

Davis, E. M. (1990), 'The 1989 ACTU Congress: Seeking change within', *Journal of Industrial Relations*, March, pp. 100–10.

Davis, E. M. (1992), 'The 1991 ACTU Congress: Together for tomorrow', *Journal of Industrial Relations*, March, pp. 87–101.

Dell'Aringa, C. and Lodovici, M. S. (1992), 'Industrial relations and economic performance', in Treu, T., ed., *Participation in Public Policy-making: The Role of Trade Unions and Employers' Associations*, Walter de Gruyter, Berlin, pp. 26–58.

Dimmock, S. J. and Sethi, A. S. (1986), 'The role of ideology and power in systems theory: Some fundamental shortcomings', *Relations Industrielles*, No. 4, pp. 738–55.

Dowrick, S. (1993), *Wage Bargaining Systems and Productivity Growth in OECD Countries*, Background Paper No. 26, Economic Planning Advisory Council, May, AGPS, Canberra.

Drago, R., Kriegler, R., Tulsi, N. and Wooden, M. (1988), *The BCA–NILS Industrial Relations Study: An Overview of the Employee Survey*, Working Paper No. 100, National Institute of Labour Studies, Flinders University, September.

Drago, R. and Wooden, M. (1990), 'The BCA report: A response to Frenkel and Peetz (II)', *Journal of Industrial Relations*, September, pp. 413–17.

Drago, R., Wooden, M. and Sloan, J. (1992), *Productive Relations? Australian Industrial Relations and Workplace Performance*, Allen & Unwin, Sydney.

Dufty, N. F. (1972), *Industrial Relations in the Australian Metal Industries*, West Publishing, Sydney.

Dufty, N. F. and Fells, R. E. (1989), *Dynamics of Industrial Relations in Australia*, Prentice Hall, Sydney.

Dunlop, J. T. (1958), *Industrial Relations Systems*, Holt, New York.

Easson, M. and Shaw, J., eds (1990), *Transforming Industrial Relations*, Pluto Press, Sydney.

Ellem, B. (1991), 'Solidarity in the nineties? The ACTU, Costa and Dufty and union amalgamation', *Economic and Labour Relations Review*, December, pp. 65–89.

Employment and Industrial Relations, Department of (1985), *Review of Australian Law and Practice in Relation to Conventions Adopted by the International Labour Conference*, AGPS, Canberra.

Evans, A. C. (1990), affidavit, Metal Trades Industry Association, 17 December (mimeo).

Ewer, P., Hampson, I., Lloyd, C., Rainford, J., Rix, S. and Smith, M. (1991), *Politics and the Accord*, Pluto Press, Sydney.

Ewer, P., Higgins, W. and Stevens, A. (1987), *Unions and the Future of Australian Manufacturing*, Allen & Unwin, Sydney.

Fightback! Fairness and Jobs (1992).

Fightback! It's Your Australia (1991), The Liberal and National Parties' Plan to Rebuild and Reward Australia.

Flanders, A. (1970), *Management and Unions: The Theory and Reform of Industrial Relations*, Faber & Faber, London.

Forbath, W. E. (1989), 'The shaping of the American labor movement', *Harvard Law Review*, April, pp. 1109–256.

Forsyth, P., ed. (1992), *Microeconomic Reform in Australia*, Allen & Unwin, Sydney.

Fox, A. (1966), *Industrial Sociology and Industrial Relations*, Research Paper 3, Royal Commission on Trade Unions and Employers' Associations, HMSO, London.

Fox, A. (1974), *Beyond Contract: Work, Power and Trust Relations*, Faber & Faber, London.

Fox, C. and Teicher, J. (1994), 'Victoria's Employee Relations Act: The way of the future', paper, Annual Conference of Association of Industrial Relations Academics of Australia and New Zealand, Sydney, February.

Frenkel, S. and Peetz, D. (1990a), 'Enterprise bargaining: The BCA's report on industrial relations reform', *Journal of Industrial Relations*, March, pp. 69–99.

Frenkel, S. and Peetz, D. (1990b), 'The BCA report: A rejoinder', *Journal of Industrial Relations*, September, pp. 419–30.

Frenkel, S. and Shaw, M. (1989), 'No tears for the second tier: Productivity bargaining in the Australian metal industry', *Australian Bulletin of Labour*, March, pp. 90–114.

Gahan, P. (1993), 'Solidarity forever? The 1993 ACTU Congress', *Journal of Industrial Relations*, December, pp. 607–25.

Gardner, M. (1988), 'Australian trade unionism in 1987', *Journal of Industrial Relations*, March, pp. 147–54.

Garnham, J. (1994), 'Workplace freedom and flexibility: fact or fiction— The Tasmanian experience', paper, Annual Conference of Association of Industrial Relations Academics of Australia and New Zealand, Sydney, February.

Gerritsen, R. (1986), 'The necessity of "corporatism": The case of the Hawke Labor Government', *Politics*, May, pp. 19–27.

Gill, H. and Griffin, V. (1981), 'The fetish of order: Reform in Australian union structure', *Journal of Industrial Relations*, September, pp. 362–82.

Gleeson Report (1991), *Australian Industrial Relations Commission Review*, Report of the Committee, AGPS, Canberra, March.

Goodwin, M. and Maconachie, G. (1990), 'Voluntary employment agreements: Labour flexibility in Queensland', *Labour and Industry*, March, pp. 21–43.

Gould, L. L., ed. (1974), *The Progressive Era*, Syracuse University Press, Syracuse, NY.

Gray, P. R. A. (1993), foreword in Ronfeldt and McCallum, eds, pp. iii–v.

Greer, T. H. (1949), *American Social Reform Movements: Their Pattern Since 1965*, Prentice Hall, New York.

Greiner, N. (1990), opening address in H. R. Nicholls Society, *Public Interest or Vested Interest?* pp. xi–xiv.

Griffin, G. and Scarcebrook, V. (1989), 'Trends in mergers of federally registered unions, 1904–86', *Journal of Industrial Relations*, June, pp. 257–62.

Gruen, F. and Grattan, M. (1993), *Managing Government: Labor's Achievements and Failures*, Longman Cheshire, Melbourne.

Guille, H. (1984), 'Industrial relations theory: Painting by numbers', *Journal of Industrial Relations*, December, pp. 484–95.

Guille, H. (1986), 'Domesticating unions with foreign ideas: Australian industrial relations 1940–80', in Bray and Taylor, eds, pp. 195–218.

Gurdon, M. A. (1978), 'Patterns of industrial relations research in Australia', *Journal of Industrial Relations*, December, pp. 446–62.

Hagan, J. (1981), *The History of the ACTU*, Longman Cheshire, Melbourne.

Haig, B. D. (1986), *The Comparative Productivity of Australian Industry*, Discussion Paper No. 142, Department of Economics, Research School of Social Sciences, Australian National University, June.

Hall, D. R. (1988), 'Deregulating the labour market in the pioneer state', *Australian Journal of Labour Law*, May, pp. 59–69.

Harcourt, G. C. (1992), 'Markets, madness and the middle way', *Australian Quarterly*, Autumn, pp. 1–17.

Harrison, J. E., Frommer, M. S., Ruck, E. A. and Blyth, F. M. (1989), 'Deaths as a result of work-related injury in Australia, 1982–84', *Medical Journal of Australia*, February, pp. 118–25.

Hawke, R. J. L. (1986), Remarks at the Opening of Meeting between Representatives of the ACTU, BCA and CAI on Work and Management Practices, Melbourne, 24 September (mimeo).

Higgins, H. B. (1915), 'A new province for law and order—I', *Harvard Law Review*, November, pp. 13–29.

Higgins, H. B. (1919), 'A new province for law and order—II', *Harvard Law Review*, January, pp. 184–217.

Higgins, H. B. (1920), 'A new province for law and order—III', *Harvard Law Review*, December, pp. 105–36.

Hills, S. M. (1993), 'Integrating industrial relations and the social sciences' in Adams and Meltz, eds, pp. 183–225.

Hilmer, F. G. and McLaughlin, P. (1990), 'The BCA report: A response to Frenkel and Peetz (I)', *Journal of Industrial Relations*, September, pp. 403–12.

H. R. Nicholls Society (1986a), *Arbitration in Contempt*, Proceedings of the H. R. Nicholls Society, Melbourne.

H. R. Nicholls Society (1986b), *Trade Unions Reform*, Proceedings of the H. R. Nicholls Society, Melbourne.

H. R. Nicholls Society (1987), *The Light on the Hill*, Proceedings of the H. R. Nicholls Society, 6–8 June, Melbourne.

H. R. Nicholls Society (1988), *Back to Basics*, Proceedings of the H. R. Nicholls Society, 19–21 February, Melbourne.

H. R. Nicholls Society (1989a), *In Search of the Magic Pudding*, Proceedings of the H. R. Nicholls Society, 5–7 August 1988, Melbourne.

H. R. Nicholls Society (1989b), *The Legacy of 'The Hungry Mile'*, Proceedings of the H. R. Nicholls Society, 19 August 1989, Melbourne.

H. R. Nicholls Society (1989c), *No Ticket No Start—No More!* Proceedings of the H. R. Nicholls Society, 24–26 February, Melbourne.

H. R. Nicholls Society (1990a), *Back to the Waterfront*, Proceedings of the H. R. Nicholls Society, 15 September, Melbourne.

H. R. Nicholls Society (1990b), *Public Interest or Vested Interest?* Proceedings of the H. R. Nicholls Society, 9–11 March, Melbourne.

H. R. Nicholls Society (1991), *No Vacancies*, Proceedings of the H. R. Nicholls Society, 12–14 April, Melbourne.

H. R. Nicholls Society (1992), *For the Labourer is Worthy of His Hire*, Proceedings of the H. R. Nicholls Society, 3–5 April, Melbourne.

Horne, D., ed. (1992), *The Trouble with Economic Rationalism*, Scribe, Newham, Vic.

Howard, J. W. (1990), guest of honour's address in H. R. Nicholls Society, *Public Interest or Vested Interest*, pp. 47–50.

Howard, W. A. (1978), 'Doctrine, theory and teaching in industrial relations' in Turkington, D. J., ed., *Industrial Relations Teaching and Research in Australia and New Zealand: Conference of Teachers of Industrial Relations*, Victoria University of Wellington, 10–12 May, pp. 25–43.

Hoxie, R. F. (1924), *Trade Unionism in the United States*, Appleton, New York.

Hulme, S. E. K. (1993), 'A constitutional basis for the Coalition's industrial relations policy', *Economic and Labour Relations Review*, June, pp. 62–76.

Hutson, J. (1971), *Six Wage Concepts*, Amalgamated Engineering Union, Sydney.

Hyman, R. (1980), 'Theory in industrial relations: Towards a materialist analysis' in Boreham, P. and Dow, G., eds, *Work and Inequality: Ideology and Control in the Capitalist Labour Process*, Macmillan, South Melbourne, pp. 38–59.

Hyman, R. (1987), 'Strategy or structure? Capital, labour and control', *Work, Employment and Society*, March, pp. 25–55.

Industrial Relations, Department of (1988), Submission by the Commonwealth Government National Wage Case October 1987–January 1988, AGPS, Canberra.

Industrial Relations, Department of (1989), Submission by the Commonwealth Government National Wage Case June–July 1988, AGPS, Canberra.

Industrial Relations, Department of (1991), 'Government guidelines for workplace bargaining' in *Review of Wage Fixation Principles, September 1991*, Vol. 2, *Exhibits Presented by the Commonwealth Government*, 15 May (mimeo), AGPS, Canberra, pp. 117–21.

Industrial Relations, Department of (1993), *Workplace Bargaining: The First 1000 Agreements*, Canberra, August.

Industrial Relations, Employment, Training and Further Education, New South Wales Department of (1993), *Women and Enterprise Bargaining: A Review of NSW Enterprise Agreements*, Sydney.

Industrial Relations: The Agenda for Reform (1990) (mimeo).

Industrial Relations Policy (1986), Liberal Party of Australia, National Party of Australia, 11 May (mimeo).

Isaac, J. E. (1971), 'Penal provisions under Commonwealth arbitration', in Isaac, J. E. and Ford, G. W., eds, *Australian Labour Relations: Readings* (2nd ed.), Sun Books, Melbourne, pp. 451–64.

Isaac, J. E. (1977), 'Wage determination and economic policy', *Australian Economic Review*, 3rd quarter, pp. 16–24.

Isaac, J. E. (1989), 'The Arbitration Commission: Prime mover or facilitator', *Journal of Industrial Relations*, September, pp. 407–27.

Isaac, J., Kates, S., Peetz, D., Fisher, C., Macklin, R., and Short, M. (1993), *A Survey of Small Business and Industrial Relations*, [Commonwealth] Department of Industrial Relations, Canberra, May.

Jamieson, S. (1990a), 'Enterprise bargaining: The approach of the Business Council of Australia', *Australian Journal of Labour Law*, May, pp. 77–82.

Jamieson, S. (1990b), 'A rejoinder', *Australian Journal of Labour Law*, December, pp. 308–9.

Jamieson, S. (1992), 'Enterprise agreements in New South Wales: A new era?' *Australian Journal of Labour Law*, March, pp. 84–8.

Jobsback! The Federal Coalition's Industrial Relations Policy (1992).

Johnstone, R., McKenzie, D. and Mitchell, R. (1993), 'The Industrial Relations Commission of Victoria 1982–92: A system under pressure', *Australian Journal of Labour Law*, August, pp. 97–120.

Keating, P. J. (1988), *Economic Statement*, AGPS, Canberra, May.

Keating, P. J. (1989), *Economic Statement*, AGPS, Canberra, April.

Keating, P. J. (1992a) *One Nation*, AGPS, Canberra, 26 February.

Keating, P. J. (1992b), 'A new charter for industrial relations in Australia', address to International Industrial Relations Association, Ninth World Congress, Sydney, 31 August (mimeo).

Keating, P. J. (1993), speech to Institute of Directors luncheon, Melbourne, 21 April (mimeo).

Keenoy, T. (1991), 'The roots of metaphor in the old and the new industrial relations', *British Journal of Industrial Relations*, June, pp. 313–28.

Kelly, P. (1992), *The End of Certainty: The Story of the 1980s*, Allen & Unwin, Sydney.

Kelman, B. N. and Coates, A. W. (1986), *Restrictive Work Practices*, submission to Economic Advisory Council on behalf of Business Council of Australia, 5 September (mimeo).

Kelty, B. (1989), keynote address, Rules and Finance, ACTU Congress, 1989, Sydney, 25 September (mimeo).

Kemp, D. (1986), 'Trade unions and liberty' in H. R. Nicholls Society, *Trade Unions Reform*, pp. 15–23.

Kemp, R. (1991), 'With particular reference to the Democrats', in *No Vacancies*, Proceedings of the H. R. Nicholls Society, 12–14 April, pp. 75–93.

Keynon, P. D. and Lewis, P. E. T. (1992), 'Trade union membership and the accord', *Australian Economic Papers*, December, pp. 325–45.

King, S. and Lloyd, P., eds (1993), *Economic Rationalism: Dead End or Way Forward*, Allen & Unwin, Sydney.

Kirby, R. (1970), 'Conciliation and arbitration in Australia: Where the emphasis?' *Federal Law Review*, September, pp. 1–29.

Kitay, J. and McCarthy, P. (1989), 'Justice Staples and the politics of Australian industrial arbitration', *Journal of Industrial Relations*, September, pp. 310–33.

Kochan, T. A., Katz, H. C. and McKersie, R. B. (1986), *The Transformation of American Industrial Relations*, Basic Books, New York.

Kochan, T. A., McKersie, R. B. and Cappelli, P. (1984), 'Strategic choice and industrial relations theory', *Industrial Relations*, Winter, pp. 16–39.

Kolko, G. (1963), *The Triumph of Conservatism: A Reinterpretation of American History, 1900–1916*, Free Press, New York.

Lansbury, R. D. and Westcott, M. (1992), 'Researching Australian industrial relations: Dawn or twilight of a golden age?' *Journal of Industrial Relations*, September, pp. 396–419.

Larouche, V. and Audet, M. (1993), 'Theorizing industrial relations: The dominance of logical positivism and the shift to strategic choice', in Adams and Meltz, eds, pp. 255–82.

Lasch, C. (1966), *The New Radicalism in America*, Alfred A. Knopf, New York.

Lee, M. (1980), 'The Industrial Peace Act of 1920: A study of political interference in compulsory arbitration', masters thesis, Faculty of Economics, University of Sydney.

Lenin, V. I. (1970) [1902], 'What is to be done?' in *On Trade Unions: A Collection of Articles and Speeches*, Progress Press, Moscow, pp. 68–142.

Leo XIII (1960), *Rerum Novarum* (The Workers' Charter), Encyclical Letter, Catholic Truth Society, London.

Lewin, D. (1987), 'Industrial relations as a strategic variable' in Kleiner, M. M., Block, R. N., Romkin, M. and Salsbury, S. W., eds, *Human Resources and the Performance of the Firm*, Industrial Relations Research Association, Madison, WI, pp. 1–41.

Lewis, P. E. T. and Spiers, D. J. (1990), 'Six years of the Accord: An assessment', *Journal of Industrial Relations*, March, pp. 53–68.

Liberal and National Industrial Relations Policy 1988 (mimeo).

Lindell, G. J. (1984), 'The corporations and races powers', *Federal Law Review*, 14 (4), pp. 219–52.

Loveday, P. (1984), 'Corporatist trends in Australia', *Politics*, May, pp. 46–51.

Ludeke, J. T. (1993a), 'The government's new charter for industrial relations in Australia 1993–96', *Journal of Industrial Relations*, June, pp. 316–28.

Ludeke, J. T. (1993b), 'The external affairs power: Another province for law and order', *Journal of Industrial Relations*, September, pp. 453–67.

Macarthy, P. G. (1969), 'Justice Higgins and the *Harvester* judgment', *Australian Economic History Review*, March, pp. 17–38.

MacDermott, K. (1993), 'Women's productivity: Productivity bargaining and service workers', *Journal of Industrial Relations*, December, pp. 538–53.

Machlup, F. (1969), 'Cost push and demand pull', in Ball, R. J. and Doyle, P., eds, *Inflation*, Penguin, Melbourne, pp. 149–76.

Macintyre, S. (1989), 'Neither capital nor labour: The politics of the establishment of arbitration', in Macintyre and Mitchell, eds, pp. 178–200.

Macintyre, S. and Mitchell, R., eds (1989), *Foundations of Arbitration: The Origins and Effects of State Compulsory Arbitration 1890–1914*, Oxford University Press, Melbourne.

Mahony, G., ed. (1993), *The Australian Economy Under Labor*, Allen & Unwin, Sydney.

McCallum, R. C., Pittard, M. J. and Smith, G. F. (1990), *Australian Labour Law: Cases and Materials*, 2nd ed., Butterworths, Sydney.

McCallum, R. C. (1993), 'The ascendancy of federal industrial law', in Ronfeldt and McCallum, eds, pp. 74–85.

McDonald, T. and Rimmer, M. (1988), 'Award structure and the second tier', *Australian Bulletin of Labour*, June, pp. 469–91.

McEachern, D. (1986), 'Corporatism and business responses to the Hawke Government', *Politics*, May, pp. 45–54.

McLachlan, I. (1986), 'Farmers, Australia's cost structures and union power', in H. R. Nicholls Society, *Arbitration in Contempt*, pp. 69–90.

McLachlan, I. (1989a), 'Terminating the Button rents on Australia's waterfront', in H. R. Nicholls Society, *The Legacy of 'The Hungry Mile'*, pp. 39–45.

McLachlan, I. (1989b), 'The live sheep dispute: Some personal reminiscences', in H. R. Nicholls Society, *No Ticket, No Start—No More!*, pp. 55–8.

McQueen, H. (1983), 'Higgins and arbitration' in Wheelwright, E. L. and Buckley, K., eds, *Essays in the Political Economy of Australian Capitalism*, Australia and New Zealand Book Co., Sydney, pp. 145–63.

Mowry, G. E. (1946), *Theodore Roosevelt and the Progressive Movement*, Hill & Wang, New York.

Mowry, G. E. (1958), *The Era of Theodore Roosevelt: 1900–1912*, Hamish Hamilton, London.

Mulvey, C. (1984), 'Wages policy and wage determination in 1983', *Journal of Industrial Relations*, March, pp. 112–19.

Mulvey, C. (1985), 'Wages policy and wage determination in 1984', *Journal of Industrial Relations*, March, pp. 68–75.

National Competition Policy (1993), Report by the Independent Committee of Inquiry (the Hilmer Report), AGPS, Canberra, August.

National Economic Summit Conference Documents and Proceedings (1983), Vol. 2, *Record of Proceedings*, AGPS, Canberra.

National Institute of Labour Studies (1989), *Employee and Industrial Relations in Australian Companies: A Survey of Management*, report prepared for the Industrial Relations Study Commission of the Business Council of Australia, March.

National Pay Equity Coalition (1993), *Enterprise Bargaining and Women*, contribution to submission to 1993 National Wage Case (mimeo).

Naughton, R. (1991), 'Transforming industrial relations in New South Wales: A green paper (Volume Two)', *Australian Journal of Labour Law*, March, pp. 89–91.

Naughton, R. (1993), 'The institutions established by the Employee Relations Act 1992', *Australian Journal of Labour Law*, August, pp. 121–39.

Neville, J. W. (1993), 'Economic rationalism: On throwing out the bathwater, but saving the baby' (mimeo).

Nicholls, H. R. *see* H. R. Nicholls Society

Niland, J. (1981), 'Research and reform in industrial relations', *Journal of Industrial Relations*, December, pp. 482–503.

Niland, J. (1989), *Transforming Industrial Relations in New South Wales*, Green Paper, Vol. 1, February.

Niland, J. (1990), *Transforming Industrial Relations in New South Wales*, Green Paper, Vol. 2, January.

Norton, W. E. and Kennedy, P. J. (1985), *Australian Economic Statistics 1949–50 to 1984–85: 1 Tables*, Reserve Bank of Australia, Occasional Paper No. 8A, November.

O'Brien, J. M. (1990), 'Regulating decentralised industrial relations: The Niland prescription', *Journal of Industrial Relations*, December, pp. 544–59.

O'Brien, J. (1994), 'McKinsey, Fred Hilmer and the BCA: The new management model of labour market reform', paper, Annual Conference of Association of Industrial Relations Academics of Australia and New Zealand, Sydney, February.

O'Donovan, J. (1977), 'Can the contract of employment be regulated through the corporations power?' *Australian Law Journal*, May, pp. 234–46.

Otlowski, M. (1992), 'The legal fallout from the APPM dispute', *Australian Journal of Labour Law*, December, pp. 287–94.

Peetz, D. (1990), 'Declining union density', *Journal of Industrial Relations*, June, pp. 197–223.

Peetz, D. (1992), 'Union membership and the Accord', in Crosby and Easson, eds, pp. 171–209.

Peetz, D., Quinn, D., Edwards, L. and Reidel, P. (1993), 'Workplace Bargaining in New Zealand: Radical change at work' in Peetz, D., Preston, A. and Docherty, J., eds, *Workplace Bargaining in the International Context*, Department of Industrial Relations, Canberra.

Pemberton, J. and Davis, G. (1986), 'The rhetoric of consensus', *Politics*, May, pp. 55–62.

Perlman, M. (1954), *Judges in Industry: A Study of Labour Arbitration in Australia*, Melbourne University Press, Carlton.

Perlman, S. (1949) [1928], *A Theory of the Labor Movement*, Augustus M. Kelley, New York.

Petridis, A. (1988), 'Wages policy and wage determination in 1987', *Journal of Industrial Relations*, March, pp. 155–62.

Pettigrew, A. M. (1979), 'On studying organisational cultures', *Administrative Science Quarterly*, December, pp. 570–81.

Pittard, M. J. (1993), 'Industrial conflict and constraints: Sanctions on industrial action in Victoria', *Australian Journal of Labour Law*, August, pp. 159–82.

Policy on Industrial Relations (1984), Liberal Party of Australia, National Party of Australia, 16 April (mimeo).

Preiss, B. and Neery, J. (1990), *Review of Occupational Health and Safety in Australia*, Report by the Review Committee to the Minister for Industrial Relations, November, AGPS, Canberra.

Proceedings of the H. R. Nicholls Society: *see* H. R. Nicholls Society.

Pusey, M. (1991), *Economic Rationalism in Canberra: A Nation-building State Changes Its Mind*, Cambridge University Press, Melbourne.

Rees, S., Rodley, G. and Stilwell, F., eds (1993), *Beyond the Market: Alternatives to Economic Rationalism*, Pluto Press, Sydney.

Reilly, S. (1989), 'An analysis of the factors influencing the second tier and its evolution', *Australian Bulletin of Labour*, June, pp. 200–22.

Reith, P. (1989), 'The evolution of the opposition's IR policy', in *No Ticket, No Start—No More!*, pp. 29–33.

Remuneration Tribunal, *Annual Reports*, AGPS, Canberra.

Rickard, J. (1976), *Class and Politics: New South Wales, Victoria and the Early Commonwealth, 1890–1910*, ANU Press, Canberra.

Rickard, J. (1984), *H. B. Higgins: The Rebel as Judge*, Allen & Unwin, Sydney.

Rimmer, M. (1981), 'Long-run structural change in Australian trade unionism', *Journal of Industrial Relations*, September, pp. 323–43.

Rimmer, M. (1988), *Enterprise and Industry Awards*, report prepared for the Industrial Relations Study Commission of the Business Council of Australia, November.

Rimmer, M. (1989), 'Transforming industrial relations in New South Wales: A green paper', *Australian Journal of Labour Law*, August, pp. 188–96.

Rimmer, M. and Zappala, J. (1988), 'Labour market flexibility and the second tier', *Australian Bulletin of Labour*, September, pp. 564–91.

Roe, M. (1984), *Nine Australian Progressives: Vitalism in Bourgeois Social Thought 1890–1960*, University of Queensland Press, St Lucia.

Ronfeldt, P. and McCallum, R., eds (1993), *A New Province for Legalism: Legal Issues and the Deregulation of Industrial Relations*, Monograph No. 9, Australian Centre for Industrial Relations Research and Teaching, University of Sydney.

Ross, A. M. (1956), *Trade Union Wage Policy*, University of California Press, Berkeley.

Sams, P. (1991), *ACTU Wages Strategy: A Discussion Paper*, 5 July (mimeo).

Schott, K. (1985), 'The consensus economy: An international overview', *Economic Papers*, June, pp. 1–22.

Shalev, M. (1980), 'Industrial relations theory and the comparative study of industrial relations and industrial conflict', *British Journal of Industrial Relations*, March, pp. 26–43.

Shaw, J. W. (1992), 'The Greiner Government's industrial relations laws: An experiment in deregulation', *Australian Journal of Labour Law*, August, pp. 158–170.

Shaw, J. W. and Walton, M. J. (1989), 'The Niland Report and labour law: A critical response', *Australian Journal of Labour Law*, August, pp. 197–205.

Sheldon, P. and Thornthwaite, L. (1993), '*Ex parte* Accord: The Business Council of Australia and industrial relations change', *International Journal of Business Studies*, October, pp. 37–55.

Sheridan, T. (1989), *Division of Labour: Industrial Relations in the Chifley Years 1945–49*, Oxford University Press, Melbourne.

Short, M., Preston, A. and Peetz, D. (1993), *The Spread and Impact of Workplace Bargaining: Evidence from the Workplace Bargaining Research Project*, AGPS, Canberra.

Singleton, G. (1985), 'The Economic Planning Advisory Council: The reality of consensus', *Politics*, May, pp. 12–25.

Singleton, G. (1990), *The Accord and the Australian Labour Movement*, Melbourne University Press, Carlton.

Skosice, D. (1990), 'Wage determination: The changing role of institutions in advanced industrialised countries', *Oxford Review of Economic Policy*, Winter, pp. 36–61.

Smith, H. and Thompson, H. (1987), 'Industrial relations and the law: A case study of Robe River', *Australian Quarterly*, Spring and Summer, pp. 297–304.

Smith, G. F. (1985), 'The High Court and industrial relations in the 1980s', *Australian Bulletin of Labour*, March, pp. 82–101.

Smith, G. G. and McCallum, R. C. (1984), 'A legal framework for the establishment of institutional collective bargaining in Australia', *Journal of Industrial Relations*, March, pp. 3–24.

Solomon, D. (1992), *The Political Impact of the High Court*, Allen & Unwin, Sydney.

Somers, G. G., ed. (1969a), *Essays in Industrial Relations Theory*, Iowa State University Press, Ames.

Somers, G. G. (1969b), 'Bargaining power and industrial relations theory' in Somers, ed, pp. 39–53.

Spry, I. F. C. (1986), 'Constitutional aspects of deregulating the labour market' in H. R. Nicholls Society, *Arbitration in Contempt*, pp. 117–30.

Spry, I. F. C. (1987), 'Constitutional aspects of deregulation', *Law Institute Journal*, May, pp. 471–73.

Stackpool, J. E. (1988), 'Industrial relations legislation in 1987', *Journal of Industrial Relations*, March, pp. 163–74.

Staples, P. (1991), media release: 'Costs of drug abuse', Parliament House, Canberra, 6 March (mimeo).

Statement of Accord by the Australian Labor Party and the Australian Council of Trade Unions Regarding Economic Policy (1983) (mimeo) (Accord Mark I).

Staunton, P. (1992), 'Unions can survive: Marketing the nurses' union', in Crosby and Easson, eds, pp. 289–95.

Stegman, T. (1993), ' "Jobsback" and the future of wages policy', *Economic and Labour Relations Review*, June, pp. 50–61.

Steinke, J. (1983), 'The long-term decline in the standard working year', *Journal of Industrial Relations*, December, pp. 415–30.

Stewart, A. (1993), 'Federal regulation and the use of powers other than the industrial power', in Ronfeldt and McCallum, eds, pp. 86–100.

Stewart, R. G. (1985), 'The politics of the Accord: Does corporatism explain it?' *Politics*, May, pp. 26–35.

Stilwell, F. (1986), *The Accord and Beyond: The Political Economy of the Labor Government*, Pluto Press, Sydney,

Stone, J. (1986a), introduction in H. R. Nicholls Society, *Arbitration in Contempt*, pp. 9–15.

Stone, J. (1986b), introduction in H. R. Nicholls Society, *Trade Unions Reform*, pp. 3–5.

Stone, J. (1987), presidential address in H. R. Nicholls Society, *The Light on the Hill*, pp. 13–15.

Stone, J. (1989), 'Closing remarks', in H. R. Nicholls Society, *In Search of the Magic Pudding*, pp. 91–4.

Stone, J. (1991), 'The wide-ranging politics of the Cook Bill', in H. R. Nicholls Society, *No Vacancies*, pp. 61–74.

Stuart, M. (1993), *United States Mission on Recruitment and Organisation: Summary Report*, ACTU Congress (mimeo).

Tannenbaum, F. A. (1952), *A Philosophy of Labor*, Alfred A. Knopf, New York.

Tarantelli, E. (1986), 'The regulation of inflation and unemployment', *Industrial Relations*, Winter, pp. 1–15.

Taylor, V. and Bray, M. (1986), 'Introduction: Directions in industrial relations research', in Bray and Taylor, eds, pp. 1–19.

Thompson, H. (1992), 'The APPM dispute: The dinosaur and turtles vs the ACTU', *Economic and Labour Relations Review*, December, pp. 148–64.

Thurow, L. C. (1983), *Dangerous Currents: The State of Economics*, Oxford University Press, Melbourne.

Trade, Department of (1987), *Australia Reconstructed—ACTU/TDC Mission to Western Europe: A Report by the Mission Members to the ACTU and the TDC*, AGPS, Canberra.

Treasury, Department of the, *Economic Round Up*, AGPS, Canberra.

Voos, P. (1993), 'Designing an industrial relations theory curriculum for graduate students', in Adams and Meltz, eds, pp. 17–42.

Webb, S. and B. (1902), *Industrial Democracy*, The Authors, London.

Wedderburn, Lord (1986), *The Worker and the Law* (3rd ed.), Penguin, Melbourne.

Weibe, R. H. (1967), *The Search for Order: 1877–1920*, Macmillan, London.

Woodward, A. E. (1970), 'Industrial relations in the '70s', *Journal of Industrial Relations*, July, pp. 115–29.

Wootten, J. H. (1970), 'The role of the tribunals', *Journal of Industrial Relations*, July, pp. 130–44.

Worksafe Australia National Institute Report (1993), *Occupational Health and Safety Performance Australia: Best Estimates*, February, AGPS, Canberra.

Zines, L. (1992), *The High Court and the Constitution* (3rd ed.), Butterworths, Sydney.

INDEX